D1430801

The Journal

of Jesus

*A Glimpse Into the Humanity
of the Son of Man*

Deborah Ayars

Edited by: David Ferris

Illustrated by: Laura M. Kardokus

ISBN: 978-1-947745-28-5

Published by: Well YOUniversity Publications
               A Division of Well YOUniversity, LLC
               5 Zion Rd.
               Hopewell, NJ 08525
               www.WellYOUniversity.com

DEDICATION

This book is dedicated to my dear friend, Father Carmen Carlone, who ignited the spark and fanned the flame of the Spirit within me; the parish family of St. Francis, especially my fellow daily Mass attendees, for the power of their prayer, encouragement and support; my many friends, Cursillo, Credo and family members, too numerous to list individually, who provided me with continual guidance and comfort on this long and oftentimes arduous journey; and last, but certainly not least, my husband, Steve, my daughters, Beth, Laura and Lisa, and my grandchildren for their constant ability to allow the light of the Lord to shine through them to me.

Lastly, and most importantly, this book is dedicated to my brother – our brother – Jesus. As mentioned in the Preface, this book was prepared through a prayer meditation – a personal form of communication in which He directed my fingers to dance across the keyboard at times, and have insights to write at other times, and to re-write and edit portions to make His word clearer.

CONTENTS

PREFACE

As I struggled through my walk with God, I found myself intrigued by our Lord and Savior, Jesus. I found myself completely absorbed by this God-man, who lived and walked the earth about 2000 years ago. I started to meditate on his everyday life and his personal journey here on earth. In so doing, I discerned a call, which I firmly believe was from Jesus himself, to record my prayer experiences in the form of a journal. This isn't a journal of my own life or experiences, but one I received through prayer representing the thoughts, feelings and daily trials and tribulations of our Lord.

Throughout this process I've been tempted to add my own feelings and ideas to this manuscript. Certainly, in the imperfections of my own humanity, it would be impossible not to be prone to such shortcomings. However, to the extent possible, I prepared this manuscript from a prayer meditation in which I envisioned speaking to our Lord, and I recorded those things, and only those things which he spoke to me.

Upon completion of this manuscript, I couldn't help but ask why? Why me? Why now? The answer was pretty simple. Jesus said He chose me because He knew I would do it. He said there were two reasons for why now. First, because too many people recognize only His divinity and ignore the fact that he was fully human as well. And secondly, because He hoped that by reading about how he examined, accepted and learned to celebrate His humanity, it would help us examine, accept and celebrate our own.

I hope and pray that at least one other person will be equally inspired by reading this manuscript as I was by being blessed with the opportunity to record it.

1 Introduction

Hello. My name is Jesus bar Joseph. I hail from Nazareth. It's a small town not too far from the Sea of Galilee. There have been a lot of amazing things in my life; monumental and incredible phenomena. I'm afraid to talk about them with anyone because some of it seems so confusing and, well, extraordinary. I believe I've been called by God to play a very special role in the history of mankind. Imagine that! Me, a carpenter's son! How can I believe God would call me at all, let alone impact the history of the whole world?

I've decided to maintain a record of my thoughts, prayers and experiences to help to understand my journey and the details of my growth. I'm not talking about a physical journey to a far-off place like Rome. It's more of an internal journey, a journey within my own spirit. In fact, I'm not sure I'll be able to effectively write about my entire journey. Some of it seems impossible to explain. That, too, is part of the reason I've decided to record it. I hope writing down my thoughts will help me sort them out for myself.

Fortunately, as a firstborn son, I was privileged to spend lots of time at the synagogue. In doing so, I learned the art of writing from the scribes. The process has always fascinated me. Even though I knew from a very young age that God wasn't calling me to serve Him as a scribe, I recognized that learning this craft was a gift God granted me for a reason. Now I'm beginning to understand the reasons behind this part of my childhood.

First, I guess I should say something about who I am and where I come from. Even my birth was a bit strange. Apparently, my mother and father had to travel to Bethlehem as part of the census for Caesar Augustus. Soon thereafter, my parents took me to Egypt because an edict was issued for all first-born male children to be killed. Rather than risk my life, my parents decided to move to a safe location.

Oddly enough, I don't remember much of my early life. I do remember a time when I was left behind on one of the family journeys to the temple. I was so entranced by the temple that I felt compelled to stay and pray. The priests were somewhat amazed at my understanding of the Scriptures and the insights I had, especially as a small boy. I somehow lost track of time and didn't realize my parents and the rest of my family had left. They each thought I was with someone else. I didn't panic because I knew I was safe. My parents soon realized what happened and retraced their steps to the temple. They were not sure whether to admonish or hug me.

My parents have been telling me for as long as I can remember that I'm special. They have always said that I'm destined to be a servant of God. I, too, realized early on that I was different from the other children. I had the same two legs, two arms, ten fingers, ten toes, but I still felt different, as if I was a foreigner at times. I wasn't content with the rowdy games the other boys would play; I especially hated the name-calling they would do to some of the girls, to the crippled boys, or to the Samaritans. I kept most of these thoughts to myself.

Without trying to sound too big-headed, I was also more gifted than others. I could easily beat almost anyone in athletic competitions, which is why I always assumed they accepted me. I could also learn the academic subjects effortlessly. I easily caught onto music and other artistic endeavors. I wasn't the best at anything, but I was always in the top few.

Shalom

2 Dad

Dad was a carpenter, an extremely talented one, too. Dad and I were close, much closer than most sons are to their dads. We spent hours in the shop daily, and he taught me while he worked; not just things about his craft, but things about life, the Torah, God, what being a good husband means, and how a man provides a good home for his family. He didn't teach me solely with words; he let his actions speak even louder.

We weren't wealthy, although Dad could have charged much more for his work because it was the best around. But Dad wasn't like that. He never charged more than what someone could afford. He was devoutly religious and was thrilled with his Jewish heritage. He taught me all the prayers. He explained that many people believed there was more than one God, while others believed there was no God at all, but Dad knew in his heart there was only one Creator, just as the Scriptures said.

I could probably spend weeks writing about Dad, but this story isn't about him; it's about me. I will close by saying my father had a lot of the same characteristics God has. He was kind, fair, generous, giving, caring, nurturing, peaceful, honest, hardworking, pleasant, conscientious, sincere, a good provider, a disciplinarian (not that I ever needed it!), energetic, and happy to be himself. His love for Mom, me, and the rest of our family was written all over his face.

It's getting really late. I'll write about Mom tomorrow.

Shalom.

3 Friends

This isn't the first time I've maintained some sort of journal of my life. I hope this time I'll be a little better at keeping it. I've decided that rather than talk about Mom today, I will talk about myself. A lot of thoughts are overwhelming me right now, and I want to sort them out while they are real and present to me. If I wait, the feelings will be less immediate, and some of them might be lost forever. The things that are really important today look so different from another point in my path.

I'm 26 years old now. I've always been like my Dad, open and honest with my friends and family, but such openness and honesty isn't always returned. I've had relationships that seemed to lack barriers, but inevitably my friends don't, or can't, respond to me at the same depth. Then I get terribly hurt, crawl into my shell and block everyone out. This leads to depression – it's as if my very lifeblood is simply sucked away. I receive little for internal growth in such moments.

It's incredibly painful. Why I allow myself to fall into the same rut time after time after time is a mystery. I guess it's because my rut is familiar and comfortable. Why should I find another rut when this one works so well? My shell can be so cozy, even if it's lifeless. I realize I NEED to eliminate these walls eventually. But I know enough to know Babylon wasn't built in a day. I have to pick away at them slowly.

Today, I find myself climbing out of my latest rut. At least it's easier this time because I didn't fall in as far and the route out is familiar. Today I had a lot of things come to the center stage of my inner self.

First, when I went to the temple today, I overheard some "friends" who were bashing me because I am not married, because I fancy myself as having a special relationship with

God, and some other things. Normally, I'm so preoccupied with my own prayers that I don't hear them. But today, their words pierced right through me. Part of me felt like running to them and making some sort of wisecrack like "Hey guys, do you think you could at least have enough courtesy to keep the bashing a little quieter so I can pray?" But another part of me felt like crying. I hate to admit it, but even though I'm a grown man, I just wanted to crawl into my hole and cry.

Soon, I realized what was bothering me. First, one friend in particular, James, seemed to be the ringleader. He is always so smug about his relationship with God, but I know it's just a cover-up for some insecurity. But that's his problem, not mine. He became my friend during my last depression. I say "friend," but he isn't exactly a true friend. Somehow, I've always kept him at arm's length. And now I'm complaining *he* isn't being a good friend.

Another friend, Thaddeus, or Thad for short, shared in the bashing, but this didn't invoke the same hurt in me. I didn't care too much about his remarks; but I took them as the normal bellyaching we sometimes do about each other's annoying habits. Thad has been a friend for years, almost like a brother. We have only had one relatively minor blow-up. We knew each other well enough to let time mend things.

I also realized I was hurt by something else. Yet another friend, Zeke and I spent the morning having breakfast, and I found out that he was getting married. His first wife died a few years back and he was devastated. With the exception of my own parents, I don't know anyone who has had as good a relationship as they did. They worshipped each other; you could see it in their eyes. After Zeke's wife died, we started hanging around together. We talked about a lot of things – his wife, how much he missed her, how he still felt her presence in his home, how wonderful she was, and how much he would always love and cherish her.

When he made friends with a wonderful woman, Anna, he was able to release his distress over the loss of his wife layer after layer and started to look at Anna as more than just a friend. Finally, he realized he would like to remarry. The wedding is a in a few weeks. Family only, because it is both his and hers second marriage, so I'm not invited. And I've just realized how truly hurt I am.

I've known for a while that something was bothering me. I knew it because I've had insatiable hunger lately. I've noticed that I always tend to "feed" my problems. So, for the last week or so I forced myself to not overeat. This always helps me uncover my problems – and now I've finally succeeded to realize what was wrong. Defining the problem isn't the same as resolving it, but once I identify what is wrong, at least three-quarters of the battle has been fought.

I could have had a lot of other responses to today's events, but I'm very proud of the course I chose. I was able to avoid a real scene with my friends.

I can't believe I've written this much today. I'm getting a bit tired, so I will pray about this some more and go to sleep.

Once again, Shalom.

4 The Human Shell

This will probably be a very short entry. I felt sick today. My head was pounding all day, so I rested. It's still pounding, in fact. Right now, my stomach feels a little upset. Mom just made me some hot herbal drink, she says it will help. At least it didn't taste too bad. I think I feel bad because last week I was working way too hard. It seemed I had something to do every waking minute and now I have to pay for it. Sometimes I don't rest enough and then I'm not at my best. I think having a day to rest is probably a good thing each week.

Things are so quiet right now. I feel as if I'm all alone. Sometimes I hate being alone. Right now, however, it's good. I can hear God talk to me best in the quiet. Sometimes before He talks to me, I get a little pressure in my ear, usually in my right ear. His voice is sometimes crystal clear, other times I'm not sure what He is saying at all. Do I really believe God talks to me? Yes, in fact, I do. He has for over ten years now.

In this journal, I want to write down some of the fascinating tales of my relationship with God, as well as keep a record of what is yet to come. I know God has something in store for me, something very special. I know He wants me to change the way of His people. He wants me to bring all of His people, not just Jews, into a deeper relationship with Him – a relationship founded on love and forgiveness. God created each and every one of His children in His image and likeness, and He calls us to be His.

I know this might seem crazy, but God has been telling me that I am His beloved Son for several years now. He has helped me recognize His power and majesty within my inner being. He's also helped me see His work in the people around me, as well as in the natural environment. I see Him in the birds in the air, the rainbows, the flowers, the mountains, and the streams.

I've been so scared lately, which is part of the reason I curled up inside myself. Although I try to blame it on others, I know the real reason is that I didn't know how to accept the fact that I'm the Son of God. I know God is calling me out of my self-created cave and back into the light. I know I will respond, although I have no idea how long it will take or where my path will lead.

Sometimes knowing I'm God's son isn't as important as knowing I'm a man first. I think it's awesome that God has given me the opportunity to live in the clothes of His children. I'm so grateful for all of the little things most humans take for granted. I welcome the little nuances of this shell of mine, called a body; how it can be tired or, sometimes, like today, feel a little bit off, sometimes it's warm or cold, and how sometimes a hug can feel so good. I cherish walking in a light, warm drizzle, splashing merrily in a river, sweating after some hard work. I thoroughly enjoy all of these sensations and more. I thank God for giving me the opportunity to be the Son of Man.

Beyond the physical body lie my emotions. They, too, are just as much a part of this human experience. Sometimes comfort, delight, joy, peace and other times pain, hurt, anger, envy. Each feeling I have fascinates me. Sometimes I've been able to simply allow myself to fully feel whatever it is, positive or negative. These are the times I know my life is most in touch with my Father in Heaven.

I know I also have a third component, my soul. This is the part of me attached to my Father. Sometimes, I'm not as aware of it. Other times, it consumes me totally. But one thing I know for certain is God has given all of His children a soul. They all possess, as do I, a conduit that links them to the Father. I've seen it at times in some of the people who surround me. I know it exists in all, even those who demonstrate no outward appearance of it.

Today, I will rejoice in the tiredness of my body and rejoice in a day of rest. I rejoice in the pain friends sometimes cause to each other. I rejoice in being alive – as a man!!!

Shalom.

5 Deborah

I was unable to write yesterday. Once again, the events of the day altered my plan for writing. Today, I will tell you a little about a wonderful person God sent into my life years ago. I met Deborah at our synagogue. It was really strange because I somehow knew with complete certainty that someday she and I would be best friends. This was peculiar because she was obviously a visitor and she was a Levite, so the likelihood of her sharing time with a carpenter's son from the house of Judah was almost nonexistent. She had her own people.

However, I knew we would be friends. As a matter of fact, I had experienced feeling this way twice before in my life, once upon meeting my cousin John, and once upon meeting my best friend Timothy. But now I experienced the same thing with a person of the opposite sex. Some may have written it off as my adolescent hormones filling me with infatuation. But I know this was different from the way my friends acted when they became infatuated with a young lady.

Deborah and I were both helping with the renovations to our synagogue, and we instantly connected. I remember all the fun we had planning the synagogue renovations and then talking afterwards about anything and everything. We quickly became friends. Her cousins lived in our village, and she came to stay with them after the death of her parents, so we could spend a lot of time together.

Then, as unexpectedly as she came, she quit speaking to me without an explanation. I would see her at the synagogue, but she never said a word. I was hurt at first; I didn't understand why she would just leave me like that. At first, I wanted to confront her, then decided it was for the best. It was obvious my feelings for Deborah were rapidly becoming that of love, and I knew she was betrothed to another, as was the custom of Levites. It was a most sacred arrangement, and no matter how I felt about her, I couldn't violate it.

A few years later, Deborah, then married, and I found ourselves helping at the synagogue again. One day, Deborah was hurt about something her husband had done, so I offered her some words of comfort. She sort of smiled, then she looked at me with the same look I would often see in my mother's eyes. Then, shock of all shock, she said, "I love you, Jesus." It hit me like the full weight of Mount Sinai falling, engulfing and burying me. I realized that I loved her, too.

My head was spinning for days. Then days turned to weeks, and weeks became a month. I was afraid to face my own feelings, but there they were, undeniably etched into my soul. I was in love with a woman I couldn't have. I was hopeless. I confided in my best friend, Timothy, who pointed out that sometimes God challenges us in strange ways, and perhaps this was one of His challenges.

This opened up a new world for me. After this, everywhere I turned and everything that occurred seemed to echo that all of it was indeed God's doing. I was scared, but I knew the only way to work through my fear was to face it, and the only way to face it was to confront Deborah.

I was able to catch her alone one evening. It was the most unusual conversation; we seemed to know things even though nothing was said. She skillfully managed to get me to talk then and there. I said, "Deborah, do you remember when you asked me what was wrong with me a while ago and I didn't really have a good answer. Then you said that you love me?"

She said "Yes, Jesus, I remember that conversation well. Have you figured out what was really wrong?"

I said, "The problem is, I love you, too."

Deborah looked at me for a few minutes and then said, "I completely understand, but I don't really have time to talk right now because it's late. Would you like to get together another day to discuss your problem?"

I felt instant relief and eagerly agreed. Once again, it was clear that a power greater and mightier than me was directing the show. I was exuberant I would soon get a chance to clear the air with her and find a resolution to this situation. How little did I know.

After our conversation, Deborah seemed to avoid me. After several months, I was so anxious to talk to her that I decided to wait for her one evening. It seemed she knew what I was up to as she lingered mercilessly. Finally, she was alone, and I walked over to her to ask her if we could talk. She pretended she had forgotten all that had been said. I sensed she was simply not ready, so I didn't force the conversation.

After another month passed, God told me I should go see Deborah, because she was ready, and we would talk. This was my first experience with a personal communication with God in such a direct way. There were no words spoken, it was more like a revelation. I was instructed to tell her that God wasn't sending her a test, but a gift of love, His greatest gift. As weird as this seemed, my only response was obedience. Luckily, Deborah instantly agreed to see me.

I started to talk, but I stumbled over my words. I couldn't say anything. After Deborah actually begged me to talk, I dutifully delivered my message, word for word how it was given. I allowed the spirit of God to work through me. For the first time in my life I felt that I wasn't anything more than a channel for God's work and God's voice. I opened my mouth, I spoke with my voice, but the words were from a source outside of me. They were too perfect to be mine.

Deborah and I talked for a long time. I, or should I say God, unwrapped her soul. It was as though she were standing there naked, with no barrier at all. Yes, I loved her intensely. I realized God had allowed me to witness another human being through His perfect eyes. I was unable to find fault, I was unable to see mistakes, and I was unable to notice any shortcomings. I saw only the beauty of her inner soul, childlike and innocent. Deborah didn't try to hide anything from me, not that she could have. We talked about her joys and her fears. I was able to help her face the things she had tried to hide even from herself.

It's getting very late and Deborah is much more than a one-night story. The reason I'm writing about it now is because yesterday she turned up at a village event. She has since moved to another village and I haven't seen her much. But I had been thinking about her for the last few weeks. I thought I no longer NEEDED Deborah in my life. But as much as I was thinking about her, this is obviously not true. I'm back to my old trick of not facing issues but burying them. Needless to say, it doesn't work.

Somehow, God in His infinite majesty arranged for me to see Deborah. I was extremely glad to see her. I will never stop loving her. It's impossible to not love someone completely after you have had the privilege of looking at his or her soul, barren and naked. After our initial hellos, I became uncomfortable. My insides tossed and turned. I know that trying to avoid acknowledging the reason for these emotions will do me no good. I must spend some time praying and talking to God about what this all means. Once again, Deborah is helping me grow. I will be forever in her debt.

Shalom.

6 Resolution

It never seems to take me terribly long to pinpoint what is bothering me once I start to look at myself honestly. As I mentioned before, the first thing I do is make a conscious effort not to eat. For me, eating is a sort of sedative, and instead of facing my problem, I feed it. My problem doesn't go away, but I can satisfy its sting and soften its edges with food. When I notice an excessive need to overeat, I can usually tell something is troubling me. When I control the insatiable hunger, things start to surface.

I've come a long way to sort out my difficulties. First, as is often the case, Deborah has little to do with what is bothering me, although her mere presence helped me look at myself. As I was so terribly uncomfortable after seeing her again, I had no choice but to really look at my inner self. I feel that just as I can look into her soul, she can peek into mine. Somehow this thought isn't discomforting; in fact, it's quite enjoyable.

I would give anything to be able to take the place of her husband, live with her, and enjoy everyday life with her, but I realize this will never happen. I'm just glad for her presence. I thank God for the mysterious ways He constantly works through her, even in her absence, and frequently without her full knowledge.

Anyway, back to the issue at hand. I realize what was really bothering me was the process of removing my walls, this time dealing with my friend James. Believe me, this is altogether a most unpleasant task. I firmly believe that this is a mandatory part of my progress on earth. I believe God allowed me to witness the beauty of someone's inner soul to provide me with a glance of how He sees the people He created. I believe I have to find a way to look at all of His creation with those same eyes. I need to see through people's barriers and shortcomings.

Of course, God always gives us a choice. I know I can pick up the challenge and face my rugged mountain or I can rest where I am. I can't even begin to see the finish line, and I'm really not sure I'm ready. But my Father doesn't make the other choices look very attractive. I know I'm destined to rise and start walking. I also know God won't abandon me; He will give me the strength I need to keep going. Actually, it's more a matter of me finding the strength I need within myself. Sometimes I wish I could just be an ordinary human; this God's son stuff sometimes seems such a bother. Only joking of course.

Shalom.

7 Wedding Prayer

I've been too caught up to write. I could use the excuse I was busy, but that would be less than honest with myself. The truth is that by speaking to my friend James, I was confronted with the pain of getting out of my own shell again. It was easier to crawl back into it. It lasted less than a week before I realized what I was doing. I've promised myself I will continue to peek out into the light no matter what. I know it's what my Father is calling me to do.

Another thing I have to do is write a wedding prayer for Zeke and Anna. While I was, and still am, a little hurt over the lack of an invitation, I know I need to move beyond the pettiness of my human shortcomings and rise to the occasion as the Son of God I am.

Shalom.

A WEDDING PRAYER*

When you truly love one another, you are able to peer into their soul without anything blocking the path.

You are able to walk hand in hand in the soul of the other, not knowing where one soul begins and the other ends.

Your lives touch, not just for an instant, but for an eternity.

You find yourself somehow incomplete unless the other is with you, and with true love you know they are always with you.

You know the sadness or joy of another, although no words need be spoken.

The ultimate joy in life can be revealed only when you share yourself completely with the one you love.

In this kind of love giving of oneself is never considered or measured, it's necessary.

This kind of love happens infrequently in life, but when it comes, it must be cherished forever.

And this kind of love can only occur when both people willingly and lovingly allow God to be an integral and significant part of the relationship.

Dear God, as your two faithful servants have presented themselves to each other with you at their sides,

May you bless them with the many joys of life that can only come from knowing each other intimately,

May they be consciously aware not to build walls around their inner soul so the other remains free to roam inside,

May you allow them to know the joy of helping complete each other,

May they always give themselves totally to one another,

May they forever cherish you, honor you, and recognize you as a vital part of their relationship,

And may they live to love and serve you together as one.

Dedicated to my daughter, Lisa, and son-in-law, Willie, on the occasion of their wedding, July 17, 2003.

8 James

I need to expound more on my discussion with James. I thought I was so much in control and so much more spiritually advanced than James because, after all, I'm the Son of our highest God. I realized I wasn't really being a good friend to James. I had never opened my soul or my heart to him; I kept parts of me very well hidden. But I realized the only way out of my self-created hole was to lower the walls and crawl out from behind them. The only person who could help me was me, and playing God wasn't the way to accomplish it. I can only pull myself out of my shell enough to allow God to play God through me.

I also realized I've allowed myself to ignore my "vision," which is why I've fallen away from being at one with God. I'm scared of the vision. The thought of being God's Son has overwhelmed me so much that I actually choked the spirit of God from my being. I allowed my human nature to bury the vision, and in so doing, bury my spirit. As I write this, I realize that it's exactly what human nature would do. I've been so frustrated with myself for allowing it to happen, but it's what I, the Son of Man, had to do.

It's part of my growth process to fully understand what being the Son of God means. I first have to completely realize and live the human, before I can realize and live the divine. I know I've been on a long path to make the Spirit of God within me more a part of my being than before. This is what being the Son means. All the frustration I've been feeling I now see as a necessary part of the process to achieve my end. Ironic.

Thank you, dear God, for James. He has been a true friend. Help me to learn and grow from him and help me to allow him to walk in my soul without any walls to block him. And thank you so much for helping me laugh at my humanity and cherish it once again. I forgot how very important it is to be truly the Son of Man. Help me humbly accept myself as the Son of God, but always sincerely cherish the part of me that is, and will always be, the Son of Man.

Shalom.

9 Gifts

I haven't done much with myself in the last week. I'm still resisting the inevitable, which is freeing myself from the walls that bind me from within in order to take my rightful place in God's plan. I'm learning not to be so down on myself as I plod along. After all, my Father wouldn't have given me the gift of humanity if I were not to experience it fully. I guess it's still not time for me to come busting out of my shell. Besides, if I burst forth suddenly, it won't feel real. I'm learning to be content with whatever pace God gives me.

I've decided to take charge of a small faith group as part of an effort to try to enrich the lives and spirits of the congregation at our synagogue. I've already had two sessions. I'm amazed at how well I'm able to handle the group, which has some diverse personalities and theologies.

Last week I challenged the whole group to consider the five best qualities God has given them. I chose this assignment because I think it's vitally important for us to look at ourselves and honestly acknowledge God's gifts. Some of the group members really struggled with this task, stating that they had no really good qualities. I personally found it easy, not because I'm conceited, but because I readily acknowledge some, maybe not all, of the gifts God has given me.

We are lying to ourselves if we say we have no good qualities. Perhaps it isn't so much of a lie but a failure to recognize God in our lives. We **all** have gifts, and I would be amazed if any one of God's children possessed but five gifts. There are so many things we can do for the glory of God; I find it amazing we can't see them. Some can sing, others dance, others tell stories, some play the lyre, some are intelligent, some are wise, and some are potters, weavers, or shoemakers. I'm a carpenter, like my Dad, which is also a glory to God. Being a loving, caring parent counts, as does listening to others. There are some that help by cooking, some who make us laugh, a few have the gift to share God by preaching. Some have the gift of making foodstuff flourish from the land, some work hard daily to provide for their families, others teach our children, and some have the gift of leadership.

My gifts? Today, I would say intelligence first. I find I'm one of the more intelligent people in the village. People frequently marvel at my ability to learn and retain things as quickly and easily as I can. Secondly, it is my honesty. I have to admit there have been times when I was unable to be completely honest with others or myself. Sometimes it's because I can't face the truth and try to hide. Other times it's because I don't want to hurt someone else's feelings. But for the most part, I'm honest with others and, most importantly, with myself.

Steadfastness is another of my prized possessions. I've had times in my life when I had to stand up for the things I believe in. Times I've been committed to a goal others have ridiculed and sabotaged. But when I *know* I'm right, I can withstand the strongest army or the most severe storm. Somehow, I know this quality will be an absolute necessity in the future. Once I commit myself to God's chosen path, I will be unable to do anything but see my way through it.

Kindness and niceness are other valued commodities. Some have told me I'm too nice. Certainly, my being nice is one of the things that allows me to get hurt, because all too often my niceness goes unnoticed, or worse yet, actually gets shoved back in my face. But I don't think anyone can be too nice.

My fifth and final quality is sensitivity. Deborah is the most wonderfully sensitive person I know. I also appreciate the feelings of others, but I sometimes get hurt when I shouldn't because I overreact. But all in all, my sensitivity is a prized possession. It's what sets me apart from others. I have the ability to sincerely feel things at depths that seem far beyond what anyone, other than Deborah, feels. I honestly believe my sensitivity is necessary for me to recognize and accept that I am a child of God.

I find it amusing that I'm writing non-stop. In fact, I frequently have to slow down my thoughts because I can't write anywhere near as fast as I think. Yet, for over a week now I've failed to utilize my journal to record my feelings. I didn't think I had much to say. It seems I needed to store it all up.

In other areas of my life God is presenting more and more situations for me to walk along my path. More and more people in my life are being reminders I haven't been open. My life will be much more joyous and fulfilling once I simply bust out from my shell and rid myself of the extra weight that burdens me and prevents me from really knowing the joy of human life. Yet, I'm almost helpless in my ability to free myself of my self-imposed bondage and simply rise – or even soar – above it. All good things will come in their own time. God's prodding will certainly not be in vain.

God is also helping me to be less tense, less nervous, less anxious and more reliant on my faith in Him. I've faced a tremendous amount of difficult situations recently that would have made my stomach wrap up in knots before, but I seem to be growing past allowing these situations to upset me. Today, for instance, I had a particularly powerful person chastise me over my work. He called my work an embarrassment. My work! My work is never an embarrassment! His criticism was biting and even downright cruel. Normally, I would have fretted for days, or even weeks, over what this will mean for the future of my business. I would have possibly even met his obnoxious behavior with some of my own. But today I just shrugged.

There is an area of my life that has been plaguing me: money. I've reached spots in my life recently where I've been unable to provide food and the necessary supplies for my mother and me. Also, due to some illness and death, I have other family members who rely on me for support right now. I used to have major palpitations when money didn't come in as expected. Even though I've come close to running completely out, I never have. Just when I really need it, something would come through somehow. I'm again going through a period when my needs seem to outpace my ability to provide. But I'm really not worried about my dwindling reserves yet. Sometimes I think God needs to challenge my faith even more each time, and I indeed may actually have to experience what it is like to run out.

It's getting late again. I've spent quite some time with this entry. Hopefully, the next one won't be another week away.

Shalom.

10 My Call from God

I know God is calling me to be the Messiah. I don't know exactly what I am to do or how He intends to accomplish it. It has been difficult throughout my early adult life knowing I need to serve God and His people. I couldn't deal with being God's son and waking each day to grow, work, be part of my family, be a craftsman and a businessman. My answer was to put my true identity into a special place, where it wasn't totally forgotten but, to a large extent, ignored.

Now, however, over the past few months, all those thoughts and feelings of my true self are reawakening with a vengeance. The internal compartment is no longer able to contain my inner self. As I look at everything God has given me in the past few months, I know my time is drawing near. I don't yet know exactly what to prepare for, but I know that waiting for God has ended.

The next step is to actively discern my call and the steps I must initiate for God's plan to materialize. I know it's my duty and privilege as the Son of God to listen intently and follow. I won't disgrace my Father. His mission for me, while seemingly impossible, will be accomplished according to His plan. It should be interesting to watch the daily unfolding of the plan and all the intricate details God has negotiated for years. My time has begun.

Shalom.

11 God's Son

Why do I doubt who I am? I know I'm God's son, I know I'm the Messiah God promised my people. My mother and father have told me so most of my life. God has also revealed it to me several years ago. So why do I doubt it?

Look at me. I'm fully human. I walk, talk and eat like a human. I get hurt and tired like a human. I cry and laugh like a human. I make mistakes like a human, too.

So, what makes me different? How am I to believe I'm God's son? God created me as His son and as Son of Man. How is this possible? It can't be. Yet, I know it is. If it isn't, my whole life has been a lie. If I'm not His son, I must throw out all of my beliefs. They are all part and parcel of the same thing.

Somehow doubt keeps creeping into my being. It's something I've struggled with for a long time. At times my position as His son is so real, and other times it seems so impossible. But I'm growing. Slowly but surely, I find God removing the doubt and replacing it with confidence. Slowly but surely, I'm moving the knowledge of my "sonship" from my head into my heart.

Shalom.

12 Confidence

I mentioned yesterday that God does amazing things to help me build confidence. A few people have told me if they were ever going to follow someone, they would follow me. People in my prayer circles tell me I don't realize how special I am. I smile and think to myself that I do.

But do I really realize how special I am? If I did, why would I doubt my sonship so much? Isn't it curious that God sends people to me at exactly the right time – people who are able to suitably verbalize how special I am? Why do I question what they see in me? I should know that they notice the face of God in me, because to know me is to know the Father within me. So, when people say they love me and tell me how special I am, they simply recognize my sonship.

I also see something in certain people. I'm always able to pick out people that are truly open to the spirit of God, not just try to simply follow all the laws and rules. If I had to put a finger on it, I would say it's in the eyes. The eyes seem to reflect the true inner self. I see a certain sparkle in some or radiance in others. So many eyes are lifeless. They have no God. The eyes are the windows of the soul, and my eyes are shining bright.

Shalom.

13 Call to Journey

I've known for almost a year that God is calling me to prepare myself for my journey. He has been preparing me all my life, but now I must also take some steps on my own. For instance, I've learned a lot about God and the Holy Book from my studies in the synagogue. I've learned about human nature through my family and friends. I've learned about leadership through the small business I run as a carpenter. Now it's time for me to leave all this behind and begin my preparation.

I'm not sure how to prepare, but I do know what I need is some time alone with God so He can help me finalize myself for the coming mission. I know I'm not to be a Rabbi, yet I will teach men about God. I know I'm to bring the good news of salvation to His people, even though I still question why people will believe me. I know my followers will extend throughout the earth someday. I will go soon.

Shalom.

14 Mom's Prayer

I don't have much to write today about my internal struggles. However, I was thinking about my mom, and how lucky I am to have her. I thought perhaps a short poem to her would be in order. I know I will be leaving soon, and I will carve this into a special piece of wood I found for her as a parting gift.

A MOTHER'S LOVE

A mother's love is strong and true

It's a love that knows no end.

A mother's love cares not with what is wrong,

But looks only at what is right.

A mother's love is blind to failures, shortcomings, and weakness.

It, however, rejoices in the inner soul of her child,

Which she sees as forever sincere and pure.

A mother's love is unselfish.

A mother would do without to provide for her child

And would give her life without hesitation.

A mother is always caring and nurturing.

Forgiveness isn't necessary,

As her child is incapable of creating any

Wrong that would warrant forgiveness.

A mother teaches her child joyfully.

She sees the world through the innocent eyes of her child,

She watches the butterfly flutter in the wind,

And she helps her child chase rainbows.

She helps them to walk ever stronger along the path,

And helps them to grow physically, mentally and spiritually.

She is always there to pick them up and comfort them when they fall.

A mother's love is special and unique in the entire world.

It's a love given by God in His likeness.

It's a love to be cherished forever.

Shalom.

15 Inner Struggles

Today I'm a bit tired and feeling a little ill. I have a sore throat and I feel sick to my stomach. I think part of my problem is anxiety; I'm afraid to speak up about my true identity as the Son of God. Who would believe a thing like that? I know my Jewish brothers and sisters believe the Messiah will come. But in the form of a simple man like me? That seems unlikely. They expect a great king, not a carpenter. I also don't believe my Father is asking me to tell people who I am right now. I guess it's something people will have to see and believe for themselves.

Recognizing my sonship is a very big part of my inner battle. At times, a part of me thinks I must be crazy to believe I could indeed be God's son since I come from simple parents and a simple life. But another part of me knows I'm completely God's son. My entire life indicates my identity as the Son of God. How could I accept only a part of God's presence in my life and leave the things I don't want to accept? No, it's either all true, or it's all utter nonsense. I'm either mad or God's son.

Shalom.

16 Loneliness

Today I'm surrounded with a feeling of utter loneliness. I wish it were not so, but it is.

I saw my lovely Deborah today. I knew I would see her, and I was hoping we would get a chance to talk, but she didn't even say hello. My heart aches as she pulls away. She is perhaps not the same person I fell in love with anymore. That person was so full of love and understanding of God. Now she seems empty. I pray for her to re-ignite the flame; it doesn't appear to be burning bright.

As much as I try to tell myself that I don't need to talk to her, I don't need her friendship, I don't need her love, I don't need to feel that oneness again, my heart still desperately wants it. I want to let her go, but I can't. I feel empty. Just plain empty. I've found my spiritual mate, a perfect match, and a wonderful gift from God, but I can't have it. I don't understand why God is doing this to me, or to her. I don't understand His plan.

I was so miserable and on edge yesterday in anticipation of seeing her. I didn't understand the source of my extreme anxiety and irritability. How can someone so wonderful stir up such negative feelings in me? How can something so wonderful be so painful at the same time? How can being with someone who helped me understand my Father and brought out the love inside my soul be so wrong? Obviously, this love is from you and therefore it is not wrong. Experiencing love at this depth has helped me grow in so many different ways and has given me the ability to love others more deeply as well.

God, help me. I feel so utterly lonely. It has been years and years. I've waited. I've endured. I've grown. But now it's enough. Lift this burden from me. Lift this burden from her. Help us both. I know it's somehow your plan for us to grow within this situation. Help us both find that growth. Help fill my emptiness. And help fill her emptiness as well.

Shalom.

17 Forgiveness

It has been about a week since I last saw Deborah. I know a lot of things now that I didn't realize before. So many things. I hope by writing them down, everything will make sense.

First, the anxieties I experienced were not just about Deborah, but mostly about her friends and family. They had hurt me so much in the past, ridiculing me, ignoring me, trying to push me away. I think I've never truly forgiven them for all the hurt. I've ignored them, tolerated them, and accepted them, but I've never truly forgiven them. I need to do that. It's only through forgiveness I will truly heal myself and be able to fully experience the love within me.

As for Deborah, I believe I've never really forgiven her for the hurt she has given me either. Some of her words and actions really pierced my heart as if it were an arrow. I pulled out the arrow, but I never tended to or healed the wound. I ignored it. This hole in my heart needs to heal. I need to forgive her. I must also forgive myself for the pain I caused her. I know she has been suffering, too. Isn't it ironic you can cause the greatest hurt to the people you love the most, even if that's the last thing you would want to do?

Father, please help me to forgive. Please help that sincere, deep, and unconditional love return. The kind of love that was able to understand what Deborah desired without her saying. The kind of love that instinctively placed her needs above my own. The kind of love that needed nothing, wanted nothing, and desired nothing in return. The kind of love that didn't place demands, that didn't strive to be returned, or even accepted. Please, Father, grant this ability to me once again.

Shalom

18 About Three Years Later

I found this journal the other day and read it again. Wow! I didn't even remember some of the things I had written. Obviously, I had a lot more growing to do. I've still not embarked on my mission, though. Sometimes I wonder if I have a mission at all, or if it is only a part of my overactive imagination.

I will comment on the events since I last wrote. Zeke and Anna have a wonderful marriage. I haven't been very close to Zeke since the wedding, but I still consider him my friend. They are busy with their family. Whenever I get a chance to talk to Zeke, he fills me in on all the joys of his life with his wonderful Anna. I believe Zeke is a very special, caring and loving man. He must possess something special within himself to be able to have had two very successful and loving relationships.

Thad and I are still good friends. I must confess I've still been very much in my shell. Therefore, my ability to be a good friend has been somewhat limited. But Thad seems to allow me to be me. He gives me space to grow. He and I still spend time together frequently. He has a great way to help me see something without being too pushy or offensive. A wonderful gift from my Father.

Timothy is one of my oldest and dearest friends and always will be. We have shared a lot together. I know he is special in God's eyes. I'm lucky to call him my friend.

James is another story. James is one of the reasons why I'm still struggling with my shell. He kept trying to push and pull me. My attempt to help him with his insecurity gave him more reason to act superior – just as he does to everyone. Thankfully, he decided to move to a different village. I would still be helplessly locked inside my shell if I had him around every day as a "friend." I see him at the synagogue when he visits. He still thinks he knows more than everyone, including the priests.

As for me, I still have a long way to go, at least I think I do. My experience with James taught me a lot, though. He helped me learn how to deal with people who are strong in their convictions. Somehow, I think this lesson will be needed in the future.

Deborah. It has taken me another few years, but I've finally gotten to the point where I can honestly say I've let her go. I also realized why I experienced so much anxiety whenever we met. Somehow, I was afraid that seeing Deborah might make me face the fact that I was a phony, I wasn't the Son of God, and that God wasn't real. I can't exactly explain why. Deborah was a part of my path and my ability to understand God. God had given me a glimpse of His love for people through Deborah.

Yes, I still love Deborah. I always will. But I no longer struggle with my feelings. I remember the time the flame was almost extinguished in her, but the last time I saw her, the flame of God was burning strong again. She is in good hands, and so am I.

Enough for tonight.

Shalom.

19 Major Changes

My life took a major change a few months ago. Since I spent a few more years lost within myself, I found that God started opening doors for me. I started to feel myself grow in my faith and understanding of life again. I found myself repeating certain lessons, only this time they seemed to be so much more a part of me.

Another strong-spirited individual came into my life. His name is Joshua, and I took him on as an apprentice to work with me in my carpentry shop. I say apprentice, but he had already learned the trade from his dad. Anyway, Joshua wanted to take over my business. He was a very good carpenter, but not a very good businessman. We had a bit of a problem at one point, as I was still unable to deal with strong-spirited individuals. Later, we talked about it, which helped me beat my anxieties and work through my problems. Unlike James, Joshua gave me space to overcome my difficulties in dealing with strong personalities.

That seemed to be the catalyst I needed to start growing in leaps and bounds. The world seems bright and cheerful again, and God seems to be a more constant companion. I had a few other lessons to learn. God, of course, was masterful in His ability for me to have the right situations at the right time. I look back over the past few months and can't believe how far I've come.

Thank you, Father, for all you have given me. I'm the clay in your hands to be molded in whichever fashion you chose.

Shalom.

20 Doubt

Doubt. The doubt of who I really am weighs heavy on my mind sometimes. In fact, it's something I've struggled with periodically throughout my life, especially these past few years. I think there were times when even my parents wondered if I could really be God's son. After all, at times, I was just like any other child growing up, not always the perfect angel.

If I were really the Son of God, would I doubt it? The fact that I doubt my own identity may prove that I'm not who I believe myself to be. I know doubts about God are normal. I don't think any human can go through life without ever questioning God's existence. To be fully human, I must also experience all the normal human emotions, one of which is doubt. Yes, even as far as sometimes questioning the very existence of the Supreme Being.

But what about doubting myself? If I can question God's existence, which I would need to do to be fully human, I would then have doubts about everything. I would also doubt my sonship. I know God's plan for me is to be human in every sense of the word. Therefore, part of my path must be to face these doubts internally. No matter how many times and how many ways I examine the doubt of my identity, I'm always drawn to the same conclusion: I am the Son of God.

Shalom.

21 Faith

I've been working on my faith lately and restoring my connection with God. I used to be able to talk with him almost daily. For the past few years, my communication all but went away. Now, however, I find it easier to connect with my Father. I talk with him almost daily, usually when I wake up and again when I lie down to go to sleep.

I can feel myself growing in leaps and bounds. I find that now that my faith has been restored, I have more energy. I also enjoy life more. I can truly open my heart to people, although I still have a long way to go. I've also found I'm more peaceful on the inside. I still get excited over things, but the frustration and anger have all but gone away.

I know my time to begin my ministry is near. I don't know how and where to start. I'm not a priest, nor am I a leader in the synagogue. I have no idea why people would listen to me. I simply know God beckons me, and I have no choice but to listen and follow.

Shalom.

22 Call to Ministry

This urge to begin my ministry is nagging me. I feel compelled to leave my home and my business and start on a journey. This will be both a physical journey as well as an internal one.

I talked to Joshua the day before yesterday. He said he could tell something had been troubling me. It seems I haven't been as attentive to my work. Before I could ask him if he would be willing to take over the carpentry shop for me, he volunteered. He also insisted that he would take care of my mother. He said it was only right, since he has been staying with us in our home. Besides, the tools and the shop were my father's.

Today I talked to my mother. She gave me a funny look. I couldn't tell if she felt my time had not yet come or if she was just caught off guard. Or maybe she was just sad at the thought of me leaving. Or was she relieved? Only kidding. Mom wouldn't like to see me go.

I wish she had been a bit more supportive of me. I would have really appreciated some words of comfort, even if she felt it was wrong. I would have appreciated her telling me she felt it wasn't my time yet. But she said nothing. Just a funny look I couldn't figure out. I can usually tell what she is thinking by how she looks. But not today. I don't understand. I told her Joshua was going to take over the shop and provide for her. I promised her I would see her soon.

Father, I know I still don't quite understand all you want of me. Please help me discern your direction in my life. Help me have the courage to follow. And finally, help me maintain and strengthen my faith so I may truly be your Son. And please help my mother. I don't understand what she is thinking, but whatever it is, help her find internal peace and comfort. Amen.

23 The Journey Begins

I got up somewhat early today, ready to go. I didn't really know where. God and I had a wonderful talk this morning. He assured me my time had come and I was adequately prepared for my mission. He also repeated he was proud of me and how well I had prepared myself by being loyal to him throughout my life. I was thinking I was very slow to learn some of His lessons and spent a terribly long time questioning and doubting Him and myself. He sort of laughed and reminded me that it was a necessary part of the process.

When I finally got out of bed, Mom had made me a hearty breakfast of fish, fruit and bread with her special pomegranate honey. A breakfast fit for a king! She was her normal, cheerful self. Not only had she made me breakfast, but she also packed some clothes, extra food and cooking supplies for me.

We talked the whole time we ate. She didn't say much about me leaving, but she said she loved me and knew I would have to follow God wherever He took me. She also said she knew she would see me again very soon. She smiled, wished me luck, and blessed me on my journey. Then she gave me a wonderful hug. She said I needed one that would last a little while.

I wasn't sure which way to go, so I just started walking. Before long, I met an older fellow who was asking for help beyond the outskirts of town. He said he had no home and had not eaten for a while. I wasn't hungry because of the enormous breakfast I had had. I asked him if he was heading anywhere, and he said he was heading into town. I decided to turn around and walk with him a bit.

He was a very interesting person. His name was Joseph. He had a few children, but his wife died young. He was so devastated by her death that he was hardly able to get out of bed and face the day. He lost his job and ran out of money. He stole some food to feed his family and got caught, so he was imprisoned. His children were with relatives. He was trying to get himself back together now that he was out of jail, but he was having trouble finding work to make an honest living. However, so far, he had not resorted to stealing again.

After a bit, I stopped and pulled some food from my bag. Mom was right, it would come in handy. Joseph ate and ate. He was obviously famished. He said he had not had a decent meal for days.

We talked some more, and Joseph started telling me he was going to let God guide him in his life. He was going to let God show him the path, and no matter how hard it was, he was going to follow. He knew that a person straight out of prison would have a very difficult time in life, but he was committed to following the right path. He was also committed to getting his children back.

By this time the sun was getting hot, and we decided to take a short nap. I had trouble sleeping because I was so impressed with Joseph. First, he shared my Dad's name. Then, he spoke of his commitment on his journey in the same manner I must be committed to my own. I'm still dumbfounded. I'm certain God sent him.

When I woke up, Joseph had already repacked my belongings and hoisted them on his back. He said it was the least he could do. I continued back into town with him, and I decided to spend the night with Mom and Joshua. Of course, Joseph spent the night with us as well. More good food and good conversation. Tomorrow is another day.

Thank you, Father, for Joseph. He helped me understand my commitment to you. I must adopt the same courage, devotion, and dedication to my journey as Joseph. He was looking for his children. In a way, I'm also searching for children, the children of God.

Shalom.

24 The Next Day

Mom prepared another hearty breakfast for me and already replenished my supplies. She seemed happier for me to leave this time. I guess seeing me return with Joseph was a sign for her as well.

This time, I decided to try the opposite direction. I met a few travelers and we started talking. They told me about a young man named John, who was baptizing people in the Jordan River. As they continued to talk about him, I realized they were speaking of my cousin. When I mentioned this, they couldn't keep quiet. They went on and on about all the wonderful things they had heard about him. They told me I should go and get baptized. I said I would.

We soon came across a person heading the other way, who had a broken wheel on his cart. Being a carpenter, I knew how to fix it, but without the proper tools, I needed more than my two hands. Needless to say, everyone helped. We all had something to contribute. The owner of the cart had a few tools, but not all. Oddly enough, one of the people I was traveling with had just the right tool that was missing. Two others helped lift the cart, while a third found the right piece of wood for the repair.

After we were finished, the cart owner treated us to some delicious fruits he was carrying in his cart. When we finished, we walked on a little further until we came to a fork in the road. I planned to continue my travels with them, but they said the way to John was the other way. I hesitated but knew which path I had to choose.

Father, thank you for this most incredible day. I know this is the journey you intend for me; the travelers talking about John, the cart owner with the broken wheel, how everyone was able to share in the repair, and the fork in the road. I'm sure that you want me to visit John. Perhaps he needs me. Perhaps I'm to help him in his ministry. Whatever it is, I'm sure you will reveal it in due time. Until then, thank you for this wonderful life you have given me.

Shalom.

25 John

Today I arrived at the Jordan River to visit my cousin John. When I first approached, I watched him for a while. He was short, had a full brown beard and long hair, wore a cloak of camel's skin and moved with such peace and dignity. I had no doubt he was filled with the spirit of God. As I was watching, I heard my Father tell me to go to him and be baptized. First, I resisted, since it seemed awkward that God would ask me, his son, to be baptized by another. After a short discussion – I really didn't argue all that much – I went down to the river.

The odd thing was that the conversation was very real. It was as if the two of us were talking out loud, although no sounds pierced the silence. It was so vibrant to me that I felt certain other people could have heard us if anyone was around. It was an extremely powerful experience! Previously, all of the thoughts and conversations I received from my Father were clearly within my own head. This, however, was an external conversation.

Upon seeing me, John walked up to me, and we hugged. It was like we were long-lost brothers, not cousins. It was also as if we knew each other's hearts. I asked to be baptized. He objected saying he wasn't fit to untie my sandals and I should be the one to baptize him. Imagine that! This wonderful young man, obviously great in the eyes of God, feels he isn't fit to untie my sandals! In keeping with God's directive, I insisted he was more than worthy to baptize me. I assured him it was God's plan to do so, and although he remained somewhat skeptical, he followed my wishes.

Then the weirdest thing happened! The sky became dark, and clouds grew rapidly upon us. Then a single solitary dove flew down and landed on my shoulder. Almost at the same time, the clouds opened, and a ray of sun shone directly upon me. Suddenly, I heard God's voice again. This time it was very different. His voice was louder and deeper, the words pierced the air around me. "This is my beloved son with whom I am well pleased." I realized almost instantly I wasn't the only one who heard those words – almost all of the people there heard it.

"This is my beloved son." Wow! I've known I was his son for so long, but I needed some reassurance this was all real, and it never came. It's so odd I had to be comfortable enough within myself, overcome my doubts, and actually begin what God called me to do, before He gave me the reassurance I longed for. May all my doubts of my true identity subside forever.

Strangely, no one talked about what had happened. I think most were too afraid they alone had heard. I know how they feel – to think God chose them for something very special is a major concern. One might think that others don't believe they are worthy enough for God's call. They see themselves as simple, plain and ordinary, not someone God would want. I've wrestled with those same fears and doubts myself.

Shalom.

26 Desert

I felt my inner spirit directing me to take some time alone to fully digest and ponder the wonderful moments of my baptism and God's call. I wandered off alone to a spot in the desert far away from everyone. I have a strong direction from God to begin my ministry, but I have little knowledge of what that really involves. I've asked Him, and I've only gotten silence for a response. If I am truly His son, why can't I hear His voice daily? Why has it gone away? I've been here for several days without food or water. I have no desire to eat or drink. My body doesn't seem to be growing weak yet, but I'm sleepy a lot. When I'm not sleeping, I'm in prayer. I'm searching for direction, for answers, for something to make sense. My mind is a whirl. I really need to sort this out.

Shalom.

27 Dryness

Lately, I've been ineffective in prayer. I spend long hours thinking, but my mind seems dry. I feel as if the world is going by, but I'm not really on it, I'm just sort of watching. I try to focus, but there are so many things running through my head so rapidly, and I can't slow down the thoughts enough to catch onto any of them.

"What am I to do for Him? Where am I to go? What am I to say?" These questions plague me. So does "Who am I really? What does it mean to be the Son of Man? Or the Son of God?" Too many questions and they just seem to spin together in a giant whirl. My day consists of sitting and trying to listen, but the questions inside me are still raging. I hope I can slow down the questions enough to be able to really start answering them one at a time.

Shalom.

28 Fears

Oddly enough, even after the wonderful experience of my baptism, I have doubts of who I am. I don't seem different from other people. I look like them and talk like them. They don't seem to notice that I'm different. The few times my mother indicated I was God's son to someone else, they all ridiculed her. After all, how could God choose the lowly son of a carpenter to be His son?

Some days when I was growing up, there was hardly enough food to eat. Wouldn't God provide His son with everything a person could need? I know now that as God's son I need to fully experience the human condition. Having a life of luxury wouldn't be helpful, I wouldn't understand the everyday trials and tribulations of man. I need to experience an average, ordinary life. However, the ridicule of the past haunts me, those times I was belittled about being a single man, being a loner, that I'd never amount to anything, that I was nothing but a dreamer, that I thought I was so holy, but God would never chose a simple man like me for anything.

Today, it isn't a doubt about who I am, but a doubt as to how anyone would believe in me. How can I tell someone who I am, and not have him think I am insane? How will I know to whom to reveal myself? And how do I ever prove who I am? Wouldn't God make His own son stand out in some way to let people know who he is? What can I say to get people to listen? I'm afraid to be God's Son.

Shalom.

29 Struggle with Inner Spirit

My fears have led to doubts again. My human desires want to push me into things that are not of God. I know several things, and I know them solidly in my heart. I'm an average person. Just like anyone else in the world. This is exactly who God created me to be. The one and only difference is that I am able to comprehend God's presence within me at a different level. God is somehow present within my being, as if we are one.

I still struggle with things that are human when my inner spirit isn't aligned completely with God. I have two forces within me: a human force, which always wants to be in control and the God part, which doesn't seem to need anything. When I allow the human part to take over, I have doubts, fears, and needs. When I allow the God part to take over, which always seems ready and able to do so, I find myself full of peace. Now that I can understand some of the struggles raging within me, I will be able to better focus on them. I already feel as if God is more in control and I have little to worry about.

Shalom.

30 Hunger

Today I felt the urge to eat. I guess it should be expected since I've been out here for a few weeks. In fact, the urge to eat was overwhelming, and, let me say, weird. Perhaps the lack of food and water has made me hallucinate. I felt the earth itself was taunting me to eat. The ache in my stomach was strong, and I was tempted to have God create bread for me. Why shouldn't He? After all, He gave manna to the Israelites when passing from Egypt. Am I not at least as important?

Somehow, in all the temptation, the answer came to me, "No! I don't need bread to live." I even remembered the passage from the Scriptures, "One doesn't live by bread alone, but by every word that comes from the mouth of God."* I found renewed strength in this message and my hunger diminished immediately.

Shalom.

*Dt 8:3 NIV.

31 Temple

I had a strange experience today. I was taking a walk and came to a place where a holy city appeared, and I found myself standing on the parapet of a temple. It was the most beautiful temple I've ever seen. I thought perhaps it was King David's temple. I felt a similar taunting as before. The temple seemed to be beckoning me to jump and rely on God to carry me down safely. A psalm came to me that God would command his angels to support me with their hands.* I should jump down and take my rightful place in this magnificent temple. I could be a king! I could teach God's people His ways. But as I stood there, I realized I'm not here for personal glory, only to bring about a change of heart in God's people. Allowing myself to be tempted by power is simply not what God has asked of me.

Don't misunderstand. The human part of me wants the power as well as the glory. A part of me wants everyone to praise and worship me. I'm God's Son. I'm special. Glory and honor be mine. However, this would diminish what I've been sent to do. As attractive as power and glory are, I know it isn't the right path; it's just the human part trying to be noticed. I couldn't put God to the test of saving me from the fall. While I'm sure He would, it isn't for me to test Him, only to follow Him. Besides, the real test isn't whether He would save me, but whether or not I could withstand the human desires to become great in the eyes of man.

Shalom.

*Ps 91:11-12.

32 Kingdom

Once again, I've struggled with my need for personal fulfillment in the eyes of man. Today I was led to a very high mountain and saw the magnificence of all the kingdoms of the world. It became obvious I could choose worldly wealth and power over all the kingdoms of the world. All I have to do is ask my Father to be the ruler of the world and it shall be. I could be the ruler of all people everywhere. King of Kings. After all, is that not what the Son of God should be? A ruler extraordinaire? A benevolent ruler, like the best of David, Solomon and Saul rolled into one? I would provide everyone with enough food and wealth. I would be fair and honest and wouldn't need to tax them outrageously. No one would lose sons to battle. Wouldn't that be what the Son of God is all about?

Part of me feels God is calling me to be a leader. However, as much as I would like to be a great king for all peoples, and it would seem in keeping with the Son of God, I don't believe God is calling me to be a king in the sense of an earthly ruler. I remembered another Scripture passage – "Fear the Lord your God, serve him only and take your oaths in his name."*

No, I won't succumb to worshipping any false God, not power or wealth. I shall serve only the Lord, my God, and I shall worship and serve Him alone.

Shalom.

*Dt 6:13 NIV

33 Desert Last

After several weeks of being alone here in the desert, I've finally reached resolve with my future. After the past few days of temptations, I felt a certain comfort last night as my hunger and thirst vanished, and my physical strength was restored. It seemed God sent His angels to comfort and minister to me.

I know God is calling me to start my ministry to change the world today. I know I have to teach the people wherever I go about God. Not the God preached by the Pharisees and Sadducees since they have seriously distorted the truth of His ways. They have gotten caught up with the law, not the true spirit of love. I'll teach people about the God I know.

I'm not sure exactly where the journey will lead. I see a road of pain for me, but the future belongs to my Father. I have to set the stone rolling down the hill. It will continue to gather speed long after I leave this earthly existence. The things I preach and the truths I realize about my Father will someday fill the hearts of people from the ends of the world, people I couldn't possibly reach, even if I traveled as far as I could travel each day.

I feel at peace. God will give me the right people to hear my message and the right people to carry it through. I know part of my mission is to heal. God will use this as a tool for the people to know my true identity. I'm confident He will provide the things I need to walk the path He has given me. Yes, I'm ready.

I must go now. "Land of Zebulun and land of Naphtali, but in the future, he will honor Galilee of the nations, by the Way of the Sea beyond the Jordan."* This verse keeps repeating in my head. I think God is calling me to Galilee. I will go there to continue the mission of my cousin. I will let all know to rejoice, for the Kingdom of God is at hand.

Shalom.

*Isaiah 9:1 NIV.

34 Return to John

I returned to visit my cousin John yesterday. I was talking with him for quite a while, so I decided to spend the night. Today two of his friends, Andrew and Zebedee, came by and John introduced me as the Lamb of God. They fell to their knees. It turns out these two men were also there a few weeks ago when I was baptized, and they saw the clouds and heard God speak. John and I looked at each other and insisted they not bow. It took us a while, but they both finally got up. They called me Rabbi. Imagine that! They considered me a teacher of God!

A few weeks ago, no one wanted to ask me about what happened. Today, these two men kept talking about it. Andrew was so impressed with me that he went to get his brother Simon. After taking one look at me, Simon knelt down and called me "Messiah." He just knelt there with his head almost buried in the ground, weeping. After he finally got up, the five of us talked almost all night. They finally got tired, as did I. However, I was unable to rest, so I decided to write.

Father, thank you for the events of these past few weeks. John is an incredible servant. I'm thankful for his presence in my life and his dedication to you and his ministry. I'm also thankful for Andrew, Zebedee and Simon. They have helped me realize I am indeed your Son, and my time to start my mission is upon me. Thank you, Father, for all you've done for me. May I humbly accept your call.

Amen.

35 Journey to Galilee

I headed off to Galilee in the morning. Andrew, Zebedee and Simon wanted me to stay. I told them to go home and I would return for them. They were reluctant, but knew it was the best thing for them to do.

On my way to Galilee, I found another young man I recognized from my baptism. He looked at me funny and was afraid to approach. I stopped and motioned for him to follow me. He wasn't too sure, so I had to repeat my offer. I waited until he came along. His name was Philip, and he was from Bethsaida, the same place as Andrew, Simon and Zebedee. While we were walking and talking about life and God and scriptures, Philip saw a friend of his. When I looked at his friend and motioned for him to join us, he ran off. Philip looked at me and shook his head, then ran off after him.

In a short while, Philip returned with his friend, Nathaniel. I immediately knew Nathaniel was a true believer because I saw no duplicity in his eyes, which were warm and inviting. I could see he had a pure heart, and he was honest, straightforward, sincere, and would always seek and accept the truth whenever he encountered it. When I told him all this, Nathaniel asked me how I knew him. I told him I had seen him under the fig tree the day of my baptism. I also told him I knew he heard the words God spoke; I could see it in his eyes.

Nathaniel dropped to his knees and called me Rabbi. He said I was indeed the Son of God and the King of Israel. I couldn't believe he was so ready to believe in me. I told him he would see even greater things if he stayed with me. It took Philip and I most of the afternoon to calm Nathaniel. He was so overwhelmed at God's presence in his life. He kept saying over and over that he was unworthy because he was a sinner.

It was getting late, so Philip started to make camp. He made a fire and went off to find some water. When he returned, Nathaniel had finally calmed down. They gave each other a long hug. I started preparing dinner. We didn't have much, but I was able to make a pretty tasty stew with the vegetables we had which we ate with some bread and wine. When Nathaniel saw me cooking, he got upset again and said I shouldn't be serving him. Philip and I simply shook our heads. Nathaniel finally came and shared dinner with us. They were both impressed I was such a good cook. After dinner I was very tired and went off to pray and rest. Nathaniel tried to follow me, but Philip held him back.

Father, you have sent me such wonderful people to share with me. They also tell me I'm the Messiah, the Anointed. They help me remove any lingering doubts I have. They help me recognize my time is indeed upon me. I still don't know what I need to do or where I will go. But I can tell I'm ready. Help me, Father, to discern the direction you wish for me to go and to have the strength and courage to follow.

Amen.

36 Visit with Mom

We arrived in Cana today for a wedding. I felt like I was riding on clouds these past few days because my connection with my Father was incredible with a lot of inner growth and reflection. I was so glad to see my mother. She seemed equally glad to see me. Joshua was doing a fine job with the carpentry shop. It seems he listened to some of my suggestions and was much better with the business side. I haven't been gone long, but it's comforting to know Mom will be taken care of.

Mom made us a wonderful dinner at our cousin's home. We all ate until we could eat no more. We sat and talked well into the evening hours. One by one, everyone went to bed. I decided to write a little.

Thank you, Father, for this day. I can feel your love welling up inside me. I find myself full of energy. The doubts I harbored about who I am have been quieted, at least for today. I find myself as if I'm in a story and I'm the lead actor. The cast is set, and the plot is already determined, so all I have to do is follow it. I'm still unsure of the direction, but I know I will rise to the challenge.

Shalom.

37 Family Wedding

Today I accompanied Mom to a family wedding. When we finally arrived, we were so glad to see some of our relatives. It seems like we never have enough time to visit all the family members we have. We are scattered throughout several villages. Families were so much closer in past times. Now we have to work so hard just to feed and clothe ourselves that we don't have time to visit much.

After the ceremony, we were celebrating with the newlyweds. Soon, I discovered all the wine was gone. Can you imagine that? All the barrels were dry, and people were still there, just getting started. Mom was nearby when the waiters were checking the vats, and she told them I would take care of it.

I was shocked at first. Here I am, procrastinating about preparing myself for a life-changing journey, and my mother wants me to help with empty wine barrels. She smiled and said, "Your time has come." I was simply amazed, not only by the awesome power of God, but also with Mom. She has not spoken to me in a while about my sonship. I almost thought she had forgotten. In fact, this is part of the reason I came to doubt so much. And now I find out she not only didn't forget, but she confirmed the time is now.

I asked Mom to join me in prayer. I raised my arms to God and prayed that the vats, now filled with water, would become wine; not just any wine, but a well-fermented sweet wine with a robust flavor – after all, this was family. They deserve the best.

A few of the waiters looked at me incredulously, as if to suggest I was some sort of a crazy person. But their look of doubt changed to a look of awe when I asked them to draw from one of the vats and they saw a rich red-purple liquid flow from the first vat. When it was tasted, the waiter was in shock.

Stories like this are few and far between in the Holy Scriptures, but here a few had witnessed it with their own eyes. Not much was said, but it didn't go unnoticed. Mom just smiled, as if to say she was pleased with me. It was also a smile of "I told you so." Mothers. Mine is a true jewel. The finest cut gemstone of all times. It's no wonder God picked her and Dad to raise me.

What an incredible feeling! I was so unsure of myself, but with Mom's support I was able to allow myself to fully connect with my Father. I can't believe I was able to turn water into wine! It seems such an odd choice for what I hope will be the first of many miracles. I am simply beside myself with the events of today.

Thank you, Father, for my earthly parents. I sometimes wonder if I can serve you as well as they have. I know Mom is right and my time has come, but I still don't exactly know what it is you want me to do. I really need some time to think and sort things out. But, let me not forget to thank you for the incredible miracle you worked through me today.

Shalom.

38 Time with Family

I spent some time with family and friends after the wedding. It felt great to simply relax and enjoy each other's company. It was also nice to have some time with Mom. I decided to head to Jerusalem this year to celebrate Passover there. Mom assured me she was well provided for and insisted I follow my heart. She knows what I need to do. Sometimes I think she is more in tune with my Father than I am.

I'm feeling more tired than I realized, so this will be a short entry. Father, please be with my mother and my family. Finally, thank you for this time with my family, and thank you for working that miracle through me. Making water into wine! Your power never ceases to amaze me.

Shalom.

39 On the Road

I have travelled about halfway to Jerusalem. Along the way, I stopped and preached to anyone who would listen. I really enjoy preaching and sharing my love and understanding of my Father with others. Most people listen intently and seem almost mesmerized by my teaching. I know I look at things a little differently from some of the other preachers, and people seem hungry for my words.

While walking and in the evening before sleep, I spend a lot of time being at one with my Father, Abba. I'm finding it easier and easier to talk with Him, but I can't quite understand what He is calling me to do. He assures me I'm doing everything He desires right now, and I should not concern myself with anything else.

It seems I spend most time each day walking. Yes, I preach some, but this doesn't seem to be much. I talk a lot with the men who are following me, sharing my love and understanding of my Father even more. But I fail to understand how this will bring about any changes in the world. My cousin John baptizes a lot of people. Me? I just walk and talk.

Abba, help me understand what you call me to do. Help me understand the plan. Help me understand how my preaching and teaching will accomplish anything. Help me find relief for my sore feet and tired body. Help me discern what you are asking of me.

Amen.

40 Money Changers

I finally arrived in Jerusalem today. I was a bit tired and was looking forward to a nice, peaceful day of prayer after preaching and travelling for so long. I find preaching drains me at times and travelling certainly does.

I went to the temple area, which was littered with money-changers and people selling animals. It was horrible. The whole scene was a defilement to God and worship. First, they basically blocked me from getting into the temple. They kept hollering at me and trying to force the sale of the animals so I would have a suitable sacrifice. One of them even grabbed me. The prices were ridiculous, and the money-changers were charging extremely high rates.

I lost my temper. I couldn't handle it anymore. I turned over table after table and admonished them. Not my best example of a loving God, I dare say. But I'm generally not at my best when I'm tired. I told the people that if they destroy this temple, I will raise it up in three days. I have NO idea why I said that. I recognized these words came from my Father, but I have no idea what He meant by them.

Father, help me be a positive reflection of you as I continue with my ministry. Thank you for helping me recognize my weaker moments, when my human side shows through more. Thank you for the response of many people who cheered my actions because they, too, were upset with the vendors and money-changers. I ask you to help me find adequate time to rest when my body tires. And please let me know what you meant with your comment about raising the temple in three days.

Shalom

41 Teachings

I've been extremely pleased that so many people are listening to me, partly because the story of my wonderful wine has spread quickly along with the fact some men are following me. I'm more concerned with what God is telling me to proclaim to His people than how He gets their attention.

First, like John, I tell people to repent because the Kingdom of Heaven is at hand. People need to be reborn in His spirit. So many of them are devout Jews, but they lack any understanding of their inner spirit. So many people see God as condemning, demanding us to follow all sorts of rules as prescribed in the Torah. But they miss the point. The point is these rules need to be written on our hearts. They are given as a guide to learn and grow in the Spirit. If anyone can see this truth, they walk in the light instead of darkness.

A surprising thing happened at the temple during Passover. One of the Pharisees named Nicodemus stopped to see me. He heard what I had said and was very intrigued by it. We talked quite a while and he listened intently. What a wonderful soul., he was so open and soaked up all I had to say.

God, I know the things you are teaching through me are new and different and exciting, yet very confusing to most. Please help me be more effective in expressing these truths and help open the ears and hearts of all who listen.

Shalom.

42 First Healing

Today, as I was preaching about forgiveness and healing, a young mother brought me her daughter. The girl was blind. I looked at this beautiful child, who had never seen the light of day. My heart was wrenched, and I started to cry. Then I remembered that God called me to heal. I prayed to God if it was His will for this child to see, let it be done.

As my tears fell on the child, she started crying, too. Her mom took her away and was a little upset with me because she came for help, and all I did was upset her daughter. The child quickly quieted down and fell asleep.

I was a little disturbed, and frankly, I lost contact with my Father for the rest of my teaching. I couldn't focus and wasn't able to let the words flow like before. I had to stop for a bit to talk to God by myself. All I could hear him say was, "Don't doubt me, my son. I'm always with you."

Shortly thereafter, the young mother shrieked in apparent delight. Her daughter woke up and her eyes were following a fly dancing around her face. The girl was moving her hands and laughing. She could see! Someone started yelling, "It was Jesus. It was Jesus. He is a true prophet of God." Pandemonium erupted. I remembered God's words. "Don't doubt me, my Son. I'm always with you."

I now have the power to heal. Praise God.

Shalom.

43 Preaching in Judea

I was preaching in Judea while some of my followers baptized people in the manner of my cousin John, until I felt that God was directing me to return to Galilee. Today I stopped for a drink at Jacob's well while my followers went to replenish our food supplies. There was a Samaritan woman there. I implored her to give me a drink. She admonished me a bit for asking her, a Samaritan woman, for a drink because normally Jews and Samaritans don't even speak to, let alone help, each other. I told her if she knew who I was, she would have begged me for living water. Of course, she had no idea what I was talking about. I pointed out if we drink of the water in the well, we will in no time be thirsty again, but if people drink the water I have, they will have a spring of water that leads to eternal life.

I heard God telling me things about the woman that I would have no way of knowing. I was amazed. God pointed out she wasn't married currently but has had five husbands. And, imagine this, the man she was living with now wasn't even one of them. When I told her what I had discerned, she called me a prophet. For me, it was yet more confirmation of who I am. Every time I start to doubt who I am, God manages to help me overcome my doubts.

She told me she heard our Messiah was coming. I was so taken up in the discussion, I told her it was me. I've never really spoken about being God's son to strangers. I haven't even discussed it much with people who heard God say it at my baptism. But this woman was so incredibly special. We had a connection. And I know God will somehow use her to further His plan.

She apparently told her village about me because they came and urged me to stay with them, so I accepted. I enjoy speaking about my Father to people who listen, and I know the message isn't just for my fellow Jews.

Father, it felt great to reveal my true self to someone today. And a Samaritan woman of all people! I know you call all people to you, not just my fellow Jews. Thank you for affirming my true identity yet again. More importantly, thank you for confirming you are God of all, and my message is for anyone who will listen.

Shalom.

44 Nazareth

We stopped in Nazareth today to visit some of my old friends and family. When I entered the synagogue, I was given the book of Isaiah to read. My Father sure has a sense of humor since it opened to the passage that reads, "The Spirit of the Sovereign Lord is upon me, because the Lord has anointed me to proclaim good news to the poor. He has sent me to bind up the brokenhearted, to proclaim freedom for the captives and release from darkness for the prisoners, to proclaim the year of the Lord's favor."* I'm so concerned with telling people who I am even though God keeps telling me to shout it to everyone.

I told them the Scripture verse was fulfilled. I went on to tell them of my understanding of God. First, they seemed to marvel at my words. Then a few of the scribes started to taunt me, pointing out I was Joseph's son, a lowly carpenter. They somehow managed to get the people to forget my words and preaching. I was a bit upset at this turn of events and told them no prophet is accepted in his own country. Things digressed from there. Basically, they ran me out of town, my own home town. I feel like I have no place to call home anymore.

Father, I don't understand. I was certain when the book opened to the passage in Isaiah you wanted me to proclaim who I am. However, when I did, they rejected me. This is exactly why I don't want to announce who I am to anyone. The Samaritans believed me and welcomed me. My own hometown rejected me and threw me out. I thought I would use Nazareth as headquarters for my ministry, but obviously, this is not a good plan. To these people, I am, and always will be, a simple carpenter. Father, I pray you help open their eyes and their hearts. Amen.

* Isaiah 61:1, 2a NIV

45 Cana

We left Nazareth pretty abruptly and journeyed to Cana, which isn't far away. The people here remembered the wine at the wedding and were quite gracious. They asked me if I was the Messiah. I told them I was unable to testify about myself since it would lack authenticity. However, there was at least one other person, my cousin John, who testified about me and his testimony was authentic. John is like a lamp that burns to give light to so many people.

I told them the very things I've done such as healing and preaching to prove that God had sent me. Most of them have never heard His voice nor seen His form. They study the Scriptures, but don't recognize that they testify about me. I told them I wasn't seeking glory, but rather desired them to find the true love of God in their hearts.

I was in the middle of preaching when a royal official interrupted me and begged me to go with him and heal his son who was close to death. I know God has given me the gift of healing, but I truly didn't want to leave my preaching. The official was on his knees, begging for his son. I prayed, and God assured me He would heal this man's son without the necessity of me actually being physically present with him. I was a bit unsure of this and asked my Father again. He asked me why I was full of doubt again. So, I helped the man rise and told him to go back home because his son would live.

What a remarkable day. Father, you are simply amazing! Your ability to find ways to humble my spirit and teach me is astounding. Sometimes I get so full of myself that I try to push your message too hard. You help me understand your people need to be guided and led, not pushed and pulled.

Thank you for your loving guidance. I would say I will never doubt again, however, I suspect my humanity isn't yet through with me.

Shalom.

46 On the Road to Galilee

I've been on the road for a long time and haven't written in a while. For the most part I've performed healing and preached a lot about the Father I've grown to know and love. I've spent some time in Capernaum, where I was asked to preach most Sabbaths.

I encountered the strangest thing today. I came upon the Sea of Galilee and I saw some men fishing. I was famished, so I implored them to stop and kindly share some of their catch. They had little, but seeing how weak and tired I was, they stopped and lit a fire and cooked some fish.

As we dined, we started talking. I simply spoke to them about the joy I felt with God. I told them how John baptized me. They had heard of him, and they had been planning to go to be baptized before they heard of his arrest. I understand he is imprisoned for his dedication to baptizing people in the name of God, and the Jewish leaders are not happy about this. I explained to them the wonderful job he was doing for God. I told them to repent, for the kingdom of God was near. Oddly enough, they both said they believed it was.

I talked for hours about the God I saw and the beauty I realized all around me. I had so much to share that I was rambling on and on. They, however, were enraptured by my talk. I say it was my talk, but it really wasn't. It was again as if someone from outside of me was talking, and I just opened my mouth to let all these words pour out – words about God's love, forgiveness, fears, doubts, and inner peace. I'm still startled when all these phenomenal thoughts fly out of me, putting into words things I know to be true, but couldn't have verbalized nearly so well.

They listened well into darkness. Then they decided to rest, for they had another long day tomorrow. I was still not tired, so I decided to write. Thank you, Father, for the words you have given me to speak. I felt your spirit fill me and flow through me. I know these men heard and understood. The words you gave me were powerful and easy to understand. I was simply the voice and the human body, but you were the one that was really speaking. I'm beginning to understand your ways more each day.

Amen.

47 Simon and Andrew

Early yesterday morning I spotted some old friends, Simon and his brother Andrew, fishing. We started talking while a small crowd surrounded me, eager to hear my words. Simon suggested he take me out in his boat so I could preach from there. After preaching a while, Simon mentioned he had work to do since he had not caught a single fish the whole night. I directed him to a spot out further and asked him to lower his nets. He objected first, but finally gave in and lowered them. When they pulled the nets up, they were loaded with so many fish they had to have Andrew's boat come help with the haul.

After coming ashore, I invited them both to join me in my preaching. They eagerly left their nets and agreed to follow me. They seemed excited about my ministry. They said they had been preparing themselves for my return since they knew I would be around for them.

In the evening, we rested and caught up with each other's lives. It turned out that Simon was also known as Peter since that was his grandfather's name. I heard he actually preferred Peter, so I told him I would call him Peter from now on.

The next day, we came upon Zebedee and two of his sons. Peter and Andrew told me they knew James and John were also truly eager to learn about God. Both had a yearning to become rabbis but were unable to do so because the laws prevented it.

Peter hollered out to them as they were fishing in their boat while their father mended nets. I asked them to come and join us in our ministry. John dove from the boat and swam to us. James and his father hauled in the net and rowed to shore. Zebedee didn't argue but simply smiled as if he knew this was coming. He was so proud to have his boys share in the ministry of God. He would have been proud to have a rabbi for a son, but I think the prospect of ministering a new and fresh concept was even more to his liking.

Zebedee was truly thrilled the four of them were going to take up preaching with me. He would have liked to join us himself, but his age and family concerns kept him. He blessed his sons and their friends. I asked him to bless me too. He looked surprised I would ask such a thing, but he smiled and blessed me. He is truly a man of God.

Shalom.

48 Preaching in Galilee

It has been a few days since Peter, Andrew, James and John joined me. My followers and I are received well everywhere we go. It seems they know the townspeople around, and they know which synagogues we should attend. The people seem so hungry for the word of God. It seems hundreds of people are coming to hear me speak. Time after time, I free my head of my thoughts and let my Father's message flow through me. Sometimes I find myself lost in a sea of words.

A woman told me I really touched her when I said I was incredibly lonely even though I have a number of people around because she found herself in the same situation. I told her that I didn't say anything of the sort. What I said was I remember being lonely growing up. But then we both just looked at each other and laughed. Somehow, she heard exactly what she needed to hear.

One Sabbath I encountered a man possessed by a demon while I was preaching. The man acknowledged he knew I was the Holy One. I was a bit startled an impure spirit recognized me when so many others can't. I suspect spirits are more in touch with other spirits then people are. When I instructed the spirit to leave the man, the man first shook violently, then soon returned to normal. Now I can add casting out demons from the possessed to my growing list of miracles and accomplishments. At times like these I find myself in total awe of my Father, who has so graciously given me so much. It is energizing and almost makes me tremble to think how much He has given me.

I'm so blessed my Father has sent some wonderful men to share my ministry. Actually, it isn't just men. Occasionally, I have women with me as well, although they tend to come and go more. My followers help with the necessities of life. I don't have to worry about finding food or cooking. They find ways to help people in the villages and are rewarded with food and sometimes a place to stay. We are all caught up in a giant whirl. I can't believe how easy it is for people to comprehend the things I thought would be so difficult. There is just such excitement everywhere we go. It's truly wonderful.

Shalom.

49 Energy

I've never had so much energy in my life. None of us have. We are up at dawn, and we are on the go all day. The really odd thing is we never seem to tire. No matter what comes up, we always seem to have the time and energy for it. The energy seems to be contagious. All who come, even those who are skeptical, seem to walk away with a little sparkle in their eye or lightness in their feet.

I think the guys work harder than I do. I do very little work, no hunting or fishing or cooking. They just tell me to preach and heal and rest if I get a few minutes.

I find my connection to God growing in leaps and bounds, as is theirs. It's too awesome a feeling to explain, as I fear words are inadequate. I can't wait to get up and get on my way each day. It's truly wonderful. Praise God.

Shalom.

50 Peter's Mother-In-Law

Today we stopped at the village of Peter's wife on our way to Jerusalem. He has not been to see his wife's family for a while. We thought we were going to have an easy, relaxing homecoming, but when we arrived, his wife's mother was in bed with a fever. She wasn't deathly sick, but she was upset she was unable to entertain us and enjoy our company.

I went in to see her and took her hand in mine. The touch of her hand was warm, but not feverish. I felt energy from her as I never have before, it was almost as if we were kindred spirits. Our eyes met, and we simply smiled and held hands for a few short minutes. She then looked at me lovingly, as if she knew my inner soul, as if she were my own mother. What a wonderful loving spirit she is. Then she rose and said she was feeling better.

She ended up tending to us that day. All of us. We dined and talked and shared some of the most wonderful stories. We laughed a lot. I can't remember when I felt so much at home and comfortable in a place not my own home. We will stay a few days. She seems to have the ability to recharge my inner spirit. What a wonderful, caring soul. Peter is so lucky. But I don't think I need to tell him that.

Shalom.

51 Healing the Leper

Today was such an exciting day for me. I felt as if I had all the power in the world as the Son of God I am. Some days the energy seems to be a little less than others. Today, it was as strong as ever.

A large crowd followed me as I walked. We came down from a mountain into a valley. As we did, a leper approached. I knew this man was sincere and good the instant I saw him. It was such a touching moment. He stretched out his hand to me. The crowd gave a collective gasp when they saw I was brave enough to touch a leper. They were undoubtedly worried I would become infected myself.

No sooner had I touched him than he was healed. The sores seemed to heal in fast motion. He started to dance around and call me Messiah, and he praised me. I told him to give all praise to God and God alone. He seemed so overwhelmed. I instructed him to go show himself to the priests so he could be judged clean and re-enter his community.

However, I could sense his priest would be reluctant to hear of this miraculous cure of mine. He wouldn't want to hear this man say how I, Jesus bar Joseph, had performed this healing act. Therefore, I instructed him to tell no one. I know, however, that he won't be able to keep it a secret. He is going to shout it out to everyone and anyone who would listen. They may think he has gone mad. Poor fellow. He may only substitute one curse for another. Well, it's in God's hands now. I guess it always was, anyway.

I'm really looking forward to a good night's sleep.

Shalom

52 Bethesda

We have been in Jerusalem for a few days. I've been blessed with the ability to teach in a few of the synagogues here. I've healed some and drove out a few more demonic spirits from others. But mostly I've spent my days celebrating the feast and preaching with my followers. Our enthusiasm seems to be contagious.

Today we went to Bethesda, a pool that is known to have healing powers. However, the healing is generally limited to only one person whenever the waters are stirred. When I arrived, I encountered a vast number of people in need of healing, some blind, some deaf, some lame and some completely paralyzed. Most had friends or family with them to help them get to the pool.

I saw an older man who was unable to walk. He was just lying there. It turned out he had been an invalid for almost forty years. He had been at the pool for over a year for healing, totally alone. While most of the others were very cordial and helped him with food and drink, they were all too busy helping themselves or their own loved ones, so no one helped him get down to the water. But this man was in wonderful spirits and smiled a lot. He harbored no animosity or bitterness because no one helped him get to the pool, and he maintained hope that he would be healed.

My inner soul was incredibly touched by his story. First, to imagine being an invalid for longer than I've been alive. Then to finally get to a place for healing, but after a year, find no one to help. And all this time maintain a zest for living with no bitterness or anger. I think I have a lot to learn.

I told him to get up, pick up his mat and walk. The results were immediate. I helped the man up to his feet for the first time in about forty years. His legs were unsteady, but he was able to reach down and pick up his mat. While holding onto me, he put one foot in front of the other. After a few steps, he released my arm. Some of my followers were there to help, but he refused, saying he wanted to walk on his own. He was slow, but he walked. I went up and gave him a big hug. I told him he gave me more that day than I could possibly have given him. He said he wasn't sure what he gave me, but he was delighted with his share of the bargain. He smiled and said thank you.

Father, again and again you use people to help me learn and grow. I've learned a lot from this man about determination and maintaining a positive outlook to life despite the most trying of circumstances. I hope this will give me strength when I need it most. I thank you so much for him.

Shalom.

53 Time to Write

We have taken our time on our journey from Jerusalem. I've been so busy with healing and preaching I haven't had any time to write. Well, that isn't entirely true because God always provides me with time for everything. The truth is, I haven't used any of the time I have to write. All my days are exciting. I meet a lot of people and heal them or preach to them. I spend time talking to my followers. We enjoy each other's company, and our lives are full and vibrant.

Father, thank you for each and every person you have sent me, the ones who come to listen, the ones who come for healing, but most importantly, the ones who have chosen to share their lives with me. Thank you for my growth in trying to balance my inner being as both the Son of Man and the Son of God. Thank you for this wonderful life and the truly incredible people you have created.

Shalom.

54 Visiting Mom

This past week we visited Nazareth on our way back from Jerusalem. We spent a few days there, and I introduced my followers to my family. We gathered and talked. Some of my relatives demonstrated their various talents, more like showed off, if you know what I mean. One cousin was a novice bard and he told a few humorous stories. Another cousin, being a fairly good acrobat, performed several stunts and flips. The best was when my aunt and her daughter sang some of my favorite Jewish hymns.

We all had a wonderful visit. Mom was Mom to everyone. She took a special liking to John, but I knew she would. She was impressed with the story of how Peter and Andrew joined me. She told me privately she could see why God chose each and every one of them. She said she could see their goodness shining through their faults. She was amazed at their loyalty and our camaraderie.

Shalom.

55 Call of Matthew

This past week I've been healing people and preaching as we returned to Capernaum. As we entered the town, we passed the place of customs. One of the local tax collectors, Matthew by name, was there. I knew Matthew. He struggled with his job. It used to be his father's, and he dutifully assumed the position when his father passed away. He was only thirteen then, and he had to grow up fast. The job paid well, and his family needed the money because he had seven siblings to care for.

Matthew and I talked about becoming rabbis when we were young. It was a dream that would not come true for either of us. However, he would offer his thoughts on the Scriptures whenever he could. Somehow this led to him being called Levi even though he wasn't from the house of Levi. Instead of letting the name bother him, Matthew embraced it.

I know Matthew hates his job. Everyone despises the tax collector. With just cause, too, because the tax system is unfair and basically amounts to little more than stealing. But Matthew has a family to take care of. He was as kind and fair as he could be, but still everyone taunted him. But I knew that his heart was good.

As we passed, I looked up and invited him to come with us. Our eyes met for a brief time. With tears in his eyes, he abandoned his post, and with that, he freed himself of the burdens. His next oldest brother would now assume his office.

We dined at his home that evening. Many of his friends, some tax collectors and other "sinners" came. I say "sinners" because it always amazes me how we call someone who does the same things we do a "sinner," but we can always justify our own actions.

The Pharisees came since they heard Matthew joined me. They mingled among my followers and kept trying to trick them into changing their mind. They tried to diminish me and my closeness with God because I was socializing with, and even accepting, known sinners as my own. Once again, I found the anger building up inside me. It seems some people know how to trigger the frustration and anger within me.

These Pharisees, these so-called "men of God," had rejected me before. Now they went out of their way to reject me again. But God's spirit filled me before I was able to utter a word of rebuke. I simply said it was the sick who need a physician the most, those who were already well needed none. I was here to help the sinners, not the righteous. They had nothing to say in return and left quietly. Again, their plans to discredit me were turned away.

I'm so thankful my loving Father was there for me when I was in my greatest need today. I'm also thankful Matthew found an opportunity to serve God.

Shalom.

56 Healing the Paralytic

There is a man I met in my hometown of Nazareth, a paralytic whom I've known since I was young. Apparently, he and his family moved to Capernaum. The last time I saw him, he was still able to hobble around with a cane. It was obvious his condition had worsened and would soon take his life. Some of his family and friends brought him to me on a stretcher. I could see his relatives expected no miracle, they just wanted him to see me one last time. As the house I was in was crowded, his family somehow managed to get to the roof and lower him down on a stretcher. What a crazy entrance, and a certain way to ensure I saw him.

We talked for a while alone, and he revealed some of the things he had done in his life, a confession of sorts of the things he had done wrong. Most were not too terrible, but they obviously troubled him greatly as he was facing his death. I felt such compassion for this man. He said he told me these things because he knew I was close to God. He said he knew that since he first met me. I told him of the Father I knew in heaven and how He was a loving and caring being who forgives all sins, no matter how significant or how small. I told him to have courage, because through his faith, his transgressions were forgiven.

He squeezed my hand with the most tender and compassionate grip I had ever known, smiled at me and said, "Thank you, my friend." He looked as if he had found a peace that can only be found through oneness with God.

By this time, a few of the scribes and Pharisees had gathered around, and they started sneering at me and accusing me of blasphemy because I dared to forgive sins. I could sense their indignation and the root cause of it. Jealousy. They no doubt had heard of my healing, which is why they were there. I actually recognized some of them from when we were growing up. They were able to become scribes, while I was a mere carpenter. And now, I became more of a known preacher and spiritual leader than they could imagine.

If they truly knew God, they wouldn't question the forgiveness of sins. I merely stated what I know to be true of God. He will forgive anyone's transgressions. But instead of jumping in with my bitterness and sarcastic remarks, as I would have done in the past, the spirit of my loving Father seized my very being. I found kind and caring words and a way to show them their error without bragging or acting superior. I simply asked them, "What is harder, to say 'Your sins are forgiven' or to say, 'Pick up your stretcher, rise and walk'?"

I turned to my friend and said, "Beloved Jason, if it is your desire to live, rise now, pick up your stretcher and go home." Again, a look of peace overwhelmed him. He tried to rise. Some of the people gave him a hand, and he was able to stand for the first time in several months. He stood for a while looking at his knees and feet. Then slowly, he moved one leg a little forward. Two of his friends grabbed his arms to help steady him. They were so amazed and ecstatic. Another friend picked up his stretcher.

After a few steps, he turned and nodded. A simple nod, but it said so much. I watched as he turned and slowly started again. You could see his strength growing with each step. He stood straighter and increased the size of his steps. I watched and said under my breath, "Go in peace, my friend."

Many others had gathered to see this. They all knew Jason had been bedridden for months and was surely on his deathbed. As he went further into town, all the townsfolk came to see this man walking home. They recognized me and joined in with Jason's family and friends to sing praises to God for the cure.

I was so relieved that people gave credit to the true source of the miracle – to God, my Father, and not me. I'm nothing without my Father. All my ability to heal comes from allowing myself to be God's channel. Too many try to deify me. It was refreshing not to have to deal with that today. Praise God.

Shalom.

57 Healing

We have started to get into a system. I preach for a bit in the morning. Then we have a general healing service. I'm amazed at the people who are coming. People have come from all over Judea, from Jerusalem, and even from beyond the Jordan. I've healed people of all sorts of afflictions, from deafness to blindness, leprosy, paralytics, headaches, and various pains and diseases. I've also healed people who were mentally ill, and people possessed by demons. It seems almost all who come are in some need of healing. Fortunately, many of them are healed at once. The rest come to us individually. I'm still amazed at how many people have heard of me and how far they are traveling.

The energy builds as we go. I can't believe the power and strength given to me by my Father. I'm even more impressed with my friends. They help the lame walk to me. They also help the blind. They take care of small children. Oddly enough, I've found I need to use some of my friends as "catchers." When I pray over a person, I touch them on their head. Sometimes they pass out right in front of me. So, we have learned to have the guys take turns when the sick come. They stand behind them, and if they fall backwards, the guys catch them and place them down gently. They seem to be of boundless energy.

To think how worried I was about what God wanted me to do. To think how long I procrastinated. What a fool I can be!

Shalom.

58 Sermon on the Hillside

Today we had the biggest crowd yet. We decided to go partially up the mountain because it helped me see all the people and allowed them to see me. Also, my voice seemed to carry better for them to hear. John knew I was keeping this journal, and he thought I should record some of my preachings. I hope the words will come as freely in writing as when I speak.

When I preach, I usually start with the inner spirit. I try to explain how I am poor in my own individual spirit. I put my human self aside to let room for the spirit of God to fill me. No one can know the Kingdom of Heaven within themselves if it's cluttered with their own spirit. Next, I express the mercy of God. God blesses every one of us in all things. God blesses those who mourn. How could one know comfort if they don't know mourning?

God blesses those who are meek. Those who are meek of their own spirit won't be filled with illusions of grandeur. They won't seek happiness in riches and power and fame. They will be content with what God gives, knowing that God gives us the entire earth and all we need.

God blesses those who truly seek righteousness. I've seen so many people truly hungry and thirsty for the truth of God, not all the legalities of our religion. Those who are true to the search will be rewarded with answers. Just as with physical hunger and thirst, God will satisfy all desires.

God also blesses those who show mercy to others. I can't believe how many people have shown my followers and me mercy along our journey. I know my Father will reward all of them.

God blesses those who are of clean heart, those who don't hide their true self. Too many people build walls around their real inner self. I know I did. They are afraid to let people know who they really are. They are uncomfortable because of past hurts. But walls don't keep people out – they keep *you* inside! How can anyone see God if the walls block His presence? Only the hearts free of barriers will ever be able to see the true God. The thicker the wall, the harder it is to see through it and the less light enters.

God blesses the peacemakers. Peace is one true measuring stick of God. A person inclined to fight can't know God. Some people can find peace in any given situation, something I'm learning to do. One sure sign of a child of God is the ability to be at peace. In fact, the only way to truly know peace is to be confident that God will provide for all our true needs. Only true children of God realize this.

God also blesses those who are persecuted for righteousness. I remember my cousin John, who has at times been persecuted for preaching God's word and baptizing people. Persecuted because he dares to challenge the hierarchy of the Jews. God truly blesses him and all like him. They shall truly find that the Kingdom of Heaven is theirs.

I think writing down my preachings will help me grow and understand things even more. But now I'm too tired to finish. I must rest now.

Shalom.

59 Salt for the World

I try to make sure all of my followers understand who they are. They are followers of God, our Father. Like me, they must become salt for the rest of men. Salt is one of the mainstay ingredients of our food. Without it, many would starve. But while salt helps preserve our food, it also helps enhance the flavor. People will starve in the spirit if there is no salt to preserve it or help enhance its flavor. Being salt for others will bring out the best in the spirit.

This is easy to say, but not so easy to do. Even I struggle with it at times. Many are flocking to me now. I heal them, but I often wonder how much salt that really is. Many people seem to be ignorant of the fact that it's Abba working through me that allows me to heal them. Many believe in God at first, but several days later the joy of the spirit wears off and some new problem takes up their time and energy. Being salt for people is difficult.

I find the easiest way to be salt is to allow the light of my inner spirit to shine through. That, of course, first requires me to have an inner light, which I know I do. So do my followers. In fact, the inner light is hidden somewhere within all people. The trick is to find it! I can't force anyone to find the light, nor can I ignite it, but I can allow my light to shine through me as brightly as possible. So, too, must those who follow me.

In fact, I think once you realize you have an inner light, you are somewhat challenged to allow it to shine. Only our bright inner light will allow us to be salt for the earth. But be careful. As we all know, if salt loses its taste through contamination, it's worthless and must be thrown out. I know that when my light goes dim, I feel downhearted, confused, hollow, and oftentimes physically sick. If we allow our inner light to extinguish, we may also become worthless.

When I find my light dimming I do several things. First, is make sure I am taking care of my physical being, getting enough rest and food. Next, I try to hear whatever it is Abba is telling me. This involves listening to others, reading or contemplating scriptures, or discussing it with someone close to God. But mostly, I try to reconnect with God through prayer.

Some people misunderstand my preaching. I haven't come to abolish the laws of Judaism. The laws are valid. God gave them to Moses and the various prophets of old. I only try to explain the meaning of the laws in new and more complete ways. For example, killing doesn't just mean taking the life of another person. It means killing anything in someone that is related to the inner spirit. We do this in many ways, like when we falsely accuse someone of wrongdoing, when children tease other children because they are tall or short or fat or thin, when we ignore people or brand them as outcasts. We constantly find ways to kill the human spirit.

If only we could spend half as much energy building the human spirit. We need to tell people their strengths, not their weaknesses. We need to fill them with encouragement. We need to help everyone find the special and unique gift God generously provides within each human being and help them use it to best fulfill God's Kingdom.

Shalom.

60 Anger

Whenever we find ourselves angry with someone, we must find a way to reconcile the situation. In so doing, we can help mend the part of the spirit we killed, and the light within ourselves will be rekindled.

My followers ask me all the time, "Is it all right to be angry?" Of course, it's all right. Just like love, it's a human emotion. Emotions are the food of the soul. We must experience all emotions, positive and negative ones. This is what separates humans from other living creatures. Anger needs to be fully expressed and acknowledged. Denying our anger will only cause our inner light to go out, or worse, we will be living a lie. We will be untrue to ourselves. It's like a disease that eats up our insides. Anger is inevitable. At times, we will do things that kill the spirit in others and within ourselves. Reconciliation is then required to rekindle the flame and reignite the spirit.

What do you do if you need to reconcile with someone, but they have yet to work through their anger? That's easy. You can only control your own self. You can't demand that they listen or understand your forgiveness or accept your reconciliation. Their acceptance should not eliminate your ability to resolve the anger within yourself.

Apologize in words, and if they don't listen, apologize with your actions. Set the truth straight in any way you can. Accept the fact that you have provided an opportunity for that person to die to the old self and break forth with a new, and even better, self. If they fail to find rebirth, it isn't your fault. Just strive to find the new and better self within and pray for them to find forgiveness as well.

Shalom.

61 Rest

I needed some rest for the past few days. I found myself tired and a little irritable. I needed a break. I like the mountains for such things. I spent all day today reflecting about some of the things going on in my life.

Everything is going incredibly well. I feel God's presence in all I do. People are starting to really recognize the part of me that's my Father. People may not always recognize me as God's son, the Messiah, but they are telling me a lot of very impressive things.

Just this week, people told me how they wanted to talk over their problem with me because they know I'm so close to God. One person said he always feels so uplifted, refreshed and closer to God every time we talk. One person commented he was getting a number of compliments from his family because they can see such a wonderful change in him, and how that's my "fault." One person was complimented on her ability to deal with the death of her infant child. When asked how she was able to remain positive instead of sliding into depression, she responded it was all me. Things like this make me feel my own sonship more deeply. I could never quite figure out how God would get people to believe in me, and all I had to do was be myself. The rest is on Him.

I'm having a big problem with my dearest friend and follower, Timothy. He has been my best friend for most of my life. He and Thad have helped me through some of my rough times. I would sometimes get angry with Timothy, because he always professed to know what I was going through. A lot of times he was right, too. At first, it was comforting to have someone so close. He was able to soothe some of my hurts and eliminate some of my fears. But then when I withdrew into myself, I wanted him to leave me alone and he usually did.

Timothy has a lot to do with me being able to be who I am. God certainly blessed me with just the friend I needed at the most difficult times of my life. He was always there for me. He consoled and comforted me, and listened.

Now things are not right between us. He disagrees with me and has even hollered at me in front of the others. He says things that seem to have no other purpose than to intentionally hurt me. He takes no active role in any part of our work. Any time someone asks him something, he withdraws into his own hole and tells them he knows nothing. Most of the others are upset with him and wish I would simply let him go. I can't do that to this man. He has helped me so much become who I am. He was there when I required someone to comfort me, nurture me, console me, and befriend me when I was at my lowest, and Timothy was such an excellent choice. He truly deserves a special place among men. I bet it was hard work for him to make the Son of Man turn into the Son of God again. He deserves all my love and none of my criticism. But when I tried to tell him this, he said he didn't want to be my friend any longer. But he still stays. I've tried everything to get him to change, but to no avail.

I think he is jealous of me. He can't accept the fact that I excel him in many things. He can't compete with me, but he should not need to compete with me at all. He is Timothy, and God has richly blessed him. God has made him one of the people who helped me, God's son, when I really needed help. God specifically picked him to nurture me. Imagine that!

Dear Father, help me get Timothy to change. Now that I write that I understand I can't get Timothy to change. Only Timothy can change Timothy. Father, help me accept Timothy wherever and whoever he is today and help me assist my other followers to respect and love him. Help me identify whatever I am doing to hurt him and change me while accepting Timothy wherever he is right now. Writing in this journal is sometimes the best gift I give myself. It gives me time to slow down and really address my thoughts directly with you. You speak to me in so many ways and help my hands write the things I need in order to tell me what I need to know. Blessed be you, Father, forever and ever.

Shalom.

62 Adultery

People often question me on marriage and adultery. I believe my Father prescribes marriage. I believe He wishes humans to live together, one male and one female, for the rest of their human existence. This will obviously cause problems because no two humans will grow together exactly the same way. No people will have the same physical, emotional, or spiritual needs. And even if they are similar, time might force them to grow dissimilar.

In these cases, emptiness or loneliness enters the heart, and the person who experiences loneliness frequently reaches out to find solace in someone else. The trick of true love, however, is to be complete. Relying on another person to fulfill your needs on any level is a form of selfishness; it isn't love. Love requires you to accept that person wherever he or she is, and place no burdens, needs, desires, demands, or strings on the relationship. True love is complete in its lack of requirements upon the other because fidelity, loyalty, honesty, and integrity within the relationship would be a natural response of love. All too often people believe they would love the other if this or that were different. But true love has no ifs or buts.

Adultery is a violation of God's ultimate plan. On a deeper level, even the man who doesn't act upon his desire for another woman has still committed a sin. He has failed to accept his wife where she is. He is looking for someone else to replace something missing from himself.

We need to free ourselves of all things that cause us to sin. If we look upon the body of another with desire, we should rid ourselves of the eyes that show us beauty in the wrong place. Physical needs are a wonderful part of our humanness, a gift of Abba, and an experience that can provide pleasure beyond most other physical activities. But our eyes are often in the way of reaching our own inner beauty. We should then throw them away. It's better not to see the physical world than have our eyes keep us from looking at the true underlying beauty of things.

All too often we utilize parts of our body to prevent us from finding the spirit of God within us. In these cases, we would simply be more complete of a person without the part that prevents us from finding the spirit God has so graciously given each of us.

Shalom.

63 Divorce

Divorce isn't a prescription given from Abba. My generous Father will see people through rough times, if only we turn to him and ask. As I said above, there will always be tough times in marriages, situations will arise which create grief in both parties. It's sometimes hard to help each other through these tough times. At times like this, the perfect union created by Abba is challenged.

Many difficulties will arise in the course of a life together. As mentioned before, people may grow at different rates and at different times. But God provides challenges for growth, and a couple can truly find a way to grow in all challenges. As they grow, their relationship will deepen. Divorce simply stops the growth and prevents the process from becoming complete. When one or both parties simply stop fighting, they give up on God, give up on life, and give up on themselves.

A divorce without a just cause makes the perpetrator guilty of adultery. Marriage is intended to be forever. Ironically, the human spirit can never escape from the problems he is facing. Certainly, running away from a roadblock that can ultimately lead to inner growth will make things appear to be better for a while. Invariably, however, the person will soon find themselves facing the same roadblock they were facing before. The person won't find happiness until and unless they accept the arduous task of getting over, under, or around the roadblock.

Now let me say a few words for the other party in such situations. They can't control you more than you can control them. If one accepts the roadblocks and is willing to look for a path to overcome the difficulty and the other is not, that person can do nothing. One can only accept, just as God must accept, that the other party is not willing to live up to their commitments, and is not ready to continue the journey of personal growth. The other, however, won't be burdened by these choices. They will be free to live their life, marry again, and journey again. Believe me, nothing can provide more opportunities for personal growth than a commitment to another person to remain with them and grow with them for a lifetime. God would never desire anyone to be limited from this wonderful and special relationship.

Shalom.

64 Retaliation

One of the hardest things for my followers to comprehend is my understanding of God's true wishes towards retaliatory behavior. Such behavior is counter to God's plan. The old teaching "an eye for an eye" is faulty. I have no right to take your eye, ever. Not even if you have taken mine! All human life is of God, and no matter what, we should respect each and every part of God's wonderful creation – even the parts that sometimes seem bad.

Retaliatory behavior is representative of "might is right" thinking. Might isn't right. The person who wins a fistfight isn't necessarily right, he is just gifted with superior strength. Once a wrong has occurred, another wrong can't fix it. Never. A wrong is always a wrong. Taking one's eye is wrong in all cases. So is taking a life. We can't find reasons to overcome God's rules. They simply don't exist.

It's the lack of true love that creates the lack of forgiveness, the need for revenge, the need for retaliation. We believe we must right the wrongs in the world, not trust God to take care of things in His own way in His own time. Revenge is wrong and purposeless. The need for revenge is like a disease that will eat us away from the insides until we can justify the wrong. Then when we get our revenge, we will find it isn't satisfactory. Our insides will continue to be eaten up. The only way to stop the process is forgiveness. The sooner a situation is forgiven, the sooner our inner torment will end.

Sure, there are times when we get angry and want revenge. There are times we want to retaliate against someone who has "wronged" us. Accept these emotions. Embrace them. Bring them to our loving and caring Father in prayer. Ask for understanding. Pray for comprehension. Be thankful for the strength not to act on your anger and pray to have it taken away and replaced with forgiveness.

Shalom.`

65 Love of Enemies

In keeping with the thoughts I wrote last night, we must love our neighbor. It isn't enough to merely be tolerant of them. Try as they might, even my closest followers have a difficult time accepting this belief. They have learned to overcome the normal response of retaliation, but to love those who harm you? How can it be?

We give people power over us any time we allow them to keep us from the goodness and peace of God. We give up our control of ourselves to others. The only way to avoid this is to love as God loves. This requires loving all of God's people, even those who harm us. In fact, *especially* those who harm us. It's hard to love someone who forces you into servitude. It's hard to love someone who kills your friend or a family member or kills your inner spirit. However, being truly in touch with the inner spirit graciously bestowed on us by our loving Father requires us to be love just as He is love. This is a difficult concept to understand or explain. In fact, I sometimes think it's only via experience one will truly comprehend love.

What is love? This is like asking, "What is God?" – God is Love. Love for humans is to be in touch with the inner spirit God has given them, to be in touch with the author of Love. The power and strength I have because of being in touch with the inner spirit of love is absolutely astounding. I also find the response of people to my love amazing. Some feel insignificant and insecure; others yearn to learn everything I can teach. Many are drawn to me, but I threaten some. There will likely come a day when those who feel threatened will try and do something radical about me.

Love isn't a feeling. It isn't simply that giddy, starry-eyed look young folks have when first enjoying the company of the opposite sex. Love is a state of being when one is in touch with the indwelling spirit of God.

In this state, one celebrates the beauty of nature – the sunsets and sunrises, mountains, fertile valleys, the animals, lakes, streams, waterfalls, even the desert. In this state you also recognize the inner beauty of other individuals. You are acutely aware of your senses. Smells are at times wonderfully luxurious, other times horribly discomforting. The same with taste. Touch, especially the warm embrace of another human, is of vital importance. The important things in life change from food, water, air, clothes, wealth, and other material things to only living each day in the fullness of God. Other needs in life such as power, glory, recognition, honor among men, and security evaporate. Life becomes a chance to be of service to God in all things.

Love is doing all things in peace with God. Life becomes a prayer. Scrubbing the floor, burying the dead, carrying water, hunting, or caring for the ill are all done with the same inner spirit of love. When you are truly in love, your inner spirit can't be hurt. If the actions of others destroy something, it can only hurt if you claim it as yours.

This isn't easy. How can a person who loses a child not hurt? If they loved the child, it will hurt; actually, the more they loved the child, the more it will hurt. This is true until your human love is replaced by true love, which is the spirit of God. At this point, you will be saddened by the loss, but you will rejoice in knowing the child has returned to God, where you will join them whenever God calls you home. You can even be in touch with the spirit of your child in a fuller way.

Love is giving selflessly. Not from need but from joy. Love is accepting all things whatever they are. Love isn't in forgiving, but in not needing to forgive. Love isn't in overcoming anger, but in not being angry anymore.

Love is in having no fear – no fear of death, no fear of the future, no fear of strangers, no fear at all. We can't be in touch with love as long as we have fear. But we are afraid of so many things. We are afraid that we might not have enough to eat tomorrow. We are afraid to die. Sometimes we are afraid to be our real self. Fear is an illness that keeps us from being in touch with our true inner spirit, our inner spirit from God. Love takes courage – courage to overcome fear.

As the Son of God, my true inner self is the part connected to God, however, I sometimes struggle to stay in touch with it. My human spirit, which I consider my ego, often takes over. I only really understand and experience the love I speak about as the Son of God, so I know that this type of love has not been experienced by many other humans, if any.

So why should someone follow this path? Well, having had the experience of God's love, I can assure you the journey is worthwhile, because only through love can we be in complete touch with joy and peace in our life. We use these words every day, but how little do we understand the true meaning! Joy is exuberance. Peace is overwhelming. Love is love.

Shalom.

66 Alms

Today Peter was asking me about giving alms. We were attending Sabbath at the local synagogue. There was such a big fuss made of giving of alms. The people were placed in rows, according to their almsgiving. Those who gave the most were treated as kings. Everyone was so impressed with how wonderful those people were. Nonsense! The person who gives in public to have recognition isn't giving from their heart. They just need to feel needed. They need to be singled out. These people won't experience anything in the form of growing towards the inner spirit.

The goal of life should not be to see how many people view you as wonderful or notable. The goal of life is to grow daily in the inner spirit, grow daily in love. However, giving isn't always a sign of growth in the inner spirit. One can recognize true generosity only when accompanied by humility. Giving humbly requires our gifts be given in secret. Someone who truly gives from the heart will find himself growing inwardly.

Also, be mindful of considering generosity solely by amount. Obviously, the wealthy landowners can give more than their tenant farmers or the harvest workers. The truly wealthy rarely give anything out of their need; they give only from their surplus. They basically obtain wealth through the toils of others, then try and look pious by returning a small portion to the people who labored for them. However, a person who gives only a few denarii out of their need has given much more than all of the wealthy put together. The ultimate judge, however, of a person giving is God. We must be careful not to judge others.

Shalom.

67 Prayer

Prayer is one of my favorite subjects. First, what is prayer? Prayer is simply a form of communication with God. We sometimes worry about the length of prayer, but it doesn't matter. We sometimes worry about how we talk to God, but that doesn't matter either. A gifted poet can write beautiful, harmonious words for prayer, while a rabbi has learned to talk in special prayer words that may seem to have mystical power. But our creator accepts any talk in its wholeness. He doesn't count the number of words or judge the harmony of the words. He hears all, even the simplest like "Father, help me." He already knows what you need.

Public prayer is acceptable, but there are too many people who think they can be holy by learning to use beautiful eloquent words in public. Again, I tell you, this is nonsense. Public prayer is like almsgiving, just done for the show and may not be real. Prayer is talking to God, listening to him, or doing something in his name. Prayer can be preparing the food, tending to the fields or anything and everything in the day, if we do it in union with God.

Prayer is true communication, which comes within the quiet of your own soul. In quiet, you can allow your inner spirit to be open to the spirit of our wonderful Father. I've found my own prayer can take many forms. I frequently find that my writings are a form of prayer. When I write this journal, I record my inner feelings. I slow my thoughts down to a point where I can really look at them with God's guidance. I often see things I previously missed. It also helps to put my thoughts into words so I can better preach and teach them to others.

My prayer is sometimes a dialogue with my Father. I speak and I hear Him speak back. His voice is strong but gentle, pleasant, and kind. It isn't always the same.

Sometimes it's deep, other times it's soft. At times, it even takes on a feminine form. Sometimes He just plants a thought into my being during prayer. It has sometimes taken me several minutes to explain the idea He has given me. Other times my prayer is in doing things. In my days as a carpenter, working became a prayer at times when I was able to work in communion with God.

Sometimes God speaks to me indirectly through other people. He tells me things I need to know by listening to others or watching events unfold. When I was in what I call the desert of my spirit, preparing myself for this ministry, I was trying to hang onto God. He told me again and again I'm His son. I struggled with that, as it seemed so impossible. I called to Him constantly and prayed endlessly, yet it all seemed useless because things didn't get better; in fact, they worsened. One day I was swimming and relaxing. I tried to pray as I drifted along. I asked God why He wasn't helping me.

As I was floating along, Joseph, my young cousin of about five years of age, grabbed me and started screaming, "Help me! I'm drowning!" He was grasping me so tightly that I was struggling to keep myself above water. I finally blurted out, "Joseph, if you would just stop grabbing me, I would be able to help you!" As soon as I uttered the words, understanding instantly filled my head. I, too, was guilty of grasping God so much that I prevented him from being able to help me. Perhaps going through a period of clinging to God is somewhat normal. If someone finds they can no longer experience God in prayer, then letting go of the desperation and simply relaxing in God may be the answer.

In prayer, use all of your being, all of your senses, and then listen in all things, for God uses everything at His disposal to give us answers. He answers everything, if only we could get used to listening.

68 A Jewish Prayer

There is a wonderful Jewish prayer I like. In fact, we can use this prayer as a guide in our own situations. It goes as follows:

> Our Father in heaven
>
> Hallowed be your name,
>
> Your kingdom come
>
> Your will be done,
>
> On earth as in heaven.
>
> Give us today our daily bread,
>
> And forgive us our debts,
>
> As we forgive our debtors,
>
> And don't subject us to the final test
>
> But deliver us from the evil one.

While I prefer a sincere, heartfelt prayer to predetermined wording, this prayer has wonderful elements in it. First, it recognizes God as a nurturing parent to us. He loves us and cares for us. We are indeed His children and we have the right and privilege of calling on Him whenever, wherever, as frequently as we need to. It further recognizes that unlike our earthly father, this Father is the ruler of Heaven. He is our supernatural creator. He is the maker of earth and all things of earth, as well as Heaven. We further recognize His dignity, give Him the reverence He deserves, and recognize that His name is hallowed.

Next, we ask for His Kingdom to come to earth as He promised. We must not forget that God's Kingdom starts within our own inner being, within our own hearts. We acknowledge His power, willingness and desire to bring His Kingdom to fullness. We also ask His will to be done. God knows what is best. We must ask for His answers in our situations, not simply seek to fulfill our own desires. We need to recognize the instances when our desire isn't aligned with His will. We pray for the ability to accept His will.

We then ask Him for our daily bread. I'm not talking merely about food for our bodies, but food for our souls as well. We must recognize God is our one and only true provider and all things are from Him. We ask Him to fulfill our daily needs. We ask Him to forgive our debts, our failings, and our shortcomings. Here we can be specific about a particular debt or transgression. We also ask for the ability to forgive others for their transgressions.

As I stated before, we should welcome the day when forgiveness won't be required, but often people fall woefully short of the ideal. Therefore, ask God to forgive you and ask Him to let you be the gift to forgive others the way He can forgive you. We can never receive the full benefit of God's forgiveness until we are first able to forgive others. If we hold on to the pain, we will never truly understand the forgiveness God has in store for us.

We close by asking God not to subject us to the final test. While this is generally taken to mean the messianic woes, I take it on a more personal level. Don't subject us to any test that would be more than what we can handle – any test for which failure to follow God would be the end result. We ask God to give us only a challenge to which we can find the courage to rise to, what we can accept and overcome.

And finally, never let us be subject to evil. I again take this on a more personal level. Evil would be defined as failing to follow God or falling short of the desired end. Help give us only things in our life that we can successfully complete.

It's truly a wonderful prescription for prayer.

Shalom.

69 Heavenly Treasure

All too often, people measure success by measuring earthly treasures. They value themselves by the amount of money or goods they own. Some value power, others value glory, but none of these can bring happiness or peace. They can fool people into thinking they are happy, but none of them are real. They can be easily taken away from anyone. What if a flood ruins your entire crop, a fire destroys your home, or a robber takes your wealth as well as the life of your family?

Most people are too tied to earthly goods, too obsessed with power, success, and wealth. But true wealth can only be measured in relation to God. The man who has God in his heart has treasure beyond belief, both on earth and in heaven. God in one's heart is akin to bringing heaven's pleasure, joy and peace to earth. All we have to do is be willing to live in harmony with God.

Many people don't really understand what the story of Job is trying to tell us. Job had earthly possessions, we all do, but his earthly possessions didn't own him. He had God in his heart. Even in the gravest of situations, he was able to rely on God, the god of Love, to pull him through. Was Job tied to his earthly possessions? It didn't appear so. Was he hurt, upset and distressed over the loss? Of course, he was. Then what is the difference? We have to recognize that whatever God provides God can also take away. Things didn't own Job – Job owned his relationship with God. This is the true treasure.

Shalom.

70 Light of the Body

As I've often stated, the eyes are the gateway to the soul, a direct corridor to the inner self. I can read people by reading their eyes. It's as if they are a light that shines brighter the closer one is to God. Certainly, even my followers have good days and bad days. I can see that in their eyes. I can tell when things are right with them and when they are not.

Today I had the great misfortune of running into a person with no light. He was almost like a walking dead man. Even people who are sad due to death or illness usually have a light. Their light may not be shining brightly, but it's there. This man was imprisoned for killing another in a fight and when he was released he found his family had died from malnutrition. He was devastated and simply gave up hope, cursed God and was completely without light. There wasn't anything. No enthusiasm, no joy, no peace, no anger, no sadness, no fear, NOTHING. This is the ultimate darkness. It was scary to see someone at such a depth of hopelessness. I wouldn't have thought it possible.

He experienced a major challenge in his life and couldn't deal with all the negative emotions, so his answer was to bury them. The more he buried them, the more he covered his light. Any light escaping would mean he would have to face those awful feelings. So, he slammed the door, put a roof on it, and now he exists, but does not live. We are all in charge of our own inner light. We mustn't bury our feelings too deep, as that is how you come to utter darkness.

If only I could do something to help him rekindle his inner light! But I failed. Not even I could find a crevice to start opening the lid. Father, I pray for you to help him. He needs you. He truly needs you. No one should ever just exist. I feel the tears welling up inside me. Please, God, help him. Amen.

71 God and Money

As I stated before, even though my followers have a difficult time understanding this, material things generally don't bring you closer to God. I see men every day who love my message, they love being near me, they love all I have to offer, but they don't love me as much as their wretched wealth. I ask them, "How many tunics do you own?" They proudly say, "Twelve." I say, "To follow me, you can only carry three." They say they can't part with any, as each one has a special significance. Ha! They have made those tunics their God.

The most obvious is money. Money is everything to some people. They brag about how they help others with all their money. But will they give it all away? They look at me as if I was crazy. Why should they give all their money away? They try to convince me the money would be "shared" with the rest of my men and me. Nonsense. They don't want to keep the money for our sake; they want it for themselves.

Just today, someone came to join me. He was willing to give up all his possessions. Or so he said. He argued for over an hour about his mule. He wanted to keep it. He argued how it could carry things. It could even carry one of us – someone who is tired, injured, or ill. I said the mule could not come with him. He eventually left, saying how crazy I was and he was almost foolish enough to follow me.

Yes, maybe I'm crazy. What other explanation could you have for someone who thinks he is the Son of God? What explanation could you have for someone who has no job, simply roams from village to village, and lives off the generosity of others or whatever he can scrounge from the countryside. Who else but a crazy person would preach of forgiving people instead of seeking revenge? Even the law says "an eye for an eye."

Yes, I must be crazy. Crazy for a God no one understands the way I do. Crazy with a love and passion for humanity few can comprehend. Crazy for these followers who seem drawn to me. Crazy to admit that I love these men. Imagine that! A grown man in love with not one, but several other men. I'm truly insane.

The world is simply not ready for me. When I say I love these men, some people are ready to call me a homosexual. They envision orgies in our camp at night. They talk and laugh behind our backs. Many listen intently and like the ideas. But then they go home and listen to others who "set them straight" again. Many people get the energy from me, and they throw it away. Yes, I'm truly a crazy person. There is no other explanation for me, the Son of God.

Shalom.

72 Dependence on God

My followers hit a low spot today. We went without much food. We were traveling and the people we met were few and far between, and none had so much as a crumb to offer. They complained all day about the lack of food.

I keep telling them to trust God in all things. He alone can and will provide for us. It reminded me of Moses in the desert. "God will provide," he said. The people first mocked him, but God sent manna. However, today we had no manna. For a brief period, the hunger pains tore through my stomach, but as I prayed, they diminished. In fact, I'm not hungry at all right now. When I think of it, the time I got hungry was when I allowed the complaints of the others to bother me.

I wanted to cry out to God for them. In a weak moment, I asked God how He could abandon all of us who followed Him the most. His answer was spoken within the confines of my own head: "My son, my beloved son. Do you not understand that I, your Father, love you more than all the birds, all the animals, and all the fish? I provide the birds with the most beautiful clothing, I dress them regally, and I protect them well from all types of weather. I provide food for all animals. I find ways to feed them all. How could you ever doubt that I, the God of Love; I, Abba; I, creator of all things will provide you with everything you will ever need? Trust in me, dear beloved Jesus, trust in me in all things."

God had a plan for us today, a huge one. The fact we had no food wasn't so much for my followers as it was for me. Sometimes I, too, lose track of my relationship with God. I think I know it all. I get caught up with being the Son of God. And today God showed me it's He who is really in charge, and the message came across loud and clear.

I preach we shouldn't worry. Then worry creeps into me and begins to overtake my inner self, while I'm blind to it. I've been worried about tomorrow and the future tomorrows. I worry about how I will keep everyone fed and clothed. How will I keep expressing everything I need to express? Today, He brought me back to His reality again. I'm still only the Son. I'm no different from His other children since they must rely on God, and so must I.

Shalom.

73 Judging Others

Today was one of the most frustrating days I've had in a while. The men were all picking on Peter. They were upset with him for his bragging. He always seems to be the first to jump in and agree with me on things, and then he tries to repeat what I have said in his own words. Yes, sometimes he makes a fool of himself because he doesn't quite get the point.

But it's not only Peter. The others complain about how James always wants to be first. Then John complains about how stingy Judas is, since Judas carries our purse. And so on and so forth. They all seem to dwell on the faults of others and ignore their own. Fools. Can they not see how much better it would be for everyone if they focused on their strengths? We can grow so much more in ourselves when people tell us good things, but we still concentrate on the negative.

Why do men always have to look for the small splinter of wood in the eye of their brother, when they all have planks of wood in their own eyes? Perhaps that is exactly why they concentrate on the splinters. I know that sometimes I perceive a small problem in someone else because I have the very same problem. What is so hard for me to see in myself becomes readily visible in another. The truth is that the more negative things we see in each other and the more we judge them, the more we have within ourselves to be judged.

Instead, we should look at each other's good qualities. This way, we would be able to find good qualities in ourselves. Just as we see the small splinter in another's eye, a positive quality could be revealed in the same way.

Shalom.

74 Pearls to Swine

Today we had a most unusual encounter. We passed a group of Levites. Believing we were on a mission similar to theirs to bring the word of God to His people, we joined them for a bit. I tried to speak to them about the beauty of my Father, all the wonders and riches He provides, the truths of His Kingdom He has revealed to me, and love, forgiveness, and peace – all the things I speak about to the crowds and my followers.

I expected the warmest and gentlest reception from these chosen people of God. Kindred spirits, or so I thought. But they argued with me. They asked me where I studied to have such fancy notions. They tried to correct the "errors" of my ways. They couldn't believe how I "distorted" God's word and His truths. They mocked and ridiculed me.

Peter jumped to my rescue and got a bit nasty with them. My whole group was ready to join in, but I had to stop them. Couldn't they see they were doing the very things God instructs us not to do? These people love God within their own understanding of love. They serve Him in a way they believe to be right. They don't have a personal relationship with God. All their truths come from what is passed on through the years. However, throwing my pearls of wisdom to the wrong people will only allow them to go unheeded. Worse, they may be turned against me and used to devour me or tear me to shreds. It's hard to believe a simple man such as myself could be such a threat.

It was a challenge for us to grow past this situation. The Levites had all the answers and wouldn't listen. I know in my heart the truths of which I speak are from a loving Father. We can't throw away all these truths, even when the pearls of wisdom fall on such deaf ears.

75 Answer to Prayers

We have prayed for rain for over a month now. It has been hot and dry. The fields are starting to wilt. The rivers are drying up. A fear is spreading that famine and thirst will lead to deaths soon. The followers now doubt our almighty Father. They are starting to question His ways. I say to them, "Ask, for God will give. Believe what you ask will be given and given generously. Don't doubt; don't put God to test. Simply ask and He will hear you and answer you. Seek and it will be given."

We all know that earthly fathers bestow wonderful gifts on their children. Can't they believe God will be even more generous? I tell them God, as any good father, won't give a snake when a son asks for a horse. I discussed this with my men for days. I believe I finally got through. John told me yesterday he knew the rains were on the way. And in answer to our prayers, today we were greeted with rain, a long, soaking rain, one that will stay with the soil for a while.

I tell my followers that they must ask for God to come into their life. Knock on the door, knock loud and long. God will open it up to all who seek Him. All they have to do is pray for God to truly enter their hearts. All too often, we complain we have knocked, but we have received no answer. But don't forget that after you knock, you must step away from the door and allow it to be open. If you are clinging to God you won't be able to recognize His presence and may keep Him from entering your heart.

Shalom.

76 Golden Rule

My followers often ask me to summarize my theory into one simple and clear statement. I've struggled with this challenge now for weeks. "If it's so simple," they say, "make it simple. Tell us how to be a follower in a simple matter." I've prayed to God to give me an answer to this question. And sure enough, He answered it today.

While eating, we started to discuss the Levites we encountered just a few days ago. Some of my followers were still irritated we didn't try to beat some sense into them. They felt that they didn't defend my honor, so to speak. Then John said I was right in leaving them alone. He reasoned they were people with their own beliefs, just like we were. We certainly didn't like one bit how they tried to forcefully change our way of thinking, so what gave us the right to try and force our way of thinking upon them?

That, of course, is true! This is the golden rule these men have been asking me to provide. And it isn't me, but one of my followers who discovers it. We must treat people the way we wish to be treated. Which one of us likes to be bullied or lied to? Who wants to be ignored or forgotten? We all like to be treated fairly, given a chance to explain ourselves, and accepted for whoever we are, wherever we are. We need to treat others the same way. This would assure living in true communion with God. A simple rule, just as they asked.

Shalom.

77 Narrow Gate

It seems people want to know what to do to ensure they obtain Heaven. They want me to make it simple and easy. Obtaining Heaven may be simple, but here on earth the way to ultimate joy isn't via an easy path. The path is winding and steep. It twists often and suddenly. One who chooses to follow the path to a fuller and richer life can be assured the road won't be short, uneventful or straight. However, only few choose the narrow gate, the one that leads to the long, winding road.

Why should they? The other gate is wide, and the path from it looks inviting. This is misleading, though. The path from the wide gate leads only to failure, destruction, and unhappiness. I say, in order to find fulfillment in life, choose the narrow gate. Choose the path that's most rugged and twisty. God will use this as a method to cleanse you of past wrongs, unforgiveness, and difficulties. We all have things in our past we need to improve. The wide gate only leads to more things that will require additional recompense. The longer we choose the wide gate, the more difficult and twisty the path away from the narrow gate will be.

If someone needs your help, the wide gate with the easy path is to walk away, while the narrow gate is to help. If a friend is having a difficult time, the wide gate would be to ignore their problems, whereas the narrow gate would lead to listening and comforting them. If a leper were thirsty, the wide gate would be to run as fast and as far as you can, the narrow gate would be to give him a drink.

If someone murders someone we love, the wide gate is to demand "justice" and fight for equity, the narrow gate is the one of forgiveness. If someone is rude to us, the wide gate is to respond in justifiable anger, the narrow gate is to treat the person with dignity and compassion. If someone betrays us, it's easy to reject him, it's difficult to accept them in their weakness. If we lie about something, the wide gate is to justify and rationalize our lie, the narrow gate is to accept our shortcomings, own up to our lie and forgive ourselves. If we are intensely hurt about something, we frequently try to pretend our pain doesn't exist, rather than take the narrow gate and try to overcome it. We constantly try to take the easy way out.

There are times we can't take the narrow gate. Sometimes we aren't ready to deal with the situation. Sometimes waiting and growing stronger in order to take the narrow gate is in order. I should know since I've done this many times myself. As long as we recognize the narrow gate as the real path to inner peace and don't outright reject it, we are on the right path. God will always provide for rest, a chance to regroup or whatever else we may need in order to enter the narrow gate and the long, windy path that leads from it. This is the first step towards obtaining Heaven.

Shalom.

78 False Prophets

Today we encountered some "prophets," so to speak. They said they spoke the word of God, but they didn't. They spoke of a God who was vindictive, vengeful, and demanding. They tried to use intimidation and fear, not reverential awe, to get people to love God. They would ask people to deny themselves of their worldly goods and possessions because God demanded nothing less.

I, too, know God doesn't want people who make possessions and wealth their God. But these so-called prophets only wanted the possessions for themselves. It is stealing, for which they have the audacity to use the name of God to justify. Woe to them! We must always look out for these false prophets who come to us in sheep's clothing to hide the true nature of the ravenous wolves they are. We must learn to recognize them.

For me, it is easy to spot them. I can usually see the insincerity in the heart. You have to look at what they say and do to tell the difference. Do they preach with love and compassion, or do they preach using intimidation and fear? A good tree will bear good fruit, while a rotten tree bears bad fruit, and so it goes with the prophets. A good prophet will speak of the good things of the loving God. He will do good works. He will help the poor, and he won't require you to give up riches while he basks in wealth. Learn to look past the voice, peek into the heart and learn to spot the good fruit, which is truly of God.

Shalom.

79 True Disciple

Today we had many people come and listen to me speak. Many cried out "Lord, Lord," as if they could gain heaven by merely uttering those words. They use the word as if it was magic but don't truly listen to and act on my words. They are like a person who builds a house with no foundation. When the floods come, the house will be destroyed. Obtaining the Kingdom of God is a decision only my Father can render. But I tell you this, the Kingdom of God is available to all those who truly give their heart in this life. But merely saying words won't do; one must listen and pray to understand the things they don't. These are people who dig deep and build the foundation for their house on rock. When the floods come, and they always do, the house will stand.

After a lifelong struggle with this humanity, I know that it isn't an easy task. I, too, struggle daily to maintain my relationship with my Father. Some days, frankly, I do better than others. But the true secret is to learn from the days that are not as good and enjoy the days when our inner spirits are in unison with God. Therein lies the true Kingdom of God in this existence.

I know those who listen to my words, strive to truly understand them, and follow them in their heart have built their home on solid rock. However, those who hear my words and don't listen have built theirs on sand. The winds will come in their life, and their house will collapse. I hope they understand that my message requires inner understanding. One cannot simply build on my words in a shallow manner.

Shalom.

80 The Centurion

Today I felt a certain closeness with God when I arose. I always feel closest to him on the days I'm given the gift of healing. I wondered who I would heal today.

The answer didn't take long because just as we entered Capernaum, a centurion came to see us. He explained his servant was paralyzed and suffering terribly. He refused to let me come and help him. He told me to only say the word, and he knew my word would be followed. I couldn't believe this man's faith. A centurion, a Roman, with faith that would put most Jews to shame. It wasn't me, but his faith in God that cured his servant. I myself couldn't demonstrate that much faith.

I was so wrong this morning. I wasn't given the gift of healing at all. It was God who healed me. I started to forget I'm nothing without God. I started to think I alone could heal. I started to revel in the glory of the reactions of people towards me. This centurion helped me realize it isn't me, but my Father, who works through me. I alone am nothing. May I never forget that again. Oh, yes, and thank you, Father, for the great gift of healing today – the gift of healing my own ego.

Shalom.

81 The Widow's Son

I was told today the centurion's servant was healed while the centurion was talking to me yesterday. I continue to wonder about my own ego. I find myself taking credit for the things God accomplishes through me. I'm proud of my ability to preach. I know it's God working through me, but at times I allow my humanity to relish in it. Why is it so easy for the Son of Man part of me to take control while the Son of God part is pushed under? I truly don't understand. I've tried so hard to stay focused on my indwelling spirit and keep my connection with my Father strong, yet this Son of Man part keeps surfacing.

When we entered the town of Nain this evening after journeying all day, we noticed a large crowd carrying out a dead person. It was a young son of a widow. The woman was beside herself with grief. I can only imagine her pain and heartbreak. I made my way through the crowd to see her. She was so young, but her beautiful face was masked with grief. As I gave her a hug, I heard my Father telling me the boy was fine. I went over to the bier and told the young man to get up.

He sat up almost immediately and began to talk. I grabbed him and carried him over to his mother. What an amazing transformation in this woman! Her incredible grief was replaced with extraordinary joy. The townspeople were full of awe. Even my own followers were amazed. And I wonder why my head gets so full of myself sometimes. It's so difficult not to accept at least some of the glory and joy for the things I do in my Father's name.

Father, help me maintain my connection with your spirit, and minimize the Son of Man part within me that seems to relish in the glory. And thank you so much for helping that young boy and his mother today. It was so nice to be able to provide them with the gift of a renewed life.

Shalom.

82 The Sinful Woman

I'm amazed at how many people live around here. I've been walking and preaching and healing in the same area and yet more and more people find me. A few join me in my ministry. I have quite a following now.

After preaching today, some of my followers and I were invited to the home of a Pharisee. He was interested in my understanding of love and forgiveness and seemed truly open-minded. While we were there, a woman of sin from the town entered with a jar full of perfume. Apparently, she was overwhelmed with my preaching earlier and was begging me for forgiveness for all the many sins of her life. She fell on her knees and her steady flow of tears actually made my feet wet. After crying for a while, her sobbing stopped, and she realized my feet were a mess with her tears. So, she poured a bit of the perfume on them and began to wipe them dry with her hair and clothes. The Pharisee muttered in disgust that if I were truly a prophet, I would know the woman I allowed to touch me was a sinner.

I asked him, "If two people owed a moneylender money, one five hundred denarii and the other only fifty, and the moneylender forgave the debts of both, which would love him more?" He replied, it would be the one with the larger debt. I said he was correct. He clearly didn't understand my message. Sometimes I wonder how people can be so smart and yet so dumb at the same time.

I told him that while he didn't give me water for my feet, this woman cleaned my feet. He didn't greet me with a kiss, but this woman has not stopped kissing my feet. He didn't put oil on my head, but she poured perfume on my feet. I told him it was obvious to me that she accepted my preaching in her heart, the love she displayed was great, she realized the many sins of her past life and was seeking forgiveness and a new start. I told him whoever has been forgiven only a little was only able to love a little, but those forgiven a lot would be able to love a lot.

I reached down and helped her up. When I looked at her, she turned her head away. I put my hands on her face, looked into her eyes, and told her that her sins were forgiven and her faith saved her. I told her to go in peace. She closed her eyes and took a deep breath, then she smiled at me. As she was leaving, she turned and said thank you.

I don't understand why forgiveness is so difficult a concept. It seems so many people want to hold onto the sins of others. For many people in this town that woman will remain a sinner. Can't they understand that if they are not capable of forgiving others, they will never begin to forgive themselves? Every one of us has the stain of sin on our soul. It's impossible to be human and not sin. But holding onto sin is like an anchor dragging behind a boat. It not only slows you down, it may even drag the boat under permanently. We need to forgive sins of others first so we can truly forgive our own. Our loving Father is always ready to forgive sins of anyone who sincerely seeks it.

Shalom.

83 Mary

A few days ago, we came to the village of Magdala. A wealthy man asked me if I would come and help his daughter because she was possessed by many demons. I was going to heal her right then and there without seeing her in person because I was in the midst of preaching. But the man was persistent I come and invited us to dine with him later in the day, so I accepted.

When I arrived at his home, I met his wife and a few of his other children. Then I went in and saw a young woman sitting on the floor pounding on something and talking loudly. Her name was Mary. When her father got her to turn around our eyes met. They were deep set eyes, the color of a raven, with an inner sparkle the unresponsive exterior couldn't quite hide. I couldn't believe it. I had the same reaction as the one I had when I met Deborah. I somehow knew we would become great friends. How odd is that?

I prayed fervently for all the demons to release her at once. She started pounding and shrieking even more at first, but then released one final ear-piercing sound and fell silent. Her parents and brothers and sisters were concerned, but I realized she had simply fallen asleep. I suggested we eat dinner while she slept, and although reluctant, they all agreed. Mary's mother turned out to be quite a marvelous cook, she prepared a feast of lamb stew with lentils, onion, leeks and beans along with some bread and a very robust wine. She even had some watermelon! What a treat!

After dinner, I was a bit reluctant to leave since I was concerned about Mary, who was still sleeping. When he noticed my hesitation, her father asked if I would stay the night. I normally return to camp with my followers, but for some reason, I felt drawn to Mary. I needed to get to know her better, so I agreed.

When I woke the next morning, my senses were aroused with wonderful aromas of breakfast. Mary was cooking with her mother. She was a changed woman. Gone were the wild eyes of yesterday and in their place, there was a soft expression. She was absolutely gorgeous! I introduced myself, and we started talking. Her family allowed the two of us to talk all through breakfast, although they added a few comments here and there. Afterwards, I asked her if she would like to listen to me preach, and she eagerly agreed.

I spent yet another evening with Mary and her family and another evening after that as well. As with Deborah, I felt I knew Mary inside and out, and she knew me just as well. The men were getting a bit annoyed since we normally spend our evenings together, and they missed our conversations and camaraderie. I knew they were right, but I was reluctant to leave Mary.

I knew I had to move on and return to my ministry. I told Mary and her family that I was leaving the following day. Without hesitation, Mary asked if she could join me. This was a bit unexpected, but then again, I did have other women travel with me, so why not? Her father didn't hesitate about giving her his blessing to come. He said he was fairly wealthy and would help us with food and provisions as well. He said he was delighted and honored I would allow his daughter to be counted among my followers.

Father, thank you so much for the gift of Mary. I've longed for a companion to share a bit more of my life with. I had forgotten how much I missed Deborah. I missed having someone truly understand the things I'm experiencing internally. Mary and I can relate to each other better than I can to anyone else. She is an absolutely beautiful gift, and I will always cherish her.

Shalom.

84 Would-Be Followers

I haven't written in a while. We've been so busy. It seems as if everyone who is possessed by demons, or sick or whatever, has discovered I'm a mighty healer. They almost claw at me, they won't let me eat. I get no peace. Most of the time they don't even let me go and relieve myself.

One evening, many possessed people gathered. I was able to cure them all at once. Afterwards, some of them came to follow me. They were more like obnoxious children. They only wanted to share in my glory, not to look at themselves. They weren't sincere in learning about God, they just wanted to be part of the excitement. A few joined us for a few days, but they quickly tired and returned home.

One scribe asked to follow, but he was unaware of the type of life a traveler like me lives. We have no place to call home, no place to lay down our heads. Another man has come to me daily for the past week, claiming to be a loyal follower. But every day I give him a chore, like getting some fish for dinner, collecting firewood, or bring the lame leper to me, he conveniently remembers he has an important chore to help with at home.

As we were preparing to leave today, I asked him to help carry some of our things. He said he would return to us soon, but first he had to bury his father. Too many excuses. I was a little short with him and told him to let the dead bury the dead, and simply follow me now. He looked at me as if I was crazy. In the end, he just walked away.

Too many of us are like that. We have many excuses for not looking at ourselves and not fixing the things that require fixing. We make excuses for not forgiving, for being angry, or for hurting others. This isn't following me, or honestly seeking God. The act of following me requires one's total commitment on the inside, lip service isn't enough. I know it isn't easy, and sometimes the excuses seem valid. But any excuse that keeps us from God is invalid.

God, please help that young man learn to be more sincere about following you, help him to truly find you, help him become the person he proclaims he desires to be.

Shalom.

85 Storm at Sea

Yesterday was simply exhausting. I had so many people coming and seeking me to heal them. I pushed myself to the limit. I had to find a way to free myself for a short rest. I could feel my internal energy draining away. I managed to get the men to retrieve Peter's boat for me.

Several of us got in the boat late last evening and got as far away as we could from the shore. We drifted most of the day today. Just taking it easy. We had some supplies we could eat, and some of the men rested by fishing.

I took a wonderful refreshing swim. Peter and John joined me. John is by far the best swimmer of all of us. He is young and strong and very fast. It almost seems he should have been born a fish. He says he used to be a giant jewfish. He says once he swallowed a whole human being, but it didn't sit too well in his stomach, so after a few days he spat him back out. Ha-ha. That's John. He does have a strange sense of humor.

After we napped a bit, we gathered around and talked about God again. Timothy asked about God's presence during the difficult times in their lives. I explained that God is all around us in everything. He is everywhere. Not a moment passes without God being in complete touch with us. The rough times in life are the times God uses to help us grow. We need to be assured and certain of God's love for us and His desire to help us during these difficult times. Praised be those who can see God even through difficulties. I explained it's during the real challenges of life we most need to rely on God and believe He is present with us.

Some people are drawn to God in the difficult times, while others think God ran out on them and left them alone. They insisted they were in the group of the former, they ALL said they found God in the difficult circumstances of life. At that moment, I felt God was toying with them to help them see the lies and dishonesty they were trying to hide.

After supper I fell asleep. Next thing I know, God sends an unexpected storm upon us. I found out after we had docked later that the storm never hit land. It was only seen in the distance and was short-lived.

The men instantly became terrified and started yelling about how they were going to perish. I was almost beside myself with the irony of the situation. Here were my men, who insisted they ALWAYS found God in difficult circumstances, and now they were crying out how God had abandoned them. It took no time for me to ask God to calm the storm. Almost as quickly as the storm arose, it subsided. They were impressed with me and how I was some sort of wizard to get the storm to dissipate.

"Fools," I told them. "This is exactly what I was talking about today. God is always with you. The difference is I turned to God in this time of trouble and you abandoned Him. How can God help us when we abandon Him?"

I think I actually saw a small glimmer of understanding in a few pairs of eyes. At last, at long last. To think God wants me to get these men to understand Him as I do. Sometimes I believe He has given me an impossible challenge. But now I wonder who it is that doubts God's plan.

Shalom.

86 Legions

After we had breakfast this morning, we started on the road to Gadara. Little did we know, but two savage humans haunted the road we chose. Reportedly, the two men were inhabited by demons. Legions of demons, we were told.

The father of one of them caught up to us before we came upon them. He warned us about his son. He explained he had tried everything, but the boy remained possessed. About this time, the boys came from the hills and their demons started to shriek and plead with me not to drive them out. They begged for mercy. There was a herd of swine grazing along the cliff. They asked me to send them into the swine.

I was sort of laughing to myself. Even though I had said nothing, they knew who I was. After some begging, I simply said, "Go then." The next thing I knew, the entire herd of swine went crazy. They started jumping about and kicking like I had never seen before. Then they started running in circles and as the circle grew larger, they all ended up running right over the cliff into the sea. Oddly enough, they almost all drowned instantly, even though swine are generally good swimmers.

I must say I was a bit taken aback by the whole incident myself, so I can imagine how it must have been for the others. The father of the one boy was ever so grateful. He was jumping up and down because I cured his son. He ran off ahead of us to tell the village.

Shortly thereafter, we saw a large body of people coming towards us. We were all smiling and anticipating a warm and wonderful reception and dreamt of the succulent dinner they would provide. However, as they arrived, we realized their noises were not ones of welcome, but shouts of anger. They begged us to leave them alone, as if they were afraid.

The boy's father pushed his way through the crowd and begged for forgiveness for his village. He had told them of the wonderful gift, but they reacted wildly. He said that the people were content with things as they were and didn't want some wizard to change things. He begged us to turn away. He promised to bring us food if we would but wait where we had originally met him.

Now it dawns on me how typical of humans the villagers' behavior is. Even me. I, too, am afraid to change. I find myself too comfortable wherever I am, and changing seems like too much work. I would rather keep a difficult situation then face the unknown. I resist change, even when I know God is behind it. Like with this entire ministry. How long did I doubt who I am? How long did I labor over what God wanted? How many times and in how many ways did He tell me His plans? I was too afraid and I had a thousand excuses.

Today, no matter the testimony of the father, the townspeople were simply not listening. They had already made up their minds. They were too afraid of the changes I would bring. Their only answer was to shut the door on me.

Today's message may be more for me than anyone else. There is certainly something God has been asking of me. I've knowingly and intentionally procrastinated about it. That may be the underlying source of my tiredness these past few days. But I'm so, so afraid. I don't know if I can do what He calls me to do. I'm comfortable right where I am. But I know if I don't do it, I will suffer continued tiredness. Oh, the choices!

Thank God we have a loving and caring Father who never stops telling us things gently and quietly, not in a pushy and forbearing manner. He keeps telling us what we need to hear. It's up to us to listen. Oh, blast it all. I guess I had better stop procrastinating.

87 Fasting

Over the past few days, we caught up with some of my cousin John's followers. It was strange to see how we differ in our approaches to life. They seek God through virtuous behavior and self-deprivation. They maintain a rigid prayer schedule, have taken a vow of poverty, and own nothing. They also use fasting as a continual form of sacrifice.

We, on the other hand, are not prone to a schedule. Some days we sleep late, other days we take a nap. If we tried to pray at set hours every day, it would seriously impede our ability to tend to the needs of the people who come to us. We pray in the time God gives us each day. Sometimes our prayer time is limited, while other times we have a free day and can pray a lot. There always seems to be enough time for me to pray quietly. It seems whenever I need to pray, God arranges a time in my schedule. Neither way is right or wrong, they are just different. But the followers of John seem to be a bit taken aback by what they perceive as our lack of devotion. I guess we don't act holy enough for them.

Finally, after three days, they had enough courage to ask the question, "Why is it that we and the Pharisees fast much, whereas you and your followers don't?" A simple enough question, but the underlying issue was much more complicated. Their real issue was that I didn't fit their vision of what they expected from the Son of God, which they heard I was. They were seeking to join me, but needless to say, they were a bit disappointed.

I told them no one puts new wine in old wineskins. If they did, the old wineskins would leak, and the wine would spill out. By "new wine," I meant my inner spirit of love for my Father, my new spirit of oneness with God, my understanding of the covenant God has made with mankind.

Trying to capture my spirit in an old wineskin would simply be foolish. If they believed me to be the Son of God, they would accept me for who and what I am as well as the new understanding I have of the covenant with God. They would understand that God intends life to be lived to its fullest with laughter and joy, not by religious somberness. A life of holy somberness could hold my spirit no more than old wineskins could hold new wine. I challenged them to be new wineskins, but to no avail. They didn't seem to grasp the obvious connection. Somehow, they were unable to broaden their views to accept me for who I am.

It saddened me because I know they are good and holy people. The problem was that they had preconceived notions about God. They were so wrapped up in their perceived truths that they had blocked out any other understanding. They couldn't accept a different answer because they thought they had the gift of complete and utter truth. After all, they obtained their truths from Scripture itself, so they could have no error. And to some degree, they are right.

Yet, because they refuse to open themselves to the fact that no one on earth, not even me, has a complete and total answer about who and what God is, they have missed a greater understanding, a deeper sense of peace, and a lot of potential joy. God is supreme, all-powerful and almighty. His love is endless and nearly incomprehensible. Our human understanding can grow daily if we let it. But once we think we have all the answers, we simply stop growing. We limit ourselves in one of the most wonderful parts of our humanity, which is to grow.

I know I've been guilty myself. Not growing internally was like a sickness for me, and it only made me depressed. I don't see depression in John's followers. They are too busy thinking how wonderful they are and too caught up in their journey to bring other people to the place they have found. I guess it's a necessary part of God's overall plan. It's similar to a baby who needs to crawl before it learns to walk and walk before it learns to run. Many people need to crawl with something akin to the understanding of John's followers before they can grow to the understanding I have. Hopefully, I will have provided a small opening to show them the light for further internal growth.

Beloved Father, thank you so much for these past few days. Thank you so much for all the people you send into my life. Thank you again for the gift of humility. I, too, sometimes think I have all the answers. Help me never lose sight of the fact that I am only whatever you give me. I'm your Son and without you I'm nothing. Help me remain true to you in all things. Amen.

Shalom, and go in peace with God, my brothers.

88 The Official's Daughter

Yesterday I wrote about John's followers. I was a bit upset when I started to write last night because I tried to explain, most futilely, how they were wrong and how they should accept my ways. Fortunately, as I look at it now, God saved me from messing things up for Him. He needs them right where they are to reach people of similar traits. And He needed to teach me the lesson of humility (yet again).

How did He do this? While I was explaining myself to John's followers, God sent a high-ranking official, named Jairus, to me. His daughter was dying. He felt certain she would live if I came and laid my hands on her. I didn't really want to go. I wanted to stay and explain more to John's followers as I fully believed God wanted me to do. But as he continued to beg and plead, John's followers dispersed. I attempted to keep them together, but Matthew and Andrew said they thought God was calling us to go with the official. I looked around and realized they were probably right. I still thought I should stay, but my friends started moving me in the other direction.

Once we were on our way, I felt something strange. It was as if my Father himself reached down and pulled on my cloak in a very special way. I turned around to see who had touched me. It was then that I noticed a woman. She told me she had been hemorrhaging for a number of years. She was lucky it had not taken her life already. I heard her say something under her breath about how she could be healed if she could but touch my cloak. I looked around for John's followers, but God pulled me back into His world again. I realized I had been fighting His spirit and was allowing myself to think I knew better than Him what needed to be done.

I felt like thanking this wonderful woman for a gift she could have never known she gave me. Instead, I simply told her to have courage, because her faith had saved her. Later, I found out that the hemorrhaging stopped.

About this time, Jairus' cousin arrived and informed him that his daughter had died, and he no longer needed to trouble me. I responded, without even thinking, that he should have faith because his daughter would be saved. As we walked on, I realized that there were many people following us to watch me, the great healer, at work. I had performed many healings, but once again, this girl was dead. The official seemed confident I could help. I felt a resurgence of inner power, a new connection with my Father after the gentle, yet warm touch of the woman, which filled me with energy.

I was so absorbed in the moment that I hardly heard the wailings and noises emanating from the official's home. They had already started the mourning process even though they knew he had gone to get me. It seems that no one had any hope other than the father.

As we entered the house, I told the friends and family to leave because the girl had just fallen asleep. They started to ridicule me. After we were able to clear everyone out, I went upstairs to see the girl. She felt a little cold to me at first, but she looked very peaceful. I took her hand in mine and stroked her head a bit. She was quite young and quite a beauty. She reminded me of Deborah when she was younger.

While I was sitting there, thinking of nothing in particular and just stroking her head, I noticed her eyes started to move and then open. She smiled the most wonderful, warm, caring and loving smile I recall. She looked as if she had just been with my Father. She told me everything was all right now. Imagine that – *she* was trying to comfort *me*! Then she rested as we talked a little, smiling at each other.

Her father was beside himself with joy. His little girl was alive. He was dancing around almost uncontrollably. Her mother was crying tears of joy. Not much later, the girl arose and went downstairs. A hush came upon the crowd as one by one they realized what had occurred. Some started to cry, while others danced.

I was still caught up in the events. When I was losing my way, my loving Father sent me not one but two wonderful women to get me back on my path. He always seems to know exactly what we need, doesn't he?

Dear Father in Heaven, you are very hallowed and blessed indeed. Help me bring about your Kingdom on earth and never let me lose sight of your glory. Thank you for your guidance to keep me on my path. I know you have no need to forgive my transgressions, but I would like to ask you for forgiveness anyway. I love you, Abba, and I always will.

Amen.

89 Healing the Blind

We have been on the road for a few days. I'm still a little numb about the whole thing. First, I try to take the matters of my Father into my own hand. I think I know what is best. I become judgmental and want to spend my time changing things that need no changing. And what does my loving Father do? He calls me back gently but powerfully to His plan for me.

I know my Father called me to heal the sick, but I want to heal those who are sick in their spirit, not just those sick physically. I resist His call, but my followers listen to God better than me. Then God sends me a woman who touches me for healing. I saw and felt my Father in her touch. I've finally realized I must continue to do His work, not follow my own agenda.

I have this gnawing on my inside because I don't quite understand what my Father wants of me, at least not yet. I believe He wants me to spearhead a true revitalization of humanity, a revitalization of the inner spirit. He wants me to show people that God is part of them, just as He is part of me. But my ministry seems to concentrate on the physical needs.

Take today, for instance. We encountered two blind men on our path. They followed us for a while, and then invited us to their home. After we ate and rested, we started to converse about God. They confirmed in their own mind that they had indeed come upon the "great Healer." They called out to me, saying, "Son of David, have pity on us." Here I go again, called to heal the physical body with little regard to the more important temple of God housed within this frame.

What was I to do? Ignore them? My healing ability is a gift from my Father. Am I to abandon it? I asked them if they truly believed I could make them see again. Of course, they believed in me. They even called me Lord. I told them it was their own faith that would allow them to heal. I begged them to look inside to further their understanding of the loving Father, the spirit of whom lies within their soul as well as mine, but they were only caught up in the fact that they would regain their vision, their precious sight.

I preached to them for a while. They held their eyes closed and cried the whole time, but I sensed they heard little of what I was saying. But when they opened their eyes, they could see! Here I was, healing the physical body yet again. I begged them to tell no one of this healing. I want to free myself of this burden. I want to pursue my dream and God's call to heal the inner spirit. This ability to heal the body seems to get in the way. I pray they listen and keep this to themselves

Shalom.

90 Healing the Mute

Today we traveled only a little further. It seems my wonderful blind friends didn't heed my request. Instead of keeping quiet, they spread the word of their healing throughout the community. I'm always impressed with the speed news can travel. It seems the words can outrun my feet. Anyway, a blind and mute person came forward today. He was possessed by a spirit.

A pair of Pharisees joined the crowd and watched the process of healing. After I drove the demon out of the man, and his sight and voice returned, I expected that the Pharisees would invite me to join them at the synagogue. I was hoping for a chance to express better the inner spirit of God that I so want to proclaim. But no, they didn't offer me a place among them. Instead, they claimed I'm driving out these evil spirits by the power of the Devil! Can you imagine that? Here I am, the Son of God, sent to help humanity find a better understanding of the Father almighty, and these self-proclaimed servants of my Father accuse me of working with the devil.

I pointed out that any kingdom divided against itself would surely not stand. They proclaim I represent Satan, yet if I heal people and preach about God, then the kingdom of Satan would be divided against itself and will surely fall. But if I cast out demons by the Spirit of God and preach of God's love for man, then surely the Kingdom of God is here.

Then God's spirit took over my very being in a manner beyond anything I had experienced before. I provided a long list of examples of how very wrong the idea of me working with Beelzebub was. A tree is either good and produces good fruit, or bad and produces bad fruit. A good man brings forth good things from the treasures in his heart, but an evil man can only bring out evil things from his heart. I went on and on for quite a while, channeling the words of my Father through me to them.

I remember one of the most powerful statements today. I said if anyone speaks against the Son of Man, it would be forgiven, however, if anyone speaks against the Holy Spirit, it would never be forgiven. I don't know if I've ever referred to myself as the Son of Man before in front of others. When I said this, a few people, many of my followers included, looked at me kind of oddly.

I'm so confused about this whole thing. Sometimes, this gift of healing seems more a curse than a way to draw people to my Father. It only seems to be creating a larger distance between the wonderful religion of my ancestors and me. But I know God still wants me to heal. If he didn't, the gift would be lessened, and the people wouldn't come. But each day seems to bring more people, not less. I still don't quite understand the whole plan. But then I guess it isn't really up to me to understand all things fully. It's simply enough to understand whatever He allows me to understand and trust in Him to lead me as He desires.

Dear Father, thank you so much for today. I felt your indwelling power and strength more powerfully than ever before. Thank you for the words, so many words, so many examples. I felt your power with every part of my being. It has given me renewed strength and energy. Also, thank you for allowing me to reveal myself as the Son of Man today. I don't know what anyone else will make of it, but it felt good to put those thoughts into words. And finally, give me the understanding of the things you require me to understand and help me not concern myself with things I don't yet understand.

Amen

91 Compassion

It has been several weeks since I had time to write in this journal. Since my last entry, the people have been flocking to me at an even greater rate. They come to listen to my words. Many seem to be touched by the things I say and the understanding of God I have. But mostly they come for healing of themselves or a loved one. A few are just curious.

Since my last period of confusion, I've been invited into a few of the local synagogues to preach. Some of the Levites and Pharisees seem to be impressed by the things I say. A few told me they are amazed at my insights. They truly seem to be touched on the inside.

I think I've accepted the gift of healing. Healing still seems to be my number one gift. I haven't again, at least yet, been called to bring a dead person back to life. I've healed lepers, the blind, mute, deaf, fevers, cramps, and the lame. I've healed burns and cuts, and even a bad case of sunburn. I even helped cure a few sick animals. It was the only source of income for one family. They were more grateful than many families who had people cured.

After all the struggles I've had with this gift of healing, God has allowed me to utilize it to further glorify him. The people look at me with some sort of awe. They are obviously akin to sheep wandering aimlessly without the guidance of a shepherd. These people seem to devour the words I give them on forgiveness, the loving nature of God, and the true meaning of peace. They think of me as a prophet of some sort.

But I feel a certain loneliness with these people. They have an almost empty existence. It seems the physical things of the world drive them. They work hard each day to exist. They are so tired when the day is done, they have little time to share with each other. Then, when they do find or make the time to relax, they try to enjoy life by going to excess with things like drinking, carousing, or partying. Some have heard my words, but they lack experience or guides. I can see God's harvest is full, but the laborers required to harvest before it all rots on the vines is lacking.

Dear Father, I see now your plan is to utilize my healing to bring about the inner healing we both know to be needed. Help me find people who can help shepherd this flock, and other flocks, into a greater understanding of your Kingdom. These people are in need of help, and I look to you for support, because I know it's my path to move on. Please find a way to bring this abundant harvest home to you. Amen.

Shalom.

92 Mission of the Twelve

I shared my concerns with my wonderful and most faithful followers today. I asked them, too, to pray that God doesn't let this harvest rot. After a while, a group of twelve of my followers came to me. They said, "We've been thinking." I knew I was in for some trouble. It was Peter, who is usually so impetuous, who spoke. It seems it wasn't his idea, but Bartholomew's. But once the idea was given to Peter, he charged into it.

They thought they, too, could help heal. They felt they had been with me long enough and God would want them to expand their service to Him. Besides, there was so much healing to be done and if they were to heal the physical bodies, I would have more time to concentrate on the inner spirits.

I didn't need to ask God for the answer. It seemed so obvious as they said it. In fact, I was even a bit embarrassed that this idea wasn't my own. I guess I got too wrapped up in the problem to look for a solution.

I called them all to form a circle and hold each other's hands, something they wouldn't have done easily in public when we first started this mission. I prayed over them out loud and called upon our loving Father to extend this gift of healing to each of them. I praised them for answering God's call. I instructed them on the type of healing they were to do. I made certain all they do would be for the glory of God, and God alone. I instructed them not to accept any earthly payments.

I thanked God profusely for these men, for without them I would truly be something less today than I am. I instructed them to help the lost sheep of Israel. I implored them to travel as we have, to continue in my footsteps. When we find a caring person, we stay with them. There has almost always been at least one. For the few villages that totally rejected us, I instructed them to carry no grudge, but to simply move on and trust God to fulfill their needs.

I further assured them they could always rejoin each other or me if and when they felt the inner spirit diminishing. I also told them to take the time to pray. It need not be like John's followers with a rigid prayer schedule each day, but to take the time provided by God. I also implored them to rest whenever they felt the need.

I spoke to these twelve for the better part of the afternoon. I warned them about fear, rejection, and, at times, even hate. Fear is their biggest enemy because fear itself will limit their ability to love and respond with love. I told them not to fear, because our Father in Heaven is truly with each of them. I implored them not to worry about the words they would need. I told them of the many times God filled me with just the right words to say. I warned them of the persecution they may be subject to, but to know in their heart that what they do is for the good of God's Kingdom.

As we were holding hands, my hands began to tingle and grow warm. The feeling traveled up my arms to my shoulders. It was a warm, comfortable burning sensation. In fact, it seemed to be some type of energy and power. I confirmed later with James and Thomas – they felt it too.

Something else occurred. Bartholomew, the quiet one, spoke up. He started to pray aloud to our Father. His words were so beautiful and eloquent. I could tell he, too, had the gift of opening himself to the Spirit of our Father. He prayed for courage to accept the challenges they would face, the strength to carry out this mission with continued vitality and the wisdom to know when to rest. He asked for inner peace and for God to be present in them.

Thank you, Father, for all the gifts you give me. Thank you for the gifts of these special men who have also answered your call. Be with them as they carry on. Allow them to find me and help me carry out my mission whenever I need them. Amen.

Alleluia.

93 Peter

I was so caught up in what I told the men yesterday and what they did for me that I neglected to write down some of the feelings I had. Today I would like to take a moment to marvel at the wonderful companions God has given me on my journey. At times, these people energize me and keep me going when I get weary. At other times, I wonder if God could have found a worse composite of people to do His work.

Let's start with Simon, who I like to call Peter. Peter is the impetuous one. I think it will be his downfall. "Act first, think later" seems to be his motto; he reacts to everything quickly, with his full spirit. Just like he did when first hearing the call to follow me. He has the makings of a wonderful leader. He was the captain of a small fishing vessel and was quite adept at getting the most out of his people.

He seems loyal, but at times he doesn't want to acknowledge his belief in me to those who don't yet believe. I don't think he will ever actually betray me, but he seems too afraid to speak up at times. Oh, perhaps it's for the best. He may only jump into quicksand and sink. Perhaps a day will come when he is more assured of his faith in God and in me as Messiah.

Once again, I'm too tired to finish. More another day. After all, there are twelve of my companions.

Shalom.

94 Disciples

Andrew is Peter's brother. I met him before Peter, when I was baptized. First, he wasn't pleased to join us. He seemed to have second thoughts about leaving his home and family and wandering around. In the beginning, I frequently told him he should make his own choices and not simply listen to his older brother. Slowly, over time, I realized Andrew stayed not because of Peter's prodding, but because he was truly drawn to me. His desire to be with me finally won out over his desire to be home with his family. He also hated fishing. I guess that also helped him choose me.

John and James, the brothers of thunder. They were always playfighting with each other and sometimes the rest of us. They are the ones who bring the most joy into camp. They laugh and tease and joke. I was certainly not surprised to see these two among the ones God chose. John especially has a heart of gold. He seems to be the one most able to open himself fully to love and be loved. He unabashedly will give me a hug or cry when his spirit moves him. James, too, will shed a tear or two, but he tries to fight them.

Bartholomew is the quiet one. He was the one who most surprised me the other day when he came up with this idea. Then the beautiful manner in which he was able to pray. He, too, found a way to open himself and allow God to speak through him. God's choice, without doubt.

Simon zealously opposes the Roman domination over us. He has been of most help with my ministry. He is of boundless energy. He always seems to know when to help out someone. He helps the blind to walk towards me. He sometimes carries the lame. He is the one who stays up late to tend to the fire. I sometimes wonder when he finds time to sleep.

Judas Iscariot, another easy choice. He carries our purse. He is thrifty and frugal with money. He is a good dealer, but always deals fairly and honestly. In fact, I've watched him pay more than he should at times, whenever he senses the person selling the product can truly use the extra money. A very kind and smart spirit, who seems most sensitive to the needs of the poor.

Matthew has had a special inner spirit aglow in him since we were young. He is a kind and caring soul. He accepts his duties joyfully. He is a hard worker. He is definitely a wonderful choice.

Next is Philip. He is a wonderful surprise. He is talented, caring, considerate, smart, pleasant, and all the things that would make him an ideal choice. But he is so insecure. He argues whenever you tell him something positive. He demands constant affirmation, even though he openly argues with you over it.

Thomas. He is the one to question everything I say. He has to question until he understands, or thinks he understands, exactly what I'm saying. He overanalyzes every word. His faith in God is strong, but he can't give up the old thought patterns without doubts and questions as to whether or not what I say is true.

James, the son of Alpheus. He is the strong, silent type. He leads by his example. He follows without question. He was the first to reach out and help a leper. He was the first to follow the official who asked for help with his dead daughter. He was the first to give his sandals to a stranger we met who had cut his foot. He seems to grasp the things I say and puts them into practice.

Lastly, it is Thaddeus, who is like a brother to me. Actually, his given name is Judas, but I've always known him as Thad, and it's easier to call him Thad to avoid confusion with Judas Iscariot. He has some physical problems he never complains about, and oddly enough, says he would rather not be healed. He says it's a reminder for him that God is with all people, not just the perfect. It helps keep him humble. He never lets his physical problem interfere, and most of us hardly recognize he has a problem any longer. But I'm a bit surprised that he joined me on this mission because of his physical limitations.

Another thing. I was pleased with the number – twelve. The number of tribes in Israel. I think that was no mere coincidence. It seems to be clearly the plan of my Father.

Shalom.

95 Visit to Bethsaida

After a few days of instruction to my twelve chosen followers, I sent them off on their own paths, two by two. I have heard from my Father that they are all doing just fine. Now I am visiting the towns of those twelve men. I remember the slightly less than enthusiastic response I received from my own people, so I decided it was best to set the stage for them.

I'm currently in the town of Peter, Andrew and Philip. The townspeople are amazed more than ever about me. I know more than a few people were questioning why Peter, Andrew and Philip followed me in the first place. Most of those doubters have vanished. A few have even told me they can clearly see my Father's presence in the things I say and do. Few have doubts any longer about why Peter, Andrew and Philip came with me, although they are quite astonished they have grown enough to become champions of the Father in my footsteps. They can't quite grasp that mere humans with their faults have been called to serve the Lord.

I assured them that God created all humans, and part of humanity is to fail and to grow. None of us are perfect creations, but through God we can slowly grow into perfection, even here on earth. They all understand this concept, but it's still hard for them to accept that these men could have grown quite that far. I had the same issue with my own hometown.

Father, thank you so much for the understanding you have given me today. I've long wondered why I was met with such hesitation and denial in Nazareth. My visit here has helped me understand more fully their reasons.

Shalom

96 John's Followers

Interestingly, a few of my cousin John's followers caught up to me today. This time, Herod imprisoned him because he denounced his unlawful marriage to his brother's wife. I have to question any leader so paranoid they have to imprison someone as harmless as John. He never hurt anyone and certainly never coerced anyone into anything. He merely talked about his love for God and encouraged people to be baptized in the name of God. I think any ruler who would imprison someone because he spoke the truth is incredibly insecure; perhaps he felt he was less powerful than John.

John sent them with a question for me: "Am I the one who is to come?" Strange question. I recall the day he baptized me. First, he insisted he wasn't fit to untie my sandals. Doesn't that suggest he already knew who I was? Then God spoke after my baptism and proclaimed, "This is my beloved Son, with whom I am well pleased." John heard it, as did a lot of others. So why does John ask this question now?

Perhaps it's because the time in prison is leading him to doubt. Perhaps he, like some of his followers, doesn't understand my methods. Perhaps he is afraid he will never leave prison, and simply wants me to confirm what he already knows to be true. Perhaps he was sent by my Father to ask the question so his followers could hear the truth again. Perhaps I need to reassure myself who I really am. Most likely, God's plan is so complete that all of the above reasons are valid, along with at least half a dozen more I can't begin to see. The depth and breadth of God's plans never cease to amaze me.

Stunned by the question, I was unable to give them a straight answer. While I know myself to be the Messiah of my people, I'm still not quite comfortable in making that proclamation. Besides, John has been imprisoned for baptizing people; I'd hate to think what they would do to the Messiah.

I told them to look around and report to John all they see and hear. I've called hundreds of people to a new relationship with our beloved Creator and healed many people, making the lame walk, the blind see, and the deaf hear. I even raised some from the dead. Look at the energy that permeates this town and the number of people interrupting their normal routine to come, listen and be cleansed. I told them to look around and observe the works I've done in the name of God, my Father.

They questioned me for a more direct response. I reminded them that their own leader had been imprisoned for baptizing and preaching in the name of God. I said, "Blessed were those who would take no offense in me." This is when they finally understood that my deeds and preaching were sufficient to have me suffer a fate similar to John, or possibly even worse. They realized to verbally claim myself as Messiah would likely have me fall prey to antagonized rulers. They smiled and nodded in understanding, and said they'd relay the message to John.

Before they left, I gave them a special blessing and my deep personal thank you for all the ways John helped me. I gave his men many accolades about their wonderful leader, all well deserved. He has been quite a noble and relentless follower of our Father. I realize he isn't long for this world. My Father is calling him to a different type of peace. He's done his job well. I hope my blessings and the answer to his question reach his ears before they can no longer hear.

Shalom.

97 The Next Day

I can't believe how good it was to announce my identity to others. John's followers, most of whom never saw or heard much of me, simply believed in me. If John could ask the question, they believed it could be true. My answer confirmed it to them, as it will confirm it to John. It appears I was more concerned with being laughed at or thought crazy than I needed to be. I feel like the weight of the world has been graciously lifted from me. I no longer have to hide who I am. I can allow myself to be me.

It is one thing for some of my own followers to believe in me. They have the benefit of long days of teaching and togetherness. They can personally discern that I'm a little different from the average person. They recognize that my closeness to God is distinctive and unique. They can feel the energy within me and witness the spirit of God shine through me. But for these men, who have only seen me once or twice in their lives, to believe in me is truly something special.

Thank you, Father, for this gift today. I'm thankful John's followers stayed an extra day before the long return journey. They rested and ate and shared fellowship with my followers and me. It was truly a day of thanksgiving. Even some of my followers noticed and commented on how I was more relaxed than usual and sensed I was genuinely more joyful. I'm ecstatic today. Again, Father, thank you. I can always trust you to do whatever it is I need.

Shalom.

98 Testimony to John

Today was a different day altogether. First of all, John's followers left. I couldn't believe how saddened I was at their departure. It was as if a part of me was leaving with them. Even though I have only known them for a few days, my heart was yanked apart. I know they were going to return with the answer to John. For that, I was glad to see them off. But a certain place in my heart lay heavy with loss. I sometimes wonder how such opposite emotions can run together at the same time.

As they were leaving, some of the townspeople mocked me by calling me the "Messiah." It was clear from their tone of voice they believed none of it. Then, to make matters worse, they even started to doubt John and the validity of his mission. More people gathered quickly. Even the ones who had seemed so content and comfortable with me quickly took on the new spirit of hatred and mocking of the rest.

I reminded them that the spirit obviously touched them since John baptized many of them and many others went out to the desert to seek John. I questioned why they had followed him. Did they think John was a mighty king, dressed in fine clothes? No, they went to see a prophet, they found one, and he baptized them.

I reminded them of the Scripture that indicates God would send a messenger to prepare the way for the Messiah. I told them I had never seen anyone as blessed as my cousin. His life was devoted to God, and God alone. He sought no riches. He dined on food most of us wouldn't think of eating. He lived simply and austerely. In the eyes of God, he was great, the greatest yet. John is the messenger. He is Elijah. All people have to do is accept it and believe in it.

I reminded them that John came to announce the Kingdom of God. He served as the herald to a new time and a new spirit. All of us have an opportunity to live and grow in the new Kingdom of God, a kingdom unlike anything the world has known. Anyone who can live in the Kingdom is greater even than John.

I told them that they were standing on the forefront of a new age, a new beginning. But they are often like children who sit in the marketplace. They play the flute, and no one dances; they sing a dirge, yet no one mourns. Why? The sounds of the marketplace overtake the sounds of the flute. The crowds, the foodstuff, the clothes and the trinkets absorb them. The children see and hear only what they want to. They are too wrapped up in themselves and too busy being righteous to do the right thing. Too busy thinking they have all the answers to listen to the truth.

They see the truth in John. They join for a few brief moments, but then return to the "real" world, and lose all they have gained. Now they doubt the identity of John because he came neither eating nor drinking and they reasoned he must be controlled by a demon. Then they condemn me because I come eating and drinking. They say I'm nothing more than a drunk and a glutton. I even have the audacity to befriend sinners and tax collectors, so I am only an example of the demon.

I challenged them to find fault or demons in the results of any of John's or my actions. I think I went on a little too much with this, but I was upset they had the audacity to mock John. Besides, I couldn't believe the speed at which these people changed from supporters to antagonists. I even went as far as complaining about some of the town and villages I visited that rejected my words.

After this chastisement, the younger members of the audience, some of them were only a mere twelve or thirteen, challenged me in my own preaching. They reminded me I should always look to forgive, even if it means forgiving those who rejected my teachings. They reminded me that the greatest gift is love, which requires accepting each other wherever we are.

They were right. I wasn't accepting or forgiving at all this day. I had gotten so wrapped up in the rejection, not just of me but also of John, my dear cousin, that I fell short of the mark myself. How ironic. I thanked them and gave praise to God, Father of us all. He sometimes hides things from men, sometimes even me, but He chooses to reveal them to the children. It's obvious I'm not alone in being able to understand God. He can reveal Himself to anyone.

Please help me, Father. Help me find comfort being the Son of Man. It's a most arduous task. I know I need your help with every step every day. Please continue to work through me and help me free myself of the humanity that seems to limit my ability to be fully and completely your Son, your representative on earth.

Shalom.

99 Yoke

My followers and I left a few days ago. We had time to rest and I had time to ponder God's magnificence. It's incredible in how many different ways He chooses to reveal His plan for me. It's wonderful how He uses other people to teach me or remind me of the truths He has given me; the truths I sometimes ignore. Just marvelous.

Today we encountered Matthew and Philip. They were complaining about the arduous task I gave them. I reminded them I didn't give them any task, they volunteered to follow God, and I merely assisted. They complained about heat, hunger, thirst, lack of a good place to sleep, and above all, deaf ears. They felt they could better endure the trials and tribulations of preaching if they could see more fruits of their labor.

I told them all who labor and are burdened should turn to me for rest. My yoke is easy; the burden I give is light. First, they thought I meant I would assist them in their task, but as I talked more, they saw the light. I intended them to give me their burdens. The fact that other people don't listen isn't for them to fret about.

My own lessons have quickly come into use. I would have been of little comfort if I were still tormenting over the same difficulties they were. I explained that their job was only to preach, to lay the framework. God will utilize the seeds we plant in His time. In the meantime, they should not judge their success in numbers. God's plan is comprehensive and complete, even if it appears a bit invisible at times. "Give me the burden of those who hear but choose not to listen, those who watch but choose not to see."

Thankfully, they left with renewed vigor and vitality to go out again to teach, and they were glad to leave me behind.

After all, I have all the burdens, so they were glad not to be with me. They still have a sense of humor.

Shalom.

100 Grain on Sabbath

Today is the Sabbath. We were walking from one town to the next. Being hungry, my followers began to pick grain and eat it. We were not too far from the next town and some townsfolk saw us picking the grain. They told the Pharisees, who quickly came to the field and chastised us for working on the Sabbath, disregarding one of God's most precious laws. Obviously, this was just one way of making me look bad. For how could the Son of God not follow one of the most sacred laws, a law given from God himself?

I reminded them that David and his men went into the temple and ate the offering. Even priests themselves were working on the Sabbath. This is one of the silliest interpretations of God's law I've encountered. The Sabbath is a day to be holy, a day of rest. But it isn't intended for humans to starve. God gives us life each day and the daily events of life should never be understood as work. Food and drink are vital to existence.

They were insinuating I couldn't be the Messiah since I broke the law. This would have the effect of turning people away from me. I decided to use their own sword against them. I told the people the Messiah is greater than the temple, and the Son of Man is the ruler of the Sabbath and all else God provides. Besides, the law also calls for mercy, so if the Pharisees themselves were true to the law, they would treat these men, regardless of who they were, with mercy.

I was again surprised at how easily the words flowed from my mouth. They were definitely words from above. I can always tell because of their special power. It was fun to watch the whole crowd turn against the Pharisees, as if a light was ignited within them.

We continued into the village and visited the synagogue. Recognizing us, the Pharisees tried to trap me again. A man was there with a withered hand. They asked if it was acceptable to heal on the Sabbath. However, it wasn't really a question of whether it was right or wrong to heal on the Sabbath – it was directed to challenge my ability to heal! This man had had a withered hand since birth and many others tried in vain to heal it. The Pharisees wanted to prove I was an impostor.

Of course, I couldn't resist a good challenge. I explained to them that we'd all help a sheep that had fallen into a well on the Sabbath. Since man is so much more valuable than sheep, it would also be required of us to help each other. Doing good is the rule for each and every day.

I prayed to my Father to heal the man's withered hand. Nothing happened right away, and the Pharisees sneered at me. But before the service was over, the man cried out almost hysterically. He had looked at his hand, which was now as strong and sturdy as the other. The people rushed over to him and looked on in amazement.

The Pharisees, who by this time had spoken so loud and long against me, were not in a position to retract their words. They had to find another excuse to chastise me. They counseled the people to beware of me because the deeds I did were of the devil, I was no man of God, and there was no answer other than death. The scene got ugly. We were afraid some of the people following the Pharisees' advice were going to stone us then and there. As the people in the crowd started to argue with each other, we left quietly.

We said very little tonight. It was as if something had changed. We were used to anger and negative words, but these people were actually ready to kill us. For the first time, I felt that I might soon leave this earthly vessel because my

Father was calling me away from all this. It's a bit confusing, and I'm sort of numb thinking about it. There's something God is trying to reveal to me, perhaps the answers I've been seeking.

I'm so caught up in the dealings of today I simply can't find a quiet space in my heart to listen. Even recapping the events of today hasn't helped. In fact, it only made me realize the confusion I'm facing. God has given me the task to change the world, but now He seems to call me to die. I'm finally comfortable in my role as Messiah, Son of Man and Son of God, and now it all changes again. It's like climbing a mountain. You go up and up, and when you think the summit is around the next bend, you discover it is nowhere near.

Dear Father, I know you are trying your hardest to reveal your plan to me. You want me to save the people you've created and to show them a new and different understanding of your love and the life you wish them to lead. Help me accept and follow you, no matter where it leads.

Shalom.

101 More Healing

It's been a few days since the Sabbath. Many of the townspeople, especially those in need of some type of healing have followed us. I've healed them all. It seems as if my gift of healing is growing stronger, but also more automatic with each passing day. I just turn to my Father and ask for His will, and if they are to be healed, let it be done. They are all healed. They, like all the others, want to shout out the wonders I've accomplished for them. I'm so absorbed with the last Sabbath and the reaction of the Pharisees I ask them to tell no one. I sincerely doubt any will listen.

In some ways this almost automatic healing is good. I have little doubt that I can heal the people who come and it involves very little effort. However, it is also a problem because I don't feel as alive and in touch with my Father.

I'm still somewhat unsure of God's plan. He allows me to heal, a wonderful gift. Yet, He allows some people to use my ability to heal against me. It's growing more and more obvious to me that His plan is to call me home. I'd like to think the time is far away, but I have an uneasy feeling it's very close. I know I shouldn't really need to know what God's plan is, but I must admit a large part of me wants to know exactly what He's doing. I pray He provides me with a glimmer of understanding.

Shalom.

102 Beelzebub

Today more and more people came to be healed. The Pharisees showed up again, too. They had obviously discussed the matter with the last group of Pharisees we encountered and exhibited the same attitude. They witnessed me heal a person who was blind and mute since birth.

The crowd started whispering amongst themselves that maybe I really was the promised Messiah. I was surely different and gifted, and displayed a spirit from God. But the Pharisees took over and "explained" to the people how I receive my power from none other than Beelzebub. I heal to turn people towards the devil himself.

The crowd, being fickle, began to look upon me as the devil's own. I felt anger well up within them again. I've still not learned to simply accept people wherever they are and allow God to work His miracles through me. I got angry because they challenged the very Spirit of my Father. I succumbed to my anger once again. I told them if they were not with me, then they were against me. There was no room for neutrality. I told them sin and blasphemy against people, even against me, the Son of Man, could be forgiven. But to blaspheme against the Spirit, which is directly of my Father, can never be forgiven.

Now as I reflect upon the situation, I realize I don't particularly like this human part of me, which is subject to anger and tends to bully people. "Be with me or against me." Not a very loving and caring thing to say. Certainly not something I've ever heard from my Father. He keeps telling me all of His creation is His. They all have a path and they all have free will. He is willing to accept them with all their shortcomings. He never stops providing them opportunities to come to know him.

I have to remember one of my old lessons: to embrace emotions. Being human, being the Son of Man, not the Son of God, is what I'm most thankful for. Being able to be fully alive is to experience the full range of emotions, some good and some not so good.

Dear Father, help me celebrate the times you give me to be fully human and fully alive. I know you are always with me, even when I may fall a little short of the mark. Help me to stop beating myself up for my shortcomings, but simply accept them as part of the human being I am.

Shalom.

103 A Tree and Its Fruit

Today my followers and I were discussing the events of the past few days. They asked me about the things I said about myself. I told them we must either declare ourselves good or bad. Just as bad fruit doesn't come from a good tree, good fruit doesn't come from a bad tree. A truly bad person can't bring about good from the inside. And conversely, how could evil things produce anything truly good?

But let me get more to the point about myself. I still feel a nagging in my soul from my Father. I know He's trying to tell me something about dying. The subject keeps repeating itself in my life. I fear He's telling me I am to die soon. The story of Jonah keeps coming back to me over and over again. Just as Jonah was in the belly of the large fish for three days, so shall I be. I'm not completely certain as to your meaning, Father; please help me place my whole being into your hands.

Shalom.

104 The Sign

We were in a friendly place today. The scribes and Pharisees had heard about my ministry and me but rather than reject me, they embraced me. It felt good. I needed a little reassurance. I know I should be comfortable in my knowledge of who I am and rely on Abba for all the confidence I need, but the weight of the rejection from His main followers, the leaders of the Jewish people, takes its toll on me. In fact, I didn't realize how much I needed reassurance until I received it today. My Father always gives me exactly what I need, no matter what.

Today, the scribes and Pharisees wanted a sign. I chastised them a little. Faith isn't about signs. It's about a firm belief in the things they can't see. What more could they want but the signs and miracles I've performed repeatedly? They want other signs. I said my sign would be like the sign of Jonah. I told them the people of Nineveh repented on fewer signs than what I had already performed. I'm sure they didn't understand it because I'm still struggling to understand it myself. But there must have been a reason God wanted me to speak those words.

At least these scribes and Pharisees were willing to listen. Woe to the ones who ignore me and condemn me. They will have to answer to my Father. These scribes and Pharisees listened intently to all my words, even the ones I'm sure they didn't understand. They seemed to find some solace in them.

They questioned me on the unclean spirits I've cast out. Where do they go, they wondered. I explained that unclean spirits wander around and usually return to the same place they left. The ones who have truly been cleansed will have no room for them, and they will be forced to leave again. But the unclean spirits will seek some reinforcements and will again try to dwell in the same place. The condition of the person will then be worse. We all have to fight the same evil repeatedly within ourselves.

I've found this in myself. Whatever within me is furthest from God is the thing I have to keep fighting. Right now, I'm again fighting my doubts. The spirit of doubt keeps returning to me, no matter how many times I cast it out. I still question if I can really be the Son of God. As a human being, this seems so outlandish. How could anyone believe I'm the Son of God, when I can barely believe it myself? I know the things God has done for me, but are they real? Reality seems to be fleeting, and it changes depending on a point of view.

Dear Father, help me overcome my doubts, and help me better realize my sonship, both the Son of Man and the Son of God, you have graciously bestowed upon me.

Shalom.

105 My Family

I was speaking to the crowds again today. I felt a certain exuberance I haven't felt in a while. The reason for this is that I'm overcoming the doubts that have been plaguing me recently. The doubts in my ministry lead to frustration. Then my preaching sounds confusing and hard to understand. Today, however, I again had the gift of clarity.

My family came to visit today. I used this as an opportunity to illustrate the point I was trying to make about unity. It was again enjoyable to recognize the precision with which my Father can maneuver all the things in this world. This was just a little coincidence, but a powerful one for me. I asked, "Who is my Mother, and who are my brothers?" I pointed to my disciples and told the crowd these men were my family. They worked with me, ate with me, prayed with me, taught with me, and healed with me. We shared our life together, just as we do with family. My family is measured not only by birth. I'm related to all who recognize the one true God and do whatever they can to follow him. We are all truly brothers and sisters in God, and all who truly follow Him recognize that.

I know I touched a lot of people with my discourse. A few of my followers started to cry and they hugged each other. Imagine the power of God – grown men were hugging other men in public! My mom and some other members of my family joined us and started to cry as well. It was an incredible outpouring of love. My mom knew I was in good hands with my followers. My followers, in turn, felt the warmth and kindness of the woman who raised me. It was as if we were all truly related to each other from birth. In a way, we are. I couldn't believe the power that permeated the synagogue today. It made my entire body tingle. My mother later said that she could feel it too.

Thank you, Father, for the incredible way you bring all things to yourself and for the restored confidence in my family, my followers, and me as well as the scribes and Pharisees in this holy place.

Shalom.

106 Parables

Lately I've been on fire with my preaching. God fills my head with wonderful stories to tell. I enjoy the preaching part better than the healing part. Healing is more physical, and people don't genuinely find God in the mere healing of their physical being. I don't think they understand that being able to truly hear involves not simply listening to the word of man but, more importantly, hearing the word of God.

Parables allow me to relate the ways of God in common language. People have to think about them and use their own intelligence to discern what God is saying. I also know parables often enable us to hear different things, depending on what angle you look at and what each individual needs to grow. Preaching definitely helps people grow to understand the Father I've been privileged to know more than healing the body.

I told the crowd a parable about God planting seeds today, using the example of a person sowing seeds. Some of the seed fell on the path and birds ate it. Other seed landed on rocky ground, where it sprang up but then quickly died in the hot sun. Other seed fell in thorns and the thorns choked it. Other seed fell on rich soil and produced fruit many times.

I was trying to tell them that my words are the seeds of a sower. Everyone needs to examine their inner self to see if they were like the path, the rocky ground, the thorns or the rich soil. I was telling them to look for the rich soil when they sow seed. Sowing seeds on rocks is a waste of time. I was also warning them not to be the birds, the rocks or the thorns. The birds represent people who think they know everything and rob the seed themselves before it can truly take root. There are several ways to understand this parable. Everyone needs to hear whatever is meant for them at the time.

My followers questioned me about the parables today. They prefer my straight talk. They like me to explain the parables to them or simply say whatever I need to say. I explained that everyone is different, and like the sower in the parable, I need to throw my seed everywhere. When the word is sown, some people are on the path and as soon as they hear it, Satan comes and takes it away. Some people are on the rocky ground. They receive the word at once with joy, but they have no root and the word lasts only a short time. Others are among the thorns, who hear the word but the anxieties of the world, the lure of riches or the cravings for power and fame choke out the word and it bears no fruit. And finally, others are rich soil. These are the ones who hear the word and accept it and bear much fruit.

Also, I need to understand my seed is a gift from God. He wants me to sow everywhere and not be mindful of looking only for fertile soil. I have to understand that some of the seed was intended for the birds all along. I have to let my Father determine where the rich soil is and where the rocks are.

I assured my followers they've been especially chosen to understand the new ideas and new thinking I've been given about my Father and His Kingdom. I reminded them about the difficulties they had before with some of the things I said. I reminded them of Isaiah's prophecy about how people will hear but not understand and look but not see. The use of parables helps facilitate the coming of this prophecy and helps heal people in a spiritual sense.

It certainly feels great, Abba, to fully realize within myself the sonship you have so graciously given me. Help me overcome my doubts forever.

Shalom.

107 Weeds Among the Wheat

Today I used yet another parable to relay a message about the Kingdom. In this parable, a farmer sows wheat. In the evening, his enemy comes and throws in weeds. When the farmer realizes it, he allows the weed to grow because pulling out the weeds would harm the wheat. He allows it to grow until harvest at which time the laborers gather the weeds first and then gather the wheat.

With this parable, God was reminding me again that it's my job to sow seed everywhere. He certainly is aware some of my good seed is being strewn with weeds. I want to go back and try to pull up the weeds. But God's plan is better. I must simply sow the good seed my Father has given me. I should not bother to get rid of the weeds around them. That's His job. They can grow together until my good seed has matured. Then, when the weeds are pulled, He'll be able to harvest the wheat.

As you can tell, I'm having many good days. I feel as if God and I are so much at one I don't have to force myself to pray. He is present with me at all times. He is a part of my ministry and me. I wake thinking of Him and I minister with Him as a constant companion. I open my mouth to speak, and the words flow out effortlessly. I've freed myself of the doubts around me. I find myself full of energy. I sleep and eat well. My days are full of joy, peace, and wonder. It's a most unusual yet incredible feeling. I can almost imagine heaven to be but an extension of this. I feel as if my entire being is in harmony with the world, my work, and my Father.

Thank you, Father, for giving me this experience. It's so hard to explain it to the others. I hope they can see it in my actions and I hope you find a way to lead them to it as well.

Shalom

108 Mustard Seed

Each day is better than the last. More and more people are flocking to hear my preaching. I heal a few, but the focus is on preaching. I'm not alone in the gift of healing – many of my followers are capable of healing too, but the preaching seems to be best left to me. I still speak with the power of my Father. My tongue burns with the right things to say. I answer questions competently and comfortably. Rarely does anyone misunderstand the answer. It's as if each response is specifically tailored to the person who asked it.

God gave me another interesting parable today. Abba seems to be using seeds quite often in His lessons. This time I spoke about the smallest of seeds, the mustard seed. We all know it grows into one of the tallest and sturdiest bushes. Many birds of the field find shelter in it and make it their home. The mustard seed is representative of the seeds God sows.

Each little seed I plant has the potential to grow to phenomenal proportions, much greater than one could imagine. It isn't the size or the number of seeds that's important. It's simply the seed. My seed is of God, and no mere human can limit the potential of a seed planted by God. Each seed has the ability to become a mighty bush, sturdy and tall. Each can provide shelter and a home for numerous other creatures of my Father, even the tiniest one.

I urge people to listen and spread the good news of my Father – the good news of His love and concern. Spread it to all their friends and family. The seed they plant could be the mustard seed. Fear not to make an error, because the only error will be in failing to sow the seed at all.

The people and my disciples were astonished again today at my ability to preach with the energy and enthusiasm and freshness I've been able to. My thoughts are rarely repetitive, and I can hold their attention for extended periods of time. I simply love it. I know with the seeds my Father has given me recently I can indeed change the world. Once the seed is planted, its growth is unlimited.

Father, I thank you for the wonderful gift of my ministry again. I thank you for the wonderful gift of my followers. And I thank you for the wonderful gift of the people, your people, who you love and cherish, and call to be yours.

Shalom.

109 Yeast

Today I was preaching, and my Father gave a wonderful parable to me comparing the Kingdom of Heaven to yeast. Women use but a little bit of yeast and work it through the dough until the entire bread rises. This is just like my Father. He only uses a small portion of His spirit. He gives it to me or to others, and then He works it and works it until the entire dough is leavened.

I needed this parable today because I have been feeling a little disengaged. It seems as if I'm not growing in the ways of my Father. It seems as if I've stagnated. I'm preaching and teaching His word. Occasionally, I will still heal someone, and all is going well. I haven't had too many disagreements from the Pharisees and Sadducees lately, but somehow, I feel a little empty. I don't feel as if I'm growing and learning.

The gift of the parable today was wonderful. The new parables God gives me help me see some new things about His Kingdom. Today the parable of the yeast was new and refreshing. God was telling me He could make so much out of so little. I don't need to save everyone, because He can use my yeast to leaven a lot of bread.

I'm also like the bread – with a little bit of yeast, the bread leavens. People eat it and are nourished. It's an awesome comparison, so simple yet so powerful. I know God's entire Kingdom follows the rules He has created. His rules are easily identified by looking at the rules of nature.

Dear God, my Father, I love you. Thank you for the wonderful gifts today. Thank you for giving me renewed enthusiasm in my ministry. Thank you for letting me know I still have lessons to learn. Thank you for showing me again that I don't have to be all things to all people. I'm only the yeast to help leaven the bread, or the bread that provides nourishment.

Shalom.

110 Buried Treasure

It's been going so well lately. I've had a tremendous amount of balance in my life. My Father is like my best friend who I can talk to at any time. He gives me enough time each day to share with Him. In the past I wasn't always able to properly identify the time He provided to be with Him. Lately, it's been easy. I wake up and say hello. We talk. I share with my followers while we eat breakfast. Then the crowds start coming. I keep my Father with me as I preach. Many times, I open my mouth and simply act as a channel for God to speak through me. Those are the most personally satisfying times. Other times I use some of the same teachings God has given me before. Every now and then even I can see a new meaning in one of the parables.

The Kingdom of God is much like a buried treasure. Once we see even the smallest glimpse of it, we will sell everything we own to find more. It's like a person who finds a treasure buried in a field and sells all he has to buy the field. Or like a merchant in search of fine pearls who sells all he has to buy a very special pearl.

I asked the crowd if they have ever found some treasure worthy of everything they own. Most have something special that means more to them than anything. This is exactly what I find with my Father's Kingdom. The only difference is my treasure is the only true treasure for each and every one of us. I wish I could give a glimpse of this treasure to everyone, yet all I can do is tell them about how wonderful it is. I asked them if they understood the things I preached today. They said they did. I was overwhelmed.

I instructed the scribes to write down what they heard, because they are like the head of a new household, who bring out both the old and the new from His storeroom. The old is the Holy Scriptures as we know them, the Torah, the law. The new is what I preach and teach, the new word from my Father that He gives me, so I, in turn, can pass it on to others. I ask them to record these words for all to know in the future.

Father, thank you so much for the gift of today and for the gift of understanding you have so generously given to these fine people today. May they know only half the joy I know, the joy that can only come from truly knowing and loving you. Please help them to love as you have taught me to love. Help them truly live the new laws you have given me and help write them in their hearts as well as on paper. Father, again I thank you for enthusiasm for life and the joy you have so amply given me. May I remain worthy to be your son, and may you be proud of me.

Shalom.

111 Return to Nazareth

I was so excited this morning. I was going home to Nazareth. I wanted to see my old friends and family so much. I was looking forward to the moment of my homecoming so much for the past week! Have you ever been gone a long time? When you return, you are full of joy to renew past acquaintances and share your life with your friends.

What a rude awakening awaited me! I preached to them about the joy of my Father. I told them about all the wonderful gifts He had given me, my gift of healing, my gift of wisdom, and the great gift of His love. I could see they were truly amazed at how much I had matured while I was away. I knew they were astounded at my preaching and the power of my words. But when I told them how I loved them all, they turned away from me.

It wasn't at all the reaction I anticipated. I expected them to open their hearts to me and allow my love to flow in and theirs to flow into me. I think I scared them. They were not ready to love at the level of my love, and they chose to pull tightly into their own inner shell. I was upset at first and spoke hastily out of the intense hurt I felt.

But now, as I ponder the events of today, I can tell the reaction I received from my fellow villagers was fear. It all makes sense. Fear. It was definitely fear. Fear of being vulnerable. Fear of being hurt. Fear of the unknown. Or maybe even panic. The thought of allowing their inside to be totally open to me – just as mine was to them – caused panic and immediate retreat. I can't expect to dance back into their life and be their number one friend. I should have moved a little more slowly and with a little more caution. I wanted them to run long before they learned to crawl. They were simply taken off guard.

This is one of the mightiest burdens my Father has given me. As the Son of Man, my feelings and awareness of God, my ability to love, the depth of my being is far greater than anyone else's. I realize I was caught up in loneliness at having no one to share it with. I long for someone in the flesh, someone I can touch, someone I can converse with, someone I can cry with or laugh with, someone who can truly recognize and appreciate the depth of my love. This is the loneliness I must bear. John and Mary are the closest to me, but his love is immature and childish, and hers is challenged by being of the opposite sex. I was hoping beyond hope that the friends of my youth would fill the gap, and I rushed into it without recognizing they, too, had the same limitations as everyone else. My openness scared these friends and family members today. Obviously, they weren't ready to be that open and honest.

Of all the challenges my Father has given me, loneliness is the worse. I can't help but wonder if, at some level, all of humanity is lonely. Can anyone really allow themselves the gift of being truly and completely open? To share all of one's self? This is the true test of love.

Shalom.

112 Death of a Friend

Today I heard of the awful demise of my cousin John. Herod was getting even with him. John had spoken against his affair with his brother's wife, so he had him arrested. Herod kept him in prison because he feared the people would revolt if he had him killed. But, alas, John died at Herod's hand. Not long ago I was expressing my loneliness, and now a fellow believer, a dear friend as well as a cousin is dead. Upon hearing this news, I needed time to pray alone. I went off by boat to a quiet place I know along the lake, and I've been here all afternoon with nothing but my thoughts.

I'm filled with a lot of different emotions. I'm angry someone as devoted and harmless as John could die in such a fashion. I'm a little confused as to why my Father allowed, or even dictated this fate. Perhaps it's all part of my growth process. Perhaps John suffered enough and worked enough, and my Father called him home. Perhaps there are a great number of other reasons I can't begin to understand.

I'm surprisingly calm now. I know John is with my Father in heaven, and the how's and why's don't seem to matter so much. I'm also somewhat comforted by death. I find comfort in knowing our existence in this earthly vessel will come to pass. John was simply called back home to His loving Father. We don't cease to be with God when we die – we realize a new and greater presence with Him. It's much like a child exiting the womb. How could any mother want to simply keep the baby in the womb forever? And so it is with my Father.

Thank you, Father, for this new vision of your love and understanding of the world. I thank you for the gift of my cousin John. I thank you for his baptism, faith and encouragement. I know you will take good care of him.

113 Five Thousand

Early this morning, many of my disciples returned along with some townspeople. They greeted me fondly. When they heard of the death of my cousin John, they knew I could use some comfort, so they came. Some of them actually arrived yesterday on foot, after what I'm sure was a long journey. Here I am, concerned with loneliness, and my Father sends not just some of my friends, but even people I don't know to share my grief with. It's truly amazing. They may not understand God the way I do or be able to love at the same depth I can, but here they are, ready to share what love they have with me.

As the day wore on, more and more townspeople arrived. They heard how I had helped their relatives and friends and they came to offer whatever they could to me, a stranger who was so helpful to them. I had to battle the tears of joy in my eyes all day. I preached and healed some as they told me their stories.

There must have been five thousand people who came for me. All common, ordinary people, most of whom I don't even know. Some walked a long way. What an intense feeling of bliss for me. The amazing thing is how my Father answered my loneliness. I was searching for God's plan yesterday in the death of John, and God uses it to help me, His son, find comfort from my loneliness.

My Father used this day to help me in yet another way. At dinnertime it became apparent we were all getting hungry and wouldn't be able to return to the villages before dark. My followers urged me to send the people away, but I thought it was already too late, especially for the children and elderly to safely reach the nearest village.

I heard my Father tell me in a voice only I could hear that I should feed them. I asked, "Feed them what?" He told me to gather whatever food we had and it would be enough. My Father really challenged my faith when my followers returned with only five loaves and two fish. We had thousands to feed, and our food wouldn't even fill a basket.

But my Father clearly said that He would provide for us. I remembered the way He sent manna and doves in the desert. He was certainly a God of His word, and I simply had to trust and believe. I raised the food and blessed it. I asked my Father aloud to make this food ample for all, just as He promised. I divided the bread and fish for my followers to distribute. All the people there, men, women and children took of the food, and all ate until full.

At the end of this hearty meal, I sent my followers to collect the leftovers. Much to everyone's surprise, they returned with twelve full baskets. Twelve, a favorite number of my Father with His definite sense of humor. It was His way of telling me He has, and always will, provide for all His people.

As I lay down this evening to rest, I looked out over this vast crowd of my fellow man. They help me grow in my understanding of my Father and of love. Here I am, deluding myself thinking I alone have the gift of true love. And my Father doesn't reveal my egotism through one or two of my fellow men, but thousands, literally thousands! He made sure I didn't miss His point. All people are capable of love, not just me. Perhaps our understanding of true love, real love, agape love is different. But it isn't a gift my Father has reserved for me alone.

Father. help me remember this day whenever I feel lonely. I'm not alone, now or ever. I am truly the Son of Man. All of mankind is my companion, friend and beloved. Amen.

114 Walking on Water

After the incredible surge of a couple days ago, I woke up refreshed. The rest of my followers have now rejoined us. We had time to share our adventures. It seems most were quite successful in their healing and preaching. Some relayed they experienced the same type of prayers I have. Andrew, Thaddeus and John indicated they heard God speak in their heads. Matthew, Bartholomew, Philip, and James told me that they had times when they opened their mouths to preach and felt as if it were God speaking the words through them. All indicated they had experienced the gift of healing at one time or another. We had much to catch up on, but the crowds were demanding our attention.

I preached to the people most of the morning. I tried to explain, the best I could, the wonderful gift they had given me. How they helped heal me of some of my inner difficulties. How they gave me renewed vigor and understanding of my ministry. I dismissed them and watched as they left. They were in such high spirits.

Oddly enough, as I watched them leave, the loneliness overwhelmed me again. These wonderful people were going back to their families and loved ones, and I was alone with my followers with no place to call home, with no one to share my life and love. I was upset with myself for returning to the negative feelings my Father had so incredibly freed me from just a few days ago. But I'm also a realist, and I've learned denying my feelings only allow them to fester. I had to admit to myself that the loneliness had already returned.

Soon, tears were streaming down my cheeks. My followers thought they were tears of joy, the ones I was fighting the last few days. As they were leaving, I asked them to cross the lake without me, as I really felt the need for some quiet time. They obliged, although I know they really wanted to stay with me. I went up the mountain and tried to sort out my loneliness. I soon realized the irony of the situation. Here, I have a number of loyal followers, people who gave up their families and lives to follow me, people who believe in me and believe in the things I preach, and I'm suffering from loneliness. Rather than share my pain and burden with them, I send them away so I can sulk alone about being lonely.

As I walked down from the mountain to find them, the weather started getting intense. When I arrived at the shore, the boat was gone. It was well offshore, and barely visible. The winds had picked up, and I could tell it was being tossed about quite a bit. They were having trouble steering it, and it seemed to be in danger of capsizing. I asked my Father to help them. He told me to help them myself. I was a bit amazed. Here they were, far out in the lake, and I had no way to get there, not even driftwood to hold onto to help me stay afloat. He said I should just walk over to them.

My being was filled with trepidation as I started into the water. I had actually gone out to my waist, and then chest deep, and then up to my chin. I stopped and again asked my Father to help. The waves were over my head at times, and I was bobbing around rather haphazardly. I heard Him again tell me to simply let go of my fears and place my trust in Him.

I went into my head and closed my eyes in prayer. I felt a lightness around me. I envisioned myself going through the water towards my friends. When I opened my eyes, I realized that the lightness I felt was real! My weight didn't cause me to sink beneath the surface. I was propelling myself, using my legs to walk towards my friends.

One of them saw me and cried out. He thought that I was a ghost. The others cried out in fear, because they saw me too. By this time, I had regained some of my composure. I told them not to be afraid, that it was only me and I came to help them.

Peter, the impetuous one, challenged me to prove myself. I told him to come to me. He leaped out of the boat and started running to me across the top of the waves, but then he realized the impossibility of this action, became afraid, and began to sink. He immediately yelled for me to help him. I was close enough to reach out my hand to his before he had completely submerged beneath the waves.

After we got into the boat, I asked God to still the waters and wind. The winds died down immediately. Peter looked at me and said, "You are truly the Son of God." Then the rest of the people in the boat said, "Amen, Amen." They all had different reactions. Some looked in amazement at me, others bowed to me, others covered their faces in tears, but they all recognized me as the Son of God.

We arrived in Gennesaret while it was still dark. We immediately fell onto the softest places we could find after securing the boat and fell asleep. We didn't rise until midday when several of the townspeople came by and asked if they could help us. Fortunately, many brought food with them, and we had a hearty meal. They sensed that we were tired and needed to rest, so they all took their leave early.

I have so much more to say about last night, but now I'm tired and need to rest.

Shalom.

115 Thoughts

Today was another interesting day. Word of feeding all those people has spread. Many came today for healing and preaching. My followers and I worked hard all day. I don't think I've ever seen so many people. I told some of my favorite parables. They brought enough food to feed an army of men, so I needed no miracle. Or should I say that God provided via a different type of miracle, one we take for granted most days?

I recognize all things, normal and abnormal, are miracles of God. The birth of a baby, the harvest, the sheep who give abundant wool for our clothes without shedding any blood, wells that bring forth good water. We take these things as granted, but everything we have God, my Father, provides.

I'm still overwhelmed with the other night. Walking on water! I recognize my Father was showing me a lesson much deeper than the physical reality. I could walk across the water because I believed in my Father totally and completely. I wasn't afraid. Peter was also able to walk across the water, but only until his belief turned to fear.

Isn't that the underlying truth in all human affairs? When we fully believe in God, we are able to meet any challenge fearlessly, even the seemingly impossible. But when we slip from that commitment, even slightly, we turn to fear. In fear, we sink – and eventually drown – in our troubles. The answer to all things is to fear not and believe in the grace of our loving Father. His love is limitless. And only within His love can we overcome our fears.

Calming the winds was another natural event that parallels our lives. When we are faced with rough seas in our lives, we must turn to our loving Father and seek His assistance. Just as my followers turned to me, and I, in turn, requested assistance from my Father. We must do the same with all things in our lives.

Shalom.

116 Something Missing

Over the past several days, many people came from all over to be healed. They want to touch my garments or even just one of the tassels. I tell them to touch and listen, because the touch only heals their bodies, but listening heals their souls.

I've been struggling these days to find energy to rise and greet these people. Their coming should make me feel wanted and important, but I find they are depleting my energy instead of recharging me. Once, my gift of healing was helpful in my own spirit, now it has become routine. How quickly things change for me. I feel like I'm riding a giant wave, up as high as I can go one second, and then I come crashing down, only to rise high again.

Something seems to be missing in my life, but I'm not sure what. I just go through the motions. I know God has something even bigger planned for me in the future. A part of me wants to skip past the present and jump right into the future. There maybe I will be re-energized. But, now I'm here, I have things to do, and I know from the support of people who come that this is still God's plan.

Dear Father, help me overcome whatever is holding me down. Help me rise each day with a gift of newness and freshness, a spirit not only willing but also eager to serve you. Help me go to sleep every night, starting with tonight, not being thankful for the time to rest, but being thankful for the day you gave me and the ability to serve you even better the next day. Help me find the gift of energy and spirit that comes only from being in complete oneness with your spirit. Help me find energy in each and every moment you give me so that I can enjoy your people, my brothers and sisters. Help me put my mind over my body and be the Son of Man you have created, one full of life and full of the Spirit of my Father.

Shalom.

117 Traditions

Today the elders and officials of the synagogue discovered my whereabouts. They came and challenged me about my failure to abide by traditions, saying that my men didn't always perform the traditional washing of hands before eating. But neither do the elders and officials when they are on the road traveling and don't have the proper facilities!

I told the crowd what truly defiles a person isn't what enters one's mouth – food is nourishment for the body. The words that come out of the mouth, however, can defile someone, because harsh words, lies or words spoken in anger can destroy the spirit of an individual. Even worse, words can destroy the spirit of God that resides within every human being.

Words come from the inner spirit. They are signs of what is truly within a person. Words of peace and harmony show a person in inner peace and harmony. Words of slander, blasphemy, anger, false witness, murder, and so on, are thoughts of a restless and unclean inner spirit. It has nothing to do with the cleanliness or the purity of the food we eat. It has only to do with the purity and cleanliness of our hearts.

At dinner, my followers told me that I had really offended the Pharisees today. I wasn't a bit worried because I only spoke the truth. They are hypocrites and they only seek ways to defile me. In doing so, they defile my Father, whom they say they serve. How can they serve my Father and deny all the things He has done for our fellow Jews through me?

I explained that the Pharisees, the scribes and some of the other elders of the church were blind. Unfortunately, whenever one has a blind person for a leader, they, too, will fall into the pit. I know the seeds my Father plants will be firmly rooted while those not planted and nurtured by my Father will simply uproot.

I know they're afraid I've angered the hierarchy of the Jews again. In so doing, they fear not only for me, but also for themselves. That group is likely to do anything to protect and maintain their identity, part of which requires complete knowledge, complete truth, and complete power. I'm a threat. But my conflict with these church leaders is part of the future my Father has for me. I know it may well spell a disastrous ending for me, but somehow the excitement returned with the ongoing conflict. Strange, but I needed them to remind me that whatever I was doing was truly of my Father.

I know I have the answers from my Father about the way the world should be. I have a better understanding than they do about love, peace, and the nature of the body, which is but a physical shell to house the inner spirit. The truths my Father has given me are lost in the teachings of the Jews. They have twisted the meaning into things that were never intended. They honestly believe the things they preach about God, but the words have long ago lost the true meaning.

I have a new and fresh understanding of what the Scriptures, God's words, mean. It's hard to be an island, all alone in a vast sea. I thank you for my followers and the many in the crowd, who – despite the words of the leaders and Jewish officials – have come to me to seek the truth. They listen. They must understand at least portions of what you have given me – my followers have remained loyal and the crowds keep coming. They come not just to be healed, but also to hear the words of a different type of preacher. Thank you, Father, for instilling this energy, the energy for the truth, into our cause and into my being.

Take care of our religious leaders, Father. Find ways to open them to your word. Find ways to end their pride and ego. It's impossible to fill them with the real truth when they are certain they already possess it. Father, they truly intend to serve you. Help them. They need you and your love.

Shalom.

118 More Thoughts

The Pharisees left me alone. I think they were angry with me but didn't know how to come out victorious, so they simply withdrew. The crowds continued to seek healing, but some came for blessings. This was a bit of a new touch. I blessed a couple that was with their first child, another couple about to be wed, and a man who had just lost his wife. He asked me to bless him and his children so that he may be a good provider for them and that they might grow up to love God. I was amazed at the simplicity of these requests. To come not for healing of some illness or infirmity but simply to be blessed to do the work my Father gave them!

Oddly enough, the thoughts of walking on water consumed me today again. I've realized that walking on water is the symbol of all physical impossibilities. We can do anything we set out to do, even the seemingly impossible, whenever we do so with our Father in Heaven. Whether it's walking on water, calming the seas, ordering a barren tree to bear fruit, or finding manna in the desert, the physical realities all obey God. It is true for all of life's difficulties and impossibilities.

However, certain things are in God's plan, while others are not. I must be careful not to overstep my ability to call on my Father to create the physically impossible. Constantly reshaping things to my way because I can is only going to limit my ability to accomplish my Father's plan.

I have much to contemplate. Father, help your children overcome the winds of trial in their life, help them grow from their trials, and help them be more understanding of your ways and mysteries whenever trials face them. Help me follow your plan wherever it leads, and follow it joyfully, without trying to change the physical realities of the world.

119 Canaanite Woman

We are now in the region of Tyre and Sidon. We have been here for a few days. Today I encountered a Canaanite woman who asked me to heal her daughter, who was tormented by a demon. First, I ignored her. When she persisted, I told her I was here to help the chosen children of God, the Israelites.

But the woman didn't leave. She paid me homage and earnestly requested I help her. I told her it wasn't right to take the food from children and feed it to the dogs. I wished I could have taken those words back immediately after I had said them. That was truly one of the most insensitive and hurtful things I've ever said to anyone in my life. I know my Father has sent me to heal the hearts and bodies of the Jews first, but that's no excuse to be so disrespectful to others.

She replied, "Even the dogs eat the scraps that fall from the table."

I looked deeply into her warm, friendly, brown eyes. They displayed compassion and the simplicity of genuine love for her daughter and God. Once again, God stripped me of my pride. The knowledge of being God's Son all too often allows me to think myself better than God's other children. Here I am, thinking God wants me to serve His chosen people, the Jews. Silly me! It takes a simple Canaanite woman to show me the real truth, the one I already knew. God's love and God's will are for all His children. His chosen ones are not only the Jews but all people everywhere. Every person alive, or who was alive, or will be alive are brothers and sisters in one God.

Needless to say, I complimented the woman on her faith, her love of God, and her love of man. I told her that her faith was great, and it was her faith, and her faith alone, that would allow her daughter to be healed. She smiled and fell to her knees and began kissing my feet. I knelt down alongside her, took her hand in mine, and again looked into her eyes, now full of tears. I whispered to her that her faith has helped me and told her it was I who should be kissing her feet. She looked at me and nodded as if she had understood the gift she had given me. I heard later that her daughter was healed.

Father, again and again I come to you with pride as my number one enemy. Help me, as you always do, overcome my haughtiness. Help me remain a servant to your wonderful people, all my brothers and sisters. Help me never think I'm above them, that I'm their superior. Being your Son means being the Son of Man. As the Son of Man, I'm the servant, not the master.

Shalom.

120 Healing of Many

We walked along the Sea of Galilee and went up a nearby mountain. I couldn't believe the amount of people who've come. They've been coming day after day for the past week. It's incredible to see so many people in need of healing. They are coming with the lame, blind, deformed, mute, and all types of other illnesses. My followers and I have healed most of them.

There are a few who simply can't believe in me. Even though they make the long journey, they return unhealed, almost as if to prove themselves correct. It's a sort of self-fulfilling prophecy. Isn't that ironic? Those who can't believe in my ability to heal block it. But it isn't my healing they are blocking – they are blocking themselves! It seems as if people can control their own destiny.

I'm again enjoying my ability to heal thoroughly. I still preach to the crowds, but I find the time I spend with each individual and their friends or family while I'm healing them to be the most rewarding part of my day. I find so much energy in their smile or in their gratitude. I tell them it's their own faith that has healed them. I'm but a mediator. I can't do anything alone.

They want to shower me with hugs and kisses. Some try and give me clothes or food. Sometimes we can use the food, but I don't need the clothes, so I turn them down. When they insist, I find it best to accept their gift. People need to give something, usually something material, to express their gratitude. I can always give these presents away to those truly in need.

Father, thank you again for reassuring me and my ministry. Thank you again for this magnificent gift of healing. Thank you for enabling these people to have a faith so strong they find the healing within themselves. Thank you for the gratitude so many have shown. These people are truly my brothers and sisters, truly your sons and daughters. Their simple faith and loving hearts have shown me they truly belong to you. Sometimes we work too hard trying to know all the right words, all the right prayers, all the right rubrics, all the right ceremonies, everything to please you. And yet you are most pleased by simple faith, the faith that can say, "Yes, Lord, I can be healed of this affliction." Please, Father, help us to simplify our lives and faith to simply allow ourselves to love.

Shalom.

121 The Sabbath

It has been several days now, and the crowd seems to be lingering. They arrived over the past few days and decided to stay and share the Sabbath with me. I told them I'm not a Pharisee, Sadducee, Levite, or scribe. In fact, I have no position of authority in the earthly temple. They seem to sense my power from God and have chosen to stay anyway. Needless to say, they didn't bring enough food for a stay this long.

Today is the Sabbath, and the crowd is hungry. The service we had was magnificent. It lasted all day. I spoke about various passages in the Scriptures. Others gave a personal witness of God in their life. I learned a lot from them. Mostly, I learned how God works in the simplest everyday things of our life.

I was expecting everyone to say how my healing of them, a friend or family member gave them an instantaneous and complete understanding of God in their life. I was wrong. They pointed out the faith they had *before* they came. After all, it was faith that led them to me. I wasn't the beginning, nor am I the end. They all recognized faith in God was something they lived each and every day. Some of them saw God in the harvest or in a much-needed rain. Some saw God in the smile of their child. All of them included my healing and my preaching in their witnesses, but it wasn't *everything* that led them to faith. This was clearly another one of God's humbling experiences.

Being God's one and only Son, sent by Him to save my brothers and sisters, I sometimes assume I'm the first, last, and only one in their lives. Not true. Yes, I may be the Son of God. Yes, following me will lead to my Father. But even in following my footsteps, God will use all things available to assist people in their individual journey. Even my own earthly journey has been one example after another of God using other people and everyday things to help me obtain a more complete understanding of my Father and His great love. Once again, my wonderful Father has humbled me from my thoughts of being so high and mighty.

I'm the Son of God, but I'm likewise the Son of Man. God sent me not to lord over my brothers and sisters. He sent me because He loves all of His children. His love is complete, total, all-encompassing and endless. It's the same love He has for me. I'm not better in His eyes. So, my pride in thinking I have a greater role than others is just wrong. My own humanity gets in the way of me being able to be fully love, just as my Father is fully love.

Another of my recurring holes is doubt. It's ironic, isn't it? I vacillate between doubt and pride. When I conquer my pride, I move into doubting the reality of who I am. When I conquer my doubt, my pride overwhelms me. One nice thing about constantly picking the same holes is I find myself becoming better and better at finding my way out of them.

I see the same thing with my followers. In fact, everyone I know well enough seems to repeat the same holes in their lives. Peter is impetuous. In some ways it's a good trait, but it's sometimes too much. I guess all of us have our own assortment of holes and we'll have to deal with them over and over throughout our lives. I hope and pray someday I will recognize a hole before I fall. Until then, I will be thankful for a loving and patient Father, who will always give me a helping hand to get out of my holes.

It's getting late, and it has been a long, eventful and energizing day. After the witnessing was complete, the people in the crowd all laid down their heads and fell fast asleep. Even the smallest children weren't complaining.

Tomorrow I will have to try my hand at feeding these people. My Father did it once, so I know He can do it again.

Shalom.

122 Feeding Four Thousand

I'm writing from Magdala. We left Tyre and Sidon the other day and came to this district. Mary was so happy to see her family again, as was I.

The day after that eventful Sabbath was exciting. Everyone woke up full of vigor and remarkably well rested. The energy was overwhelming. We gathered early in the morning for prayer, and they asked me to preach. I shared some of the things I wrote the night before. They were so impressed. Everyone chimed in about his or her own holes. Some had holes of lack of faith, others had lack of courage, one even admitted to being drawn to unfaithfulness. Incredible.

The next thing I knew, it was already nearing evening. We had not eaten much for a few days, and no one had anything since the morning on the Sabbath. I remembered my last thought of the night before. I would again rely on my Father to feed these people as He had done once before. I asked my followers how much food we had left. We had but seven loaves and a few fish, certainly not enough to feed these people. I looked at them and smiled. Peter realized the meaning of my look immediately. He reminded the rest about the last incident, and they all helped me seat the crowd and quiet them down.

I raised the food and blessed it. I again asked my Father to provide for us, His children, as He had done so amply throughout the ages. I broke the bread and fish and placed it in baskets and my followers passed them around. It took quite some time before they made their way through the entire crowd. After everyone had taken, we also ate. Then we took the baskets and went around again. Some of the people took only small portions at first, fearing there wouldn't be enough. This time, everyone ate their fill. Once again, the fragments we collected were seven baskets, more than I originally blessed.

Some in the crowd thought we must have hidden the food and became a little frustrated we were so selfish. However, some of the people in the front were watching closely and realized the original food was all there was. They passed this word along, and several of them even got up to share what they witnessed. After about the fifth witness, the crowd started believing a true miracle had occurred. They all prostrated themselves to pay homage to me. Even my followers joined in laying prostate, paying homage to me. No wonder I get feelings of pride.

But this time, I recognized the hole in front of me, and I was able to ask my Father for a little assistance in illuminating my path. He responded quickly and thoroughly. I shared the parts of my thoughts I withheld earlier. I was comfortable with sharing my hole of doubt, and many shared they, too, had that hole. First, I was much too ashamed of myself to admit my prideful behavior, but when I did, others also admitted they had a hole of pride, including many of my followers. Some admitted they also had a hole of shame.

When I said a closing prayer asking God to give them a safe journey home, one of the women followed up and said, "Thank you, God, for honesty, humor, humility, and FOOD." What an incredible chain of events.

Shalom.

123 Sadducees Demand a Sign

As customary, some of my first visitors in a new place are the religious leaders. I've found they come not to pray with me or pray for me, or, in fact, to pray at all. They come to challenge me. This group demanded a sign. I told them God gives signs for everything. They learn to read the signs given for the things like the weather, but they can't read the signs of the times.

They've heard the stories of healing, feeding so many with so little, walking on water and commanding the winds. They won't believe in me no matter how many signs I provide. Besides, as I've seen so many times before, if I attempt to heal someone who doesn't believe, the healing won't occur. It isn't me, but the faith of the individual that heals. It's the same with signs. The religious leaders see no signs because their own faith doesn't allow them to witness them. I told them no sign would be given except the sign of Jonah.

I better watch myself. Every time I get around these self-professed "holy" people, I tend to find my way into pride. Father, thank you for allowing me to recognize the hole in front of me. Keep me from slipping into this hole again. Thank you also for placing this hole in front of me. I will never be able to overcome this particular hole if you don't place it in my path. The challenges you place in my path are gifts that assist me in growing to a fuller, deeper and more complete understanding of your love and allow me to be more spontaneous and complete in my love for others.

Shalom.

124 Restlessness

The past few days more villagers have come, but nowhere near as many as before. I'm having great difficulty getting my mind to focus on my work. I find myself preoccupied with something else. I have no idea where my mind is going; it just seems to be wandering around a lot.

I think the answer is for me to leave and find some time to rest. I think if we go out to the sea again I will be able to take time in the boat to simply think about what is bothering me. I'm certain I'm not alone in feeling lost in my mind as I see similar behavior in some of my followers. I noticed a few weeks ago Matthew's head wasn't really with him. Come to find out he received word his brother died. It was difficult for him since he was the oldest and was supposed to be the caretaker. I talked to Matthew and comforted him about his role in the family.

Anyway, the point is while he was having the problem, Matthew was also preoccupied. My difficulty is I'm not yet sure of the source of my discomfort. I imagine it would be best for me to just pray. However, I'm finding it impossible to pray here. I don't know why, but I think I need to get away, be alone and have some time to myself. I think I will have Peter bring me to the other side of the lake so that I would have the opportunity to be alone.

Father, I ask you to help me recognize the source of my discomfort. Please, Father, help bring it clearly into focus so I can understand and grow from it. Help me resume my journey to serve your children.

Shalom.

125 Leaven of the Pharisees

We arrived at the other side of the lake today. I was no more aware of the source of my discomfort today than when we left. I found myself unable to focus in prayer. When the men told me they had forgotten to bring any bread, I blurted out, "You should beware of the leaven of the Pharisees and Sadducees." That was certainly a creative way for my Father to let me know what has been bothering me.

I wasn't concerned about the bread they left behind. Our Father has always found ways to feed us and nourish us. I'm concerned greatly with the Pharisees and Sadducees. They are the chief shepherds of God's chosen people and the leaven they use for spiritual bread for their flock is nothing but nonsense. They don't preach the goodness, wonder and mercy of my Father. They teach everyone to be afraid of Him. We should not fear our loving earthly parents, nor should we fear our heavenly creator.

But this wasn't alone the source of my difficulty. I know my Father is trying to tell me something about the Pharisees. I know I threaten them. They are afraid there are too many people who follow me. They are afraid they are losing control. I also think, at some level, they honestly believe they alone possess the complete truth. Therefore, I'm a menace to their people.

Ironic. God sends me, His son, to help His chosen people gain new insights into His love and His purpose. However, the people He has chosen to guide His children are the last to listen. It's dangerous when we think we have all the answers and all the truths. All people, including myself, need to realize that life requires us to grow. If we think we have all the answers and know all there is to know, we are not open to learn any more. Growth, hence life, I mean spiritual life, ends.

Anyway, I know my Father is trying to tell me something about the future. My comment about the sign of Jonah keeps repeating in my head. It seems Abba is telling me that I, like Jonah, will be in the belly of a large fish, and I, too, will rise again after three days. My followers will reject me, which seems unbelievable since they have been so much a part of who and what I am. It seems the plan also calls for me to die.

My death seems premature. I haven't accomplished enough to change the course of mankind. I haven't been anywhere near effective enough in my preaching. People seem to listen intently, and some leave in a state of bliss like they've been given the gift of ultimate prophecy. But I see them later in the same old distressful bodies they previously had. The bliss and peace are gone. My talk usually rejuvenates them, but I know it isn't for long. I even see this with my closest followers.

Even the simplest messages and simplest truths I teach seem to be forgotten easily. Take the bread today. Can't they realize we have a loving Father who has always provided for us? Why must they worry? And worse yet, why must they blame each other? This only leads to friction amongst us and eliminates any possibility of inner peace. I explained this to them, and they looked at each other sheepishly. They say they've learned and understood. Peter swears he will never doubt God again, but I know "never" for him isn't a long time. I'm almost certain it will only last until the next crisis arises.

Thank you, Father, for the wonderful methods you have to help us understand your ways. Please, whatever your plan is about my future, allow me to understand it in your time frame and don't let it keep me from being effective in my service in the meantime.

Shalom.

126 More Prayer

I've still not completely resolved my inner distress. There is much more to it then I originally recognized. For one thing, my Father is again confirming that I'm His Son. Every time I pray, I say, "Hello, Father." He says, "Hello, my Beloved Son."

In trying to overcome my pride, I have tried to minimize my role as His Son, the Messiah. I recognize we are all His children and we are all created equal, but I'm still somehow different. I have a very special and unique role to play in the history of mankind. But I still need to somehow confirm with my followers I'm indeed the Messiah. I'm worried they won't understand. I'm sure they see me as a special prophet, and they are glad to be in my presence, but to ascend to the role of the Son of God? This is a bit presumptuous.

I know the time is near when I must speak something to these loyal followers. They are not simply followers; they are friends, almost like brothers, and very dear companions. I think perhaps *disciple* is a better definition of what these men are for me. Perhaps if I give them a new title and new role, they may have a lot of prideful thoughts about who they are. Or worse yet, they may be so full of doubt God would ever pick them for such a role that they will simply leave.

I don't think telling these people I'm God's Messiah, sent directly by Him to help in the salvation of the world is a good plan. I know I will have to tell them eventually, and I've been procrastinating long enough. I'm even starting to feel ill, my back hurts, my feet hurt. It seems every time I deny God or fail to follow Him, my body has some sort of negative reaction. I know I will ultimately do whatever God sets in front of me, so I guess the sooner the better. But all the nagging questions remain. How will I tell them? What will they say? Will they ever believe in me? Will they ever believe in themselves? How will they overcome pride? How can someone they've known for so long, someone who they have prayed with, traveled with, laughed with, cried with, and suffered with be the Son of God?

Dear Father, I ask for your help as I struggle through revealing to these wonderful brothers of mine my role as Messiah. I ask you to help prepare them for this truth and help them to accept it as they accept me.

Shalom.

127 Revealing as the Messiah

It only took about another week of praying and procrastinating. Actually, I never did quite muster up enough courage to exactly tell them who I was. Instead, I asked them who people say I was. Some of them said I was a prophet, some even said John the Baptist, some said Elijah or Jeremiah. I asked them who *they* thought I was, not who others thought I was. Peter blurted out, "You are the Messiah, the Son of the living God."

I could hardly believe my ears. I could immediately see that all my worries were needless. I wasn't going to tell them anything God hadn't already prepared them to hear. I also knew my own ministry wouldn't last much longer, so I told Peter he was the rock upon whom I would build my church. I commissioned all the disciples to be a part of the new church and to help Peter.

I was so overwhelmed by this moment I'm certain I can't describe it adequately in words. The presence of my Father was obvious in all of the disciples. Their faith was so simple and their obedience so complete. It was clear God carefully chose each of them, and they were well deserving of the role God gave them. They all have their shortcomings, as we all do. But they are able to listen, observe, follow, and believe in God. They don't have doubts in themselves or the pride I anticipated. They've simply accepted their role and mine.

Once again, God humbled me. In my pride I thought I always have to be the teacher, the leader and the source of strength and understanding. Wrong again. These men, each and every one of them, taught me a lesson, one I hope I will never forget. These men listened to God directly. They followed not just me, but the spirit of God. They accepted whatever the Spirit offered. The Spirit offered I'm the

Messiah, so they readily accepted it. No one challenged me, no one doubted me. Why was I so afraid? Didn't I know that all along?

Tears filled my eyes by the power of that moment. Peter gave me a hug, and everyone else followed. I stood in stunned silence for the longest time. I wasn't sure what to say. I told them their faith was very strong and they were very open to the spirit of God. I felt for the first time that these men would be just fine when my time to leave comes. In their simplicity and humanness, they may have a better chance to bring my message and understanding of God to the rest of the people. They were so beautiful standing there. I assured them I would give them the keys to the Kingdom of Heaven, and that whatever they would bind on earth would be bound in heaven, whatever they loosed on earth would be loosed in heaven. I know they all possess a very special and open relationship with God, even if they are not fully aware of it.

I'm almost certain my claim to be the Messiah will accelerate a confrontation with the Pharisees and Sadducees since my threat will be even greater. In their eyes, the need to "protect" the Jews from someone so obviously deranged will be more apparent. Therefore, I asked the disciples for confidentiality. Father, again and again you reveal your presence to me in everyday people, places and things. Today, you allowed your spirit to completely overwhelm all my disciples and me. I know we all felt it because we were laughing joyfully and full of peace for the rest of the day. We were able to accomplish more healings and preach at a level that encompassed the entire crowd with a feeling of wonder.

I love you, Father, I love you with all my heart and soul. I love you with my entire being. I don't yet understand all the intricacies of your plan, but I thank you for days like today, when you reveal so much to me and help me overcome the fears which keep me from being in complete unity with you.

I found my love was taken to another level today: it enabled me to overcome my pride and doubt. Will they ever return? Possibly. That's part of my humanity. I, unlike my Father, am subject to the distractions and difficulties all humans are subject too. These limit humans from being the pure essence of love, which is God. I need to experience this level of love so I can better understand you, and better understand my role in salvation. It's like food for the starving or drink for the thirsty.

Father, I do love you. Thank you for today and thank you again for sending me here. And above all, thank you for these wonderful men, my disciples.

Shalom.

128 Understanding My Future

The little boy in me has been asking Abba to be more explicit about my future for a while. "How will I save these people? What significant role will I play in this human existence? Please, Abba, tell me, it will help me continue." Today, my Father gave me a more definitive vision of my own future. It's very difficult to understand.

Last night, after I wrote the journal entry, I lay down to sleep. Then, I heard His voice within the confines of my own head. He said, "How are you, my beloved Son? You have been patient with me for not giving you a complete picture of my plan. I'm proud you finally addressed your true identity with your disciples today. I, therefore, will give you the vision you desire." Instantly, my head was filled with knowledge of the future and of God's plan for me.

The plan is both wonderful and challenging, with a certain element of fear in it. I will go to Jerusalem on the next Passover. By this time, the Jewish leaders will have amassed much sentiment against me, since they say I claim to be the King of the Jews. It appears the word of me being the Messiah will escape our small band of loyal followers. One of my wonderful followers will deceive me and turn me in to the officials. I will be tortured and put to death, a death by the cross. But I won't be truly dead, for God will raise me up after three days, like He did with Jonah. This time, however, people will recognize I'm truly the Messiah. This, in turn, will help me bring about the changes in the Kingdom of God I'm here to do.

I have to admit that it makes so much sense. But look at the things I will have to endure – betrayal, extreme physical pain, and death. Part of me protested the plan because of those challenges and the fear I may not be able to fulfill it completely. Actually, I'm more afraid I'm not the Son of God at all. Perhaps I'm someone who has gone mad. Fear always seems to accompany my doubt. But the only logical explanation with all I've been through is I'm truly the Son of God and the things God revealed to me last night are fully true.

I've been troubled all day doubting one moment and believing the next. I think sometimes God shouldn't allow days like this at all. Things like this are certainly no way to allow the human part of me to find peace. But then again, no man knows the future and maybe that's a very good plan. Here I am, the Son of God, Son of the Father, and even I can't deal with knowing my own future. How would man deal with such knowledge?

Father, I thank you for the gift of knowledge. Help me find peace with it. I know that through your love, I will again be able to find the peace in my life that has been so elusive.

Shalom.

129 Predicting My Death

Today, like the past few days, I've been very preoccupied with the thoughts of the future. It's almost as the "gift" of knowledge has become a curse. Peter and John were asking me what was wrong. I kept telling them nothing. Then, after dinner tonight, all of the men gathered together for prayer. Peter opened and prayed for understanding. John followed and prayed for love. Matthew prayed for honesty. Judas prayed for openness, and so on. It was obvious they wanted me to share my burdens with them. I also felt the power of God upon me again, urging me to be open with them.

I told them I must go to Jerusalem, where I would suffer at the hands of the elders, chief priests and scribes. I will be put to death, but on the third day, I will rise again. They looked at each other in stunned silence. I thought it was because the understanding God gave me was overwhelming them. Later I found out that the silence was from confusion and lack of understanding.

It was Peter who came to me later this evening and asked about the future I expressed to them. I expected him to be full of loving understanding, but he was full of fear and confusion. He said he and the others would forbid such a thing from happening to me. He said I was the Messiah, and they would let no man put me to death. I was in shock they couldn't understand this was God's plan of salvation. It was, in fact, a marvelously ingenious plan, and I had to follow it.

I rebuked him, telling him he was simply an obstacle to me. I told him he sees the world as humans do and not as God does. I was a bit harsh with him, but only because I was expecting him to understand the plan. After all, God called me to share it! Peter of all people should have understood. Yet, he didn't. None of them could, and I displaced my frustration onto him. I should have been grateful that he had the courage to speak to me about it. After all, it's this boldness in Peter God will use in the future to build His church.

Perhaps I should have anticipated this reaction. Even I had some reservations about the plan. Part of it is terribly scary. I can only imagine how difficult it must be for them to accept the fact I must leave them. But my Father asked me to share His plan with these men. For whatever reason, they need to know. Perhaps without this knowledge, the one who will betray me wouldn't do so. Perhaps this is another way God challenges them to grow in their faith. Perhaps this knowledge given in advance will assist them in fully understanding the truth about my presence with them on this earth.

Thank you again, Abba, for this day, for these men, for their faith, and for their love for me. I understand it's out of love for me they reject the plan. I understand that they will ultimately follow me in spite of the dangers and fear they have. And thank you for boldness. Peter is certainly a good choice to lead the new church after I'm gone.

Shalom.

130 Conditions for My Disciples

I apologized to Peter today for the anger I displayed last night. He was more than gracious in accepting my apology. However, God's plan still didn't make sense to any of them. They were all a bit more capable of speaking their mind today. Peter said I was the Messiah, and I was needed to make God's plan work. He questioned whether this plan was one from Satan. I assured him it wasn't, but none of the men seemed too convinced.

I finally told them I was as certain of this plan as I was of anything, since everything I received from my loving Father has come in the same manner. If I were to deny it, I would have to deny everything else. I can't separate the parts I like and the parts I don't. I told them that if they wished to follow me, they, too, would have to pick up a cross. It seems God always finds the cross we each individually need to carry, but He also provides the means to lighten the load if we trust in Him.

This burden for me to suffer in Jerusalem and be physically attached to my cross will be difficult for all. But knowing that this is part of the plan of our loving Father should ease the burden. In order to follow me, these men must deny themselves, their doubts and fears. John protested again that they wouldn't allow anyone to take my life, the very life that has provided them life to the fullest for so long.

I explained that if my Father wishes for me to suffer this fate, I must do so, for whoever tries to save his life by running away from God would only lose his life. In order to gain life, true life, life in the spirit, life full of love, I must submit my free will completely over to my Father. I must put myself in His loving hands and be assured and confident of His love. True freedom can only come from complete submission to the Father, who is love. Perhaps by refusing this path, I could gain the whole world to my understanding someday. But by trying to put forward my own plan, and not follow His, I could actually lose the life my Father has given me.

They looked at each other in stunned silence. I know they still didn't truly understand. Again, Peter was the one who came to me afterwards and told me they simply couldn't quite grasp all of this. The plan made no sense to any of them. I somehow missed providing them with any glimmer of understanding God so generously gave me. They only had the fears and confusion. However, Peter assured me they agreed whatever it was, it must be "real." They no longer saw it as being from Satan but being truly of God. They agreed they would follow and accept the things I described.

Abba, as I thought about the plan you gave me, questions and confusion reigned in my own head. Perhaps this is why I was unable to provide sufficient understanding to others. You tell me I must die one of the most grueling forms of death imaginable. You tell me we all have our crosses to bear, but I never thought of the real cross, the kind that kills.

But it isn't merely the death that bothers me; it's the mockery, the humiliation, and the inability to prove you are my powerful Father by overcoming these trivial games and the betrayal. Your plan is both crystal clear and terribly hazy at the same time. I'm truly confused. My mortal self is still fighting the same battles within. There is a part of me that recognizes the value and benefit of simply giving my entire being over to you. There is another part that wants to hold on so I can still be me. I can see the same battle raging in most of my disciples, even though most are unaware of it.

Why can't I simply give up my human self, my human life and allow your spirit and my true life, which is simply love, to take over. Why do I struggle so much? Why can't I simply let go of the part of me that is afraid, prideful, selfish, hurts others, and is unloving? I know I find the true spirit of joy when I'm with you fully. Well, that's hardly true because if I were truly with you fully, the human side would simply vanish, and I would no longer have this struggle.

This makes my question even more pertinent. I have no real idea of how wonderful it must be to allow my spirit to simply die and allow only your spirit to remain. I've had but mere glimpses into this type of reality, and all of those glimpses were full of peace, joy, energy, and love. How much better would complete union be?

Father, I know it's your desire to have all my brothers and sisters enter into this type of union with you as well. You would never desire anything less for your creation. Help me in any way you can to provide guidance to people everywhere to understand that they, too, can enjoy the full extent of a relationship just as I can. You play no favorites amongst your children. We are all equals, and you wish only the best for us all. Help me send this message to the ends of the world. And one last thing. Father, thank you for my life, for my family, for my friends, for my understanding of your power and presence in my life, for love, and mostly, thank you for you.

Shalom.

131 Disciple's Love

I've been struggling lately, as we all have, with the words I spoke to my disciples over the past few days. I've been pretty much resting and contemplating alone. The men have gone off in groups. Peter has been staying with James and John. Mary and John alone have come to me in quiet times. They have no questions. They ask for no further explanation. They simply sit and talk. Mary talks about her life, her family, and her dreams for her future. She tells me she is there to listen if and when I want to talk. John talks about the weather, fishing, his family, and some things in his past.

They simply demonstrate their love for me, each in their own way. They both let me know they would listen when and if I wanted to talk, but they don't push me or crowd me. They just let me be me. They help me laugh and relax. John and I have even played a few games. He has gotten quite strong, and we were fairly even in our wrestling matches. I used to have to let him win.

As he was leaving to go to sleep tonight, John said, "I love you." He's said it before, and so have most of the others, but there was something different about these words tonight. His eyes met mine and I could see the love in his eyes, again as if they were windows to his soul. I could hear the love in his voice. I could feel the love in his embrace. Most men would question such things. A man loving another man? This is most unacceptable. But I do love John. I love all of these men and women. Why do I feel ashamed and afraid of that? People don't understand that love and sex aren't the same thing. They seem to equate the two as if you couldn't have one without the other.

Wrong. Love is a wonderful state of being. Sex is a physical act. Love of another person, any other person, be it man, woman or child, is something to strive for. Love of another human is the substance of life. Without love, we are nothing. And when you find love for another human being, it would be impossible to stop at just one.

What is love? This may be the most difficult thing to put into words. Explaining what love isn't is a lot easier than defining what love is. Many think of love as a feeling. And sometimes that's part of it. When John said "I love you" to me tonight, I felt warm from the inside out. I felt like crying, and in fact, I did shed a tear or two. I felt a little like I was floating on a cloud, which was lifting me off my feet. But love is much more than a feeling. Love is fearless, caring, understanding, kind, sensitive, joyful, and peaceful. But these things only tell you qualities of love – they don't tell you what love *is*.

Love is God. Love is the full spirit of God within, being in touch with the inner spirit, and seeing the same spirit in the other person. Love is life. Love grows and matures. Love is energy, endless energy. Love is the inner power of God. True love isn't forgiving, because true love has no necessity for forgiveness. I'm not sure any words could describe the type of true love God has graciously allowed me to glimpse. Love can't be explained, but it will be fully realized whenever it's found. And believe me, it's worth looking for.

I pray, dear Father, that people accept loving another and accept being loved by another, for this is the true secret to life here on earth.

Shalom.

132 Walk to the Mountain*

When I rose this morning, John brought me breakfast. The others had already eaten. He laughed and called me a sleepyhead. I guess I stayed up longer than I realized last night. I was so full of energy after I finished my journal that I couldn't sleep. This morning I smiled at John as he was turning to leave and said, "I love you, too." We just stared at each other a while, and then he winked at me and said, "I know." He started to leave, but I beckoned him to stay.

While I was eating, Peter and James came to talk with me as well. I always enjoy my food more when it's accompanied by conversation with good friends. I'm feeding the mind, body, and soul all at once. After we finished, I had an urge to go for a hike. I hibernated the past few days with nothing but my thoughts, and after John helped lighten my load a bit, I felt a little stiff, and needed some exercise.

We walked and talked for a while. The next thing I know, we were heading up a fairly high, steep, and treacherous mountain. James suggested we turn back, but I said I needed the challenge. Peter chimed in delightfully, running ahead a short way. John took off after Peter because he was the youngest, and he wasn't about to let an "old man" like Peter beat him. Peter put out a stick as John ran by and tripped him. John fell and started play-acting a serious injury. We walked past him, as if we didn't see him. He lay there howling for a while. We couldn't hold back the laughter. He finally got up and ran to catch us.

We were close to the top of the mountain when we spied a ledge large enough for all of us to rest. We had been walking quite some time. The sun was already past center. We stopped and our talk turned a little more serious. I was now comfortable enough to express my love for each of them individually as well as collectively with the rest of the disciples. They all responded by expressing their love for me. I was genuinely touched from the inside out that these three men were able to express their thoughts, feelings and love so eloquently. They each told stories about the things I did for them, most of which I had no idea. They revealed their true self, the inside part we usually keep hidden for fear we will be laughed at, humiliated, or even hated. Some of their deepest, darkest secrets only made me love them more.

After we talked, I felt this warmth developing deep within me. It began in my chest, and as they talked, I could feel the warmth flow throughout my entire being. It was like I was in the hottest furnace, yet not hot or sweaty, just peaceful. Apparently, this warmth must have been real because the three of them started looking at me with amazement, as if my whole being was aglow.

About this time, I noticed Moses and Elijah standing next to me, and we began to converse. I wasn't certain if they were visible to the others or just me, when Peter asked if he should make three tents for us, one for me, one for Moses and one for Elijah. Then a bright cloud seemed to come from nowhere and cast a shadow over the ledge. Other than this single cloud, the sky was clear.

For the second time in my life, I heard a voice come from above, as if it came from the cloud itself. It said the same thing as before, "This is my beloved Son, in whom I am well pleased." This time the voice added, "Listen to him, my children." All three of them immediately fell prostrate and were filled with fear. They were concerned because no one can see God and live. I went to each of them to comfort them and told them not to be afraid. John was the first to rise; he buried his head in my chest and held me for a while. I stroked his head and simply repeated that I loved him. James was next to rise, and we repeated the process. Peter refused to rise. He insisted he was unworthy of God, unworthy to be chosen, unworthy to even tie my sandals, let alone be my friend.

James and John sat and watched quietly. Peter cried. He was so caught up in his unworthiness that he refused to see his worth. He saw all of his faults and none of his strengths. He begged for us to go so he could simply die of starvation, dehydration, or wild animals, as he was unfit to be with me. It was my turn to repay Peter. I told him of the gifts he had given me. The times he lifted me up to comfort me, the times he helped me learn a difficult lesson, the times I could see the spirit of God in him, and most of all, what his love meant to me.

Uncharacteristically, Peter stopped arguing and simply listened. He didn't question any of what I said, he just buried his head in his hands again. John and James came over. They both hugged Peter and told him they loved him. John expressed his thoughts of his own personal unworthiness to Peter. He pointed out that however weak he (John) was, he knew long before today I was truly God's son, the Messiah. Today was simply a special affirmation and awakening of this fact for him. It was obvious that God had truly chosen him as well as everybody else in our group. James said it was all right to doubt ourselves, but we should not doubt God, and God sent them with me today.

Peter finally relinquished. He rose and came to me sobbing, telling me of his love for me, telling me how he will do whatever God calls him to do, how he will never again doubt, how he will never again fail, and so on. I guess you just can't take the Peter out of Peter, which is one of the things I love about him the most.

Afterwards, they all wanted to set up tents and stay on the mountain. I knew our mission didn't call for us to segregate ourselves from the others. As we left the mountain, the sun was already starting to set. We walked in silence a long while, each contemplating the day's events. I was thankful that God had found ways to eliminate my doubts again. I was impressed at the power of the moment and the fortuitous circumstances that led to the entire event.

As we neared camp, I asked them not to tell anyone what happened today, not until the Son of Man had been raised from the dead. They were still unsure what I meant exactly, but they agreed, as long as they could talk freely with each other. I assured them that was fair enough. I also told them not to forget they could talk to me, too.

I'm still overwhelmed with today's events. John said I was actually aglow, my face was shining, and my clothes turned white. I still feel like the day I walked on water. It felt as if my body wasn't really touching the ground, just sort of gliding across it.

I feel different inside, too. I feel as if God has again granted me a state of pure love. My doubts are gone. I'm full of energy and life. My senses seem to be extra sensitive. My body still feels warm from the inside out. I've never felt more loved, more a part of this group, and more a part of the world. I'm so glad to be the Son of Man, to be given the opportunity to prove my love for my fellow brothers and sisters. I'm grateful for the senses, my ability to see, taste, smell, touch, and hear. These are all wonderful.

I look out over the night. The fire is dimming, the stars are shining, and a few of the lights are mirrored on the still waters of the lake. The smell of the fire, the feel of the cool breeze, and the sound of the crickets all combine to provide a wonderful opportunity to be fully alive in this body. I can't thank my Father enough for this wonderful gift.

Please, Father, help all mankind to experience the joys this human shell can offer. Thank you for allowing me to return some of these gifts to people, return sight to the blind or hearing to the deaf. Help the rest of my brothers and sisters not take these gifts for granted but help us value them. And above all, help everyone recognize they are all, each and every one of them, truly worthy of your love.

Shalom.

---

* This passage is especially dedicated to my fellow Cursillistas, dear friends, and prayer partners, Shirley, Jacques, Sonya, Gerry, Sister Mary Paul, Mary, Terri, Linda, Maryanne, Marisel, Roseann, Renee, Teresa, Chris, and especially Val, on the occasion of their personal and internal "transfiguration" into the spirit of God. Alleluia.

133 Disciple's Faith

Today we encountered a fairly large crowd. A man approached me and knelt in front of me. He asked me to have pity on his son, for he was a deaf and mute lunatic who would throw himself into fire or water. He said he had already brought the boy to several of my disciples, but they were unable to cure him.

I was a little upset at the time because I was thinking about the events of the past day and my thoughts were interrupted. I was basking in the glory of the love, warmth, peace, and joy I found with Peter, John and James on the mountainside. Who did this man think he was to come to me uninvited? First, I retorted a bit harshly first, but then I told him to bring the boy. I cured him and we walked along further.

The disciples asked me how it was possible that they couldn't drive this demon from him, even though they had cured so many people in my name before. I told them the only missing ingredient was their faith – or lack of it. Faith in our Father in heaven alone can cure. If they had faith the size of a mere mustard seed, they would be able to move mountains.

James came to my aid. He told them that when we were all wrestling with the predictions I made a couple of days ago, they all, each and every one of them, rejected my prophecy. They had no faith at all in the things God gave me. They were limited by their own thoughts and ideas and wanted things their way. He told them I was right, they lacked the type of faith that would allow them to walk through the fires of Gehenna without fear if God so directed them. The type of faith Abraham displayed when he took his son Isaac and placed him on the altar. They had all been chosen by God to be companions of the Messiah, and yet, when I challenge them to walk a difficult path, they resist.

I was so impressed with James today. I've never heard him speak so convincingly. He was obviously still filled with the spirit of God from the mountain yesterday. John and Peter merely echoed agreement with James, but they allowed him to do the speaking today. They, too, were obviously impressed by his speech. James was usually the life of the party; even though he had a sensitive side, he usually tried to hide it. He wasn't much of a leader and rarely spoke out in public.

But today he was different. He was fighting for me. He understood whatever I prophesied, no matter how difficult, came from God, because I was from God. Therefore, no matter how impossible the plan was, it had to be accepted. To James, rejecting my plan was the same as rejecting me. It was as simple as that. He himself still didn't understand, but he believed. He challenged each and every one of them to believe, too.

There is one other thing about James. He respected my wish to be silent about our extraordinary visit to the mountainside yesterday. He really didn't need to tell anyone. He may have gained the faith and insights he had today because of it, and he simply used his energy and allowed himself to be the channel for our Father. It was inspiring to listen to him today. I got a little glimpse of what some people experience when listening to me when I'm a channel for a voice directly from God.

Before I finish tonight, let me not forget to seek forgiveness for being so short with the father of the boy today. I ignored one of my first rules of life, to live in the moment. I was totally caught up in my thought about yesterday and blocked out the rest of life. I could have missed helping that poor boy; I could have scared his father off and lessened his faith. Thank you for sending me a man whose faith was strong enough to believe in me, even when I was a little less friendly than I should have been.

Please help me overcome my need to close myself off from the world. I find this is another of the ruts I easily slip into. Oh, and don't let me forget, thank you so much for James and the gift of your spirit working through him today.

Shalom.

134 Traveling to Galilee

Last night I couldn't sleep even after walking almost all day. I was lying there, trying to still my inside. I was rewarded with a special discussion with my Father. He was talking to me, just as I talk to other people, only the silence remained unbroken. I know I've experienced this before, but it's always so special when we converse in this manner. This time, his voice was a little stronger and deeper, although still very kind and peaceful.

"I am pleased with you, Son."

"I know, Father."

"I hoped so, because I am was running out of ways to get my message through to you." At this, both of us laughed.

"I am so proud of James, Father. You chose my disciples well. Thank you so much."

"What else would you have expected?" I had to chuckle again.

He then reassured me His plan for me in Jerusalem was real. He would be by my side the whole way and would never leave me. He again told me not to fear the pain and suffering or even death, because this is how He wanted to prove His love for people. He told me He would return me in three days, thereby expressing His power. He told me I needed to try to get my followers to understand the message.

It won't be easy because I don't fully understand it either, even though He assured me I understood enough. The plan makes sense to me, but the words don't seem to follow. I've been chosen to show God's people a new way. It's as if the little children of God are now ready for a newer and deeper understanding of God. Love of God and love of fellow humans is the only law required. It's our heart that really counts. Somehow, through my death, my Father will remove some of the weight that holds people down.

People are convinced they are not worthy of God's love because of sin. I'm here to take away sin. People are worried about death. I'm here to show there is life after death. People have an elementary understanding of God and His love. I'm here to bring them to new life, a life in the full spirit of God. God isn't just on the outside; He is within us as well. I'm here to bring this new message. Jerusalem will be the ultimate expression of God's love. My suffering will show them God loves me beyond imagination, and we both love all of mankind as well.

Shalom.

135 In Galilee

We gathered today in Galilee and met up with a few past friends and companions. This evening, however, we were alone at supper. Matthew asked about my predictions about Jerusalem. I repeated my understanding to them, as directed by my Father. I must have been a little more convincing this time, because they didn't reject the notion as much. None of them said it was from Satan. They listened quietly and seemed to recognize this was coming from my Father. They were still overwhelmed with grief at the thought of my suffering, but the arguments were gone. They accepted the plan even though they were repulsed by it.

I can't imagine how my Father managed to turn each and every one of these hearts around. Perhaps James had a much greater impact than I realized. Perhaps they saw something in my being. The truth, however, lies in the fact that my loving Father found a way into each man's heart. I find the manner my Father can gently but convincingly turn people's hearts totally amazing. I know they have to be willing to listen and to be persuaded, but He also knows which people are ready to listen. He knows exactly what to do and say and He can manipulate circumstances so everyone can garnish whatever they need.

My Father never plays favorites between His children. In all circumstances, He provides answers, situations, and outcomes where everyone involved can learn and grow. In some cases, it may not be readily obvious because someone or other may seem to have "won." But in reality, my Father is just allowing the "loser" to learn a different lesson, one he or she desperately needs to learn.

I'm more and more in awe of my loving Father. I'm nothing compared to Him. I only have whatever He cares to give me. While He chooses to lavishly bestow gifts upon me, my humanness limits my ability to totally absorb all of the magnificence of my Father. He is able to manipulate and maneuver thousands of people. His power and control overwhelm me at times. Is there any end to His abilities? Of course not!

Thank you, Father, for the power of understanding you have given my disciples and thank you for removing some of my pride again.

Shalom.

136 Paying the Temple Tax

I've felt so light again. Ever since I explained my Father's plan to my disciples again and they accepted it, I've been on fire. I have this inner peace and warmth inside me. I feel excited about life, excited about love, excited about everyone I meet. I have so much energy and enthusiasm within me. I feel like I did after the day I went to the mountain. I know I don't glow the same way as I did then, but my insides feel the same warmth. I'm unable to say the wrong words or be nervous or upset about anything. I'm very calm and assured about the future my Father has planned for me, my disciples, and all of His people.

Today we visited Capernaum and went to the temple. I knew the collectors were going to use my inability to pay their tax against me. So, as I entered the temple, I asked Peter, loud enough to make sure everyone heard, "From whom do kings collect taxes, from their subjects or from foreigners?" Peter made the obvious response in saying, "Foreigners." I then pointed out that Peter and I were subjects, not foreigners, so we were exempt.

However, I also told Peter he should go drop a hook in the sea and extract a coin from the first fish he caught. The collectors and Pharisees were somewhat in awe when they followed Peter to the sea where he found a coin worth double the tax in the first fish he caught. Peter later asked me how I knew they were going to challenge me on the taxes. I smiled and told him my Father had warned me. He simply nodded back. He, too, was amazed at God's powers.

Although my Father didn't exactly speak to me about the tax, the thought somehow popped into my head and I just knew. He didn't exactly speak to me about the coin in the fish. I again just knew. I have no doubt my Father placed those thoughts in my head and the proof is obvious. My life has been full of these special moments when I somehow have full knowledge of circumstances surrounding me.

Abba, Father, I love you. Those words don't seem sufficient to express myself, but they are the only words that come close. I don't think people understand the true intent, meaning, and depth of the word *love*. Love is this state of being in control of oneself, without fear, full of energy, full of life. Love is being in control by having given up control to one's loving Father – this is the paradox of life, the truth behind love. Amen.

Shalom.

137 Disciple Squabbles

Today I had yet another situation arise which could have proven disastrous. The disciples were squabbling again over who was the greatest. Peter thought it should be him. Matthew thought it should be him, and so on. I was quite proud of Thad, Bartholomew and James, the son of Alpheus who didn't engage in the discussion. They didn't think they wanted to be the greatest, after all, I was the Messiah and my fate was to suffer on a cross.

There had been days when such meaningless, ridiculous squabbles would have frustrated me and I would have found myself unable to cope with them. But today I was able to respond to the challenge easily and effortlessly. I called one of the nearby children over and sat him upon my knee. He was so adorable. His face was full of mud because he had been playing in a puddle. His hair was curly and windblown – he probably had not combed it in days. He was barefoot and scantily clad. But when he looked at me with his big, brown, glistening and inviting eyes and smiled, you could feel the love of Abba flowing through him.

I told the rest of the disciples this young boy, with his free spirit and lack of concerns of worldly things, was greater than all of them in the Kingdom of Heaven. Unless we learn to be more like this child, innocent, without fear, without the need to be important, and without the need to be above others, we will miss the beauty and wonder of the Kingdom here on earth. I told them whoever is humble like this child is the greatest in the eyes of Abba. Whoever receives children such as this in my name will receive their own child within themselves.

We all have a child inside of us, one who loves and needs love. As we grow, our inner child is lost largely to hurts and fears found along the road of life. However, to be truly able to find fulfillment in this life, we have to return to our inner child. We need to be open and unafraid. Past hurts will never go away, and new hurts will never stop coming, but we need to look at all of these through the eyes of our Father's love, our Father's embrace, and our Father's guidance. We need to find ways to overcome them just as I did with the temple tax and the arguments.

In both situations I could have easily become trapped and lost, which would have led to hurts, frustration, anxieties and a feeling of lack. Instead, I used both situations to energize the people around me, and in so doing, to let myself rely more and more on Abba. Just as a child relies completely on his parents for support, so too, must we all rely on our loving Father. I've been able to hand over all responsibilities for myself to Abba, and in so doing I've become more responsible for myself. I find that the more I give to my Father, the more I have. This is the paradox of our faith.

Shalom.

138 Sin

One of the things my disciples keep asking me about is sin. They don't really understand the true definition of sin. It isn't defined as a list of things, such as in the Ten Commandments. They are defined in the heart. Simply put, sin is anything against the will of God. To some degree, I've been unable to sin because I've given my life over to my Father. Anything I've done, both the good and the not so good, has all been a result of my Father. The times I've fallen short, my Father needed me to fall short so He could teach me even bigger lessons.

Not so with the disciples. They haven't yet achieved the ability in their life to turn all their shortcomings into lessons and move on to a new, richer and fuller life with God. Sometimes they brood over injuries, other times they hurt with intent, other times they refuse to forgive. They carry the hurt and pain within themselves until it eats them up from the inside.

Any time we move further away from a relationship with God, it's sin. Any time we fall short of the mark, the mark being to align our entire lives with God, we sin. Whoever causes anyone else to sin would be better off if they were drowned. It's bad enough to cause injury to our own being, but the greatest of all sins is to keep someone else from fully realizing the love, kindness and fullness of life that comes from knowing God.

Sin causes a separation from God in this life. We are unable to fully experience peace, love, and joy in our lives when we have the weight of sin bearing upon us. We must always seek ways to forgive ourselves and others for the sins we have committed. In order to free ourselves of the chains of past sins, we need to look at each transgression, learn from it, grow from it, and then discard it as useless. Once we have learned and grown, anything remaining is indeed useless.

I don't think my disciples quite understand the concept of sin as I've defined it. Even good things in life, such as the prayerful front of the Sadducees is sin in a way, since it manages to keep them from understanding the true meaning of God and love. Their pride prevents them from being truly free from sin and in communion with God. They act righteous and appear to live a life full of good. They flaunt it to others to be worshipped as if they had found some miraculous method to fool God. It simply doesn't work. Even good deeds done with the wrong inner spirit can be a form of sin. Everything is sin that keeps someone from truly experiencing the grace, wonder and beauty of God.

Father, help everyone understand that sin keeps people away from truly experiencing you in their life. Help everyone learn that the only way to true happiness in this lifetime is to learn and live through sin, and by seeking communion with you.

Shalom.

139 Lost Sheep

It's been a long day. The Pharisees mocked us and put us to the test again. They proclaimed their own holiness and used their lives as examples. They kept pointing out they followed all the "rules," but I don't. They pointed out that we broke the "rules" of the Sabbath again. I kept trying to explain to them my understanding of sin, my understanding of the spirit of God, and the indwelling spirit. They weren't listening. I used parable after parable, story after story, to no avail. I thought I detected a glimpse of understanding from one of them at one point, but the others found a way to draw him back to their way of thinking.

My disciples then questioned me at dinner about why I spent so much time and energy on the Pharisees today. They saw them as enemies. I asked them how many shepherds they knew who wouldn't leave their flock to go assist one lost sheep. They all agreed it was the duty and responsibility of the shepherd to care for all his sheep equally. They even agreed finding the lost sheep would create much joy for the shepherd.

I just looked at them for a while. It was Matthew who first grasped the meaning. He pointed out the same principle is applicable here. He said I was the greatest of all shepherds. He stated our Father, God in heaven, sent me to tend to the people He created. Therefore, it was my job and responsibility to herd all people back to the Father. He pointed out that the Pharisees were not necessarily evil, simply lost. He said he understood I would try my hardest to bring each person back to the flock. He further indicated it wasn't just my responsibility, but his and all the disciples to bring the lost back to God.

I smiled at Matthew as our eyes met. I saw tears gather in his eyes. I told him I couldn't have explained it better myself. Peter, of course, also praised him mightily and proclaimed he would never again allow a lost soul to go without attempting to find him. Everyone looked at Peter with a singular stare. We all realize that Peter never quite lives up to all his promises. He really means whatever he says, but his spirit, while willing, is weak.

I was still somewhat baffled at Matthew's tears. I asked him if he'd go for a walk with me. He agreed. As we walked, I put my arm around his shoulder. He started to sob. I asked him what was wrong. He said that he was upset because he had ignored his brother, his own flesh and blood, not that long ago. Here I was, trying to help anyone and everyone who was lost, even those I knew would eventually seek to bring harm to me, and Matthew didn't make any effort to help his brother.

We talked a long time about the situation. Apparently, his oldest brother was killed over gambling debts he couldn't repay. His next oldest brother took over the position of tax collector and discovered Matthew had hidden away a fairly good amount of money, which if Matthew had spoken up, they could have used it to pay off the gambling debts and his oldest brother would still be alive. Matthew said he originally saved the money because he always remembered lean times when he was growing up. When he took over as tax collector, he decided he would put away some money for those lean times. Then he joined me and was so absorbed in my ministry, he actually forgot about the money. Also, while he knew his brother liked to gamble, he didn't know the debts were enough that someone would try and kill him over them.

I assured him making mistakes was human. In fact, even if he had remembered the money, it may have been enough to pay off the gambling debts this time, but what about when his brother gambled again. He didn't make a mistake with hatred in his heart. He first had to learn from the mistake, second had to grow from it, and third had to forgive himself for it. After that, he was free to return home and try to repair the damage.

I offered to help him, but he said he would work his way through it himself. He asked me if God could truly forgive him for turning his back on his own brother. I assured him God's forgiveness was so complete that it was forgiven as soon as it occurred. I placed both my hands on his head and prayed he would learn from his past mistakes, grow from them, and most importantly, understand, recognize and accept that forgiveness was already his. I prayed he would be able to forgive himself. Matthew said he was feeling better but was still not ready to go back home. I assured him that he could take whatever time he needed. After all, it's better to be fully prepared or else he would risk making yet another mistake.

We went back to camp and Matthew thanked me. He said he would pray for me. I asked him what he meant by this. He said he would pray for me to continue to learn and grow, follow the path God has given me, and preach and teach the love and joy of God to everyone, not just those who were willing listeners. I told him he made a major leap towards forgiving himself that moment. I pointed out he had already started to look past his own mistakes and reach out to help others in prayer. He smiled. No words were necessary; his smile said it all.

140 Forgiveness and Love

I'm simply overwhelmed with the events of yesterday. When I went to lie down, it was quite late. However, I found myself full of energy and simply couldn't sleep. I was astounded with Matthew and the love, commitment and leap in spirit he experienced last night. I loved Matthew fully and completely yesterday, akin to very few times in my past. I recognized his ability to look inwardly and acknowledge a negative part of him, his ability to share those insights so willingly with me, and his ability to cry. He feared talking about his inner failings would make me turn away from him in disgust, but the exact opposite was true. I found myself loving Matthew at a deeper level.

I can't help but realize how this reflects God's love. I wasn't the least bit angry about the misgivings of Matthew. I was, however, deeply touched by his ability to recognize it and struggle through it. Awesome. I can only imagine how God must feel for all of His children. Even though I'm God's son, my understanding of love is limited somewhat by my humanity. Matthew has taught me love at an even deeper level than I was previously aware of. Extraordinary.

Matthew feared revealing his shortcoming to me. Worse yet, he was afraid to reveal his shortcoming to himself. It was almost as if denying the shortcoming made him a better person, and he was exonerated and justified in denial. But the only true freedom came via the admission of error, working through the pains of guilt, and then seeking forgiveness. He was very wise to realize forgiveness needed to wait until he worked through the guilt because a premature request for forgiveness from his brother would have only resulted in disaster. Matthew made such a major leap in freeing himself from sin yesterday. Not the sin of hurting his brother, but the sin of denial, the sin of guilt.

I, too, learned and grew from last night. I learned more about love, true love, and much more about the true nature of forgiveness. God really didn't need to forgive Matthew. Forgiving someone for being human and demonstrating normal human failings isn't necessary. Love doesn't really need forgiveness, just acceptance. Love rises above all the negatives and dwells on the positive. Love is complete.

Abba, Father, thank you for loving me so much that you constantly work to teach me your ways. I will share Matthew's prayer for me to remain open to learning and not allow myself to be so full of my own "godliness" that I lose track of the fact that the Son of Man still has a lot to learn.

Shalom.

141 A Brother's Sin

Matthew left today to reconcile with his brother. His spirit was high. He didn't ask me to go with him even though I would have gladly done so. The other disciples all felt the rift between Matthew and his brother could and should have had a better solution. I assured them that we all make mistakes, which is simply part of being human. When we do, we may not readily understand, accept and admit the mistake because we all have a tendency to justify our position, regardless of how wrong it is.

I assured them that in most cases the full and complete fault doesn't rest solely with one person. Any and all discussions will be much more productive if the aggrieved person first recognizes their own shortcomings and admits them. However, if none of these things are successful, it's time to allow my Father to help open the heart of the person. In time, things will generally work out. In the meantime, we should treat the person as we would any lost sheep – kindly, lovingly and with respect. Even when being lost, Matthew has been a wonderful addition to our flock.

Matthew smiled and gave me a long, lingering hug before he left to make amends with his brother. We all wished him the best. I think I know how a father must feel when his own son grows up to be a man. My pride was bursting out. I had more than a few tears to blot from my eyes. Isn't it curious how emotions, good or bad, can create tears?

Father, thank you for tears. Tears are a sign of emotions. Emotions are a sign of spirit. We cry when we are sad or happy – both emotions make us more alive. I can't remember the day I last felt this full of life. Help us all recognize each day is a precious gift and let us truly live it to the fullest.

Shalom.

142 Forgiveness

Today we were all talking about Matthew. I reiterated why Matthew left and how proud I was of him. Peter, of course, didn't quite get it. He was concerned forgiveness from Matthew's brother may not be forthcoming. After all, he wasn't certain he would be able to forgive his brother if he felt his brother caused the death of another brother. I insisted he would have to forgive his brother, regardless of the offense, if his brother was truly sorry for what he had done.

Peter still questioned me and asked how often would he need to forgive his brother. He felt seven times would be enough, seven being the number representing completeness. I laughed a little. Peter still didn't get it. He was trying to quantify forgiveness into a specific number. I told him he would have to forgive not seven times, but seven times seventy-seven times. I used this number to demonstrate forgiveness must be complete in the heart and inner soul. We have to forgive again and again until there is nothing left to forgive.

I told them a story about a king who forgave a debtor of a huge amount of money. However, when another person owed a fraction of that amount to the debtor, he refused to forgive the debt. Upon hearing this, the king reinstated the debt and threw the debtor into prison.

Peter didn't quite understand the parable. John asked if he could have a hand at the explanation. John is the youngest of my disciples but has the greatest depth of love in his heart. He told Peter that the King was like God. He always forgives us of any wrongdoing, no matter how great. But if we can't learn from His forgiveness and we refuse to forgive others, our own wrongdoings will imprison us.

He told us one of the village children would always torment him and beat him up when he was young. John was small and timid. He didn't like to fight, and the bully took advantage of him. His brother James finally found out what was happening. Thankfully, he was able to put an end to the tormenting, but John carried the anger in his heart for a long time. He was unable to forgive the bully. He even admitted he tormented someone younger and smaller than himself out of anger once. He thought it would make him feel like a man. But it didn't. He apologized for what he had done, and the youngster hugged him with tears in his eyes.

John then realized he, too, needed to forgive, because until he did, his heart was weighted with guilt. He immediately went to the bully and forgave him. But the bully laughed and tormented him some more. John realized his forgiveness wasn't yet real. He said the words, but he didn't feel it in his heart. He had to forgive the bully over and over. Each time a little more pain and anger would go away. He was only free of the "debt" when he forgave it. Even though his prison didn't have four stone walls, he was a prisoner to his anger and pain until he forgave and forgot.

I smiled to myself. I can't believe the understanding these men have. I sometimes think I alone have the truth, I alone know the ways of my Father. And then I hear things like this. I hear Matthew struggle through his problem then take action to correct it. I hear Peter question the things he can't understand until he can really grasp them. I hear John turn my parable into real words. I think I'm so smart with these stories, but John's understanding was just as great as my own, or in some ways even greater.

I understand some things because my Father has given me a gift of understanding. John understood because he lived it and learned it. I think this may be what human existence is about. God calls us to grow, each in our own way, and in so doing, society grows. I understand things because He reveals them to me. I understand, but I don't always live them, I don't always feel them, I don't always grow through them.

People question why our Father, if He was truly so loving, wouldn't simply give us all the understanding I have. If He did, it would make it unreal and, in some ways, meaningless. The true joy of life is in living each day, making mistakes, then learning and growing from them. It's like a runner in a great race. What would it be like if he suddenly found himself at the finish line without any struggle? The real joy is in the race itself. We will all get to the finish line, since we have no other choice. But we need to learn to enjoy life; we must enjoy the race, each and every step of the way.

Shalom.

143 Feast of Tabernacles

I've been quite energetic lately. The past few days made me feel full of life. I understand the journey better, and now I'm looking forward to each new day as a challenge and a gift. My entourage has grown tremendously. It's almost as if I have a whole village following me. But unfortunately, as my following grows, so do the petty squabbles. My closest followers are still jealous of Mary and each other. They all want to be my first. Mary, though, lacks jealousy. She merely loves me and cherishes our every moment together. I'm so honored to call her my friend and thankful my Father sent her.

They fight over who is going to cook, where they are going to sleep, who is going to clean, when we should get up, who is going to sit closest to me at dinner. You name it, and they fight. Recently, some of my family joined us. This has started a whole new set of arguments. For the most part, my family doesn't really believe in me and have come more to satisfy themselves as being right than to truly follow me.

The Feast of Tabernacles is going to be celebrated soon. Today, the dispute was whether we should go or not. My family urged me to go. They said I should expand my ministry, but in their hearts, they still can't accept who I am. They still see the son of a carpenter, a simple, ordinary person. I challenged their unstated concerns over me, which at times almost rises to the level of hatred. The debate continued with many of my followers as well. Some were arguing we should go while others were arguing we should not. In the end I told them I didn't really want to go since my time has not yet come.

Father, please help all my brothers and sisters find peace in their heart. I'm so tired of these petty rows, which I allow to unsettle me all too often. I'm also not quite myself when my family comes. I'm fine with my mom, but the rest have a way of getting under my skin. I wish Mom would have come; it would have been nice to see her. She has a way of calming me. I know you are calling me to Jerusalem, and I find myself anxious about it. Part of me doesn't think it is time, yet, I've been urged to go. Do I reject this idea solely because of my inner anxieties? Please, Father, help me be open to your plan, whatever it is.

Shalom.

144 Journey to Judea

After a good night's sleep, I realized God was calling me to celebrate the Feast of Tabernacles in Jerusalem. My family was right. I should go to Judea. Again, I find I'm guilty of the same thing I see in others. I know I should always look for the plank in my own eye. It never ceases to amaze me how God uses other people to point out my own shortcomings, of which, it seems, I have many.

We started on the road, and even though it's a long walk, I hardly noticed. It seems my physical strength was as great as my spiritual strength. Unfortunately, not all the disciples were in the same place as me. Peter once again had to be the spokesman for the group and tell me to slow down. I think some of the others were afraid to say anything to me, but Peter blurted it out loud. Sometimes being impetuous is a good thing.

When we slowed down, some people gathered around me. Apparently, some of them had been following me for a while, but most were too ill to keep up, let alone catch up. It seems this is another lesson for me. We should enjoy each day, but it's a little hard to enjoy things if we are moving too fast.

Anyway, when we slowed down, the crowds returned, and I found myself in awe once again. My Father touches so many people. I'm overwhelmed such a positive word has spread about me. Sick people, dying people, and lost sheep everywhere find a way to seek me. I can't believe how many people come. Some don't really believe, but they are curious, or they want to prove me wrong. Still, my Father gets them to come.

One man came today carrying his wife, who was weak and couldn't walk. He carried her for over two hours. Here,

I thought I had great physical strength, but he had the power of hope behind him. He was hoping for a miracle, I guess mostly so that he wouldn't have to carry her home again. But even after I healed her, she was still much too weak to walk. She will be gaining back her strength over the next week or two and will soon be back at full strength.

Another couple brought their elderly parents on a mule. They were dying of malnutrition. The children found them only a few days earlier; the elderly couple was too proud to ask for help. By the time they realized they needed help, they were too weak to make the journey to their daughter's home. They were so weak they couldn't even eat. My blessing gave them the strength to start eating. Their children brought plenty of food and water so they will surely recover.

A few were crippled, a few were blind, a few couldn't hear, one was mute. But all of them had hope, a belief in God and they believed in me. They didn't even know me, but they believed in me. Incredible. I'm certain they will wonder why my eyes were so full of tears. I was crying because I discovered that in my hurriedness to find life, I almost passed it by. Praise God for slowing me down.

About this time, some of my followers returned from a Samaritan village. They went ahead to make preparations for us to spend the evening. We had stayed at one of the villages before and expected we would be received well. However, this village wasn't as open and asked us not to come. James and John asked if I wanted them to command fire to consume them. I rebuked them immediately, telling them I didn't come to destroy but to save. I sometimes wonder how I will ever get my message across to people. John and James, two of my closest disciples, still have no understanding of the things I've been preaching. No, my time has clearly not yet arrived.

Father, thank you for this day. Every day you give me is a true blessing. You not only showed me the plank in my own eye today, but you made me put my anxieties aside. First, you help me slow down to find so many people still in need of me. Secondly, you show me my disciples are not yet ready for me to go. Thank you.

Shalom.

145 Humility

Our journey continued today, and more people came. I guess we are not easy to miss since my following is quite large.

One of the young men we encountered today told me how he would follow me wherever I go. He was way too young, and his parents were looking at me shaking their heads in dissent. I appreciated this young man's enthusiasm, but clearly, he was too young to leave. I called him over and talked to him a while.

I told him I greatly appreciated his gesture and knew he would be a mighty fine champion of God and a friend for me. I told him that foxes had holes, birds had nests, but I had nowhere to lay my head. He asked me what I meant. I told him God gives animals families to share with and homes to live in, but my family wasn't with me any longer, and I had no place to call home. He thought about this for a bit and then gave me a big hug and returned to his anxious parents.

I overheard another person bragging to his friends that he was just as gifted a preacher as I was. Another came and said he thought he was an even better preacher. They didn't realize I was near. I stepped in and said they should join me since I could use all the gifted preachers I can find. One replied that he had to first go and bid farewell to those in his house. I told him anyone who had his hand on a plow and decided to look back wasn't fit for the Kingdom of God. His friends couldn't hide their smiles.

Father, again I thank you for this day. I'm glad you sent me to Judea, the walk and the new people I'm meeting are comforting for my soul. Please take care of those young men today. It's always good to have people serve you by preaching, however, they needed a lesson in humility, as I do at times. I truly hope they will learn.

146 Sabbath Teachings

Today is the Sabbath. My Father always seems to have a synagogue for me where I'm welcomed to preach. Today was no different. When entering the synagogue, I noticed a woman who was bent over and unable to stand up straight. Apparently, she has been like that for about eighteen years, but she still managed to keep going and being the best mother to her children she could. She also came to the synagogue every week and every feast day and helped wherever she could. But it was getting to the point when her infirmity was going to prevent her from doing anything. She was no longer able to even get to the synagogue without help.

I went to her and said she was loosed from her infirmity. I put my hands on her and felt energy surging between us. I knew she was a true believer and an honest, compassionate soul. I held her hand and stared into her eyes. They were so warm and friendly, full of joy and full of life. She slowly straightened up, free of pain. She was so grateful. After giving me a warm hug and kiss, she thanked me and started proclaiming her thanks and glorifying God to everyone who entered the synagogue. What a true and kind spirit!

Then, the ruler of the synagogue came out to see what the commotion was. When he realized I had healed this woman, he was indignant because I healed on the Sabbath. He told the crowd that work was only to be done on six days, but the seventh day was for rest. It's so comical that these so-called leaders of God can't see the fallacy of their own preaching. How would God ever be against healing on a Sabbath? Can something so right and clearly done with the power of God ever be wrong?

It seems I have to repeat myself Sabbath after Sabbath. I called him a hypocrite, since every one of them would loosen his ox or donkey from the stall and lead it to water, even on the Sabbath. So, shouldn't this woman, who was a daughter of Abraham but was bound by a spirit of infirmity for eighteen years, be released from her bond on the Sabbath?

I went on and on about building the Kingdom of God, repeating many of the things I had said before. After the encounter with the ruler of the synagogue and the reaction of the people, I felt energized. They asked what the Kingdom of God is like. Like I'd done in the past, I compared it to a mustard seed, which a man planted in his garden. It's one of the smallest of seeds, yet it grows into a large tree and the birds of the air can nest in its branches. I compared it to leaven that a woman uses in meal until it all grows full. The people here were open to my teachings and understanding of God. I'm sure God will bless this village greatly.

Shalom.

147 Sending Followers

We are still on the road. I'm truly amazed at the number of people who find us. We often have to stop and preach or heal. While I'm thankful that they come, it's obvious I won't arrive in Jerusalem in time for the festival if our journey continues at this pace. Mary mentioned that I had sent twelve of my followers to help preach and heal before, so I should ask if anyone wanted to preach and teach to the surrounding villages instead of going to the festival with me.

I was reluctant to ask since I was certain most would prefer going to the festival with me. What a shock was in store for me! At least seventy men volunteered. I gave them similar instructions as I did with the twelve that had gone out before. I blessed each and every one of them individually. Most will leave in the morning since it was already getting late by the time I had finished blessing them all.

Thank you, Father, for these men. So many lessons and gifts all at once. The bickering will stop, well maybe not completely. The size of my entourage will be smaller, making it easier to find places to eat and sleep. Our journey will move along more quickly, so I can arrive in Jerusalem before the festival, and my mission will be expanded. Father, sometimes I wish I was as in touch with your plan as some others are. Mary seems to be almost as in touch with you as my mother. She is truly a wonderful companion and I thank you for the gift of her presence.

Shalom.

148 Journey

We've made good time ever since I sent others out to minister in my name. Even with the quicker pace, I didn't arrive in time for the beginning of the festival; it started today. However, I will get there sometime tomorrow evening.

A few days ago, we encountered ten lepers who stood afar, trying to listen but avoiding getting too close to anyone else. They cried in unison for me to have mercy on them. I didn't see them standing there before, I guess I had been too wrapped up in my preaching to notice them. I asked them to go show themselves to the priests. Today, one of them, a Samaritan, returned and threw himself on the ground in front of me and glorified God. I was a bit dumbfounded that out of ten lepers who were healed, only this man, a Samaritan at that, returned to thank me. It seems to me that the Samaritans can understand God as well as my fellow Jews.

It has been much quieter, for which I'm thankful. In fact, I found myself celebrating the more intimate following that remained with me. My Father knew exactly what I needed, a little time to rest and recharge my inner being. Thank you again, Father, for knowing more about my needs than I do myself. I know this is a short entry, but I think my physical body needs some rest as well.

Shalom.

149 Jerusalem

I was able to teach in the temple tonight. So many of my fellow Jews marveled at my ability to preach and the messages I had. I find I preach many of the same lessons over and over, but while they are old to me, they are new and fresh to these people.

I overheard one person asking how I knew so much. I explained my doctrine wasn't my own, but my Father's, who sent me. I further explained anyone who chooses to do the will of God would know that I don't seek to gain personal glory. Everything I teach is to honor God and encourage people to do the same.

There was still a lot of grumbling amongst the leaders, so I boldly I asked them why they were trying to kill me. Healing on the Sabbath came up and everyone was angry with me. I don't understand why circumcising boys on the Sabbath is different from healing. The argument escalated and some tried to seize me but were unable to. The Pharisees even sent guards to arrest me, however, they, too, were unsuccessful. I was right; it isn't yet my time.

Thank you, Father for sending me here. I know the majority of people listen to me and understand at least some of my message, although none, not even my disciples, understand my message at the core of their being. I don't fully understand why the Pharisees are determined to kill me, but I know all things are according to your plan, and I must follow.

Shalom.

150 The Adulterous Woman

I was preaching again today. A few people came for healing. Early in the day, I saw some scribes and Pharisees coming towards me, dragging a woman. They just threw her down in front of me. Calling me teacher with some animosity, they informed me the woman was caught in the very act of adultery. They stated Moses' law commanded that she should be stoned, but they wanted to know what I thought. Another trap. If I throw stones, it would undermine the very essence of all my teaching. If I didn't, I would undermine the Law of Moses.

Again, God put the answer in my mind. I stooped down and wrote sins on the ground, some of which I knew applied to them. Greed, jealousy, cheating, stealing, pride, and many more. Lastly, I wrote adultery. Then, I rose up and said to them, "Whoever is free of sin should be the first to throw a stone."

Mary was the first to walk away. She is such a genuine soul. My disciples and some of the people who were listening followed her. Finally, the scribes and Pharisees started to leave one by one. I looked around to be sure they had all left and told the woman I wouldn't condemn her either and she was free to go. She smiled and nodded a thank you. I admonished her a bit and recommended she should commit this sin no more.

Shalom.

151 Final Day of the Festival

Today is the final day of the festival and my final day to preach. I again explained my teachings of love, peace and forgiveness and re-iterated that the lessons I have are all from God. I told them if they thirst for knowledge, understanding, a fuller life, and inner peace, they should come to me and drink my words. If they believe in me, they will find rivers of living waters will flow from their hearts, as indicated in Scripture. Once again, the majority of the crowd recognized me as a prophet, but others doubted that I was the Christ because I hailed from Galilee and not Bethlehem.

One of the scribes tested me by asking what he should do to inherit eternal life. I asked him what was written in the law, since he was a scribe and should be well versed in these teachings. He responded he should love God with all his heart, soul, strength and mind and love his neighbor as himself. I was actually a bit surprised – this sounded like *my* teaching, not the typical teaching people get from the law. I told him he was right, and if he did all this, he would live.

He challenged me further by asking who his neighbor was. I was so impressed with the Samaritans I've encountered in my travels that I told the following parable involving them: a priest was walking along the road from Jerusalem to Jericho when some robbers wounded him, took his clothing and all his possessions, and left him for dead. Another priest came down the road and saw him but crossed to the other side of the road and passed by. Likewise, a Levite came along and saw him but also crossed to the other side and passed by.

Finally, a Samaritan came along. When he saw the priest, he was moved with compassion. The Samaritan tended to the priest's wounds and then helped him onto his mule and brought him to an inn in the nearest town. When he left the next morning, he gave money to the innkeeper and asked him to tend to the priest with it, and if more was needed, he would repay him upon his return.

I asked which of the three was the neighbor – the second priest, the Levite or the Samaritan? The scribe acknowledged it was the one who showed mercy, being unable to even say the word Samaritan. I also forced him to acknowledge that the priest and the Levite were not being good neighbors despite their self-proclaimed goodness and holiness. I told him that actions spoke louder than words and being neighborly involved action. Understanding the Scriptures isn't the answer unless the lessons are written on one's heart and applied in everyday life. I told the man he needed to go and do likewise.

Father, thank you again for the wonderful parable today. What a brilliant way to demonstrate that the answers don't reside in knowledge of the law but the ability to act with a heart of love, mercy, compassion and forgiveness.

Shalom.

152 Martha

When we left Jerusalem, we traveled to Bethany to visit my friend Lazarus. He wasn't there, but his sister Martha invited me to dine with her and their young sister, Mary. They are both lovely women and I care for them as much as Lazarus. Martha busied herself with preparations for dinner while I chatted with Mary and some of my companions. Even though Mary is young, I'm amazed at how eager she is to listen and learn. She has a wonderful open heart, and her inner spirit is enthusiastic and pliable. She is like clay that I can mold and shape with my direction.

After a while, Martha became a bit perturbed that she was doing all the work while Mary was listening to me. I told her that the most important thing for us is to learn about God. Mary has chosen what was best for her, and I asked Martha to not take it away. In fact, I invited Martha to take a break and listen a little as well. I could see she was torn between the work to finalize preparations for dinner and the idea of listening.

I think we all do this at times. We all get so wrapped up in the many seemingly important things in our life. Yes, it's important to cook because without it, our bodies wouldn't survive. However, at times we get so wrapped up in our daily activities that we don't allow time for prayer or learning about God. We don't make time to sit and reflect or to simply enjoy the world around us. I know it because I'm guilty of this myself at times. Martha chose to join us and listen for a while, and then we all helped her finish the preparations while our discussion continued well into the evening hours.

Father, help me fully learn the things I preach. I've been so busy lately preaching and healing and travelling, I've been guilty of not taking time to simply be in your presence and fully immerse myself in your love. I haven't noticed the sunrise or sunset or the birds in the air or the smell of the flowers. Please help me never to take the marvelous world you have created for granted.

Shalom.

153 A Blind Man

Today I encountered a man I healed from blindness. I say encountered, but the truth is I was looking for him. I heard the Pharisees had banned him from the synagogue because he stood up for me. I asked him if he believed in the Son of Man. He eagerly asked who he was so he could believe in him. I told him it was me, and he immediately fell to his knees. I had to coax him to stand. I told him I wanted to thank him for remaining true to me despite the Pharisees. I told him he was always welcome to join us. He said he wasn't worthy to join me, his blindness proved how unworthy he was. I told him I came into the world so the blind could see, but those who were able to see would become blind.

I added the second part because I knew some Pharisees were standing near, eavesdropping. When the Pharisees heard this, they challenged me if I was saying they were blind. I told them if they were blind, they wouldn't be guilty of sin. But if you claim you can see, the guilt remains. They said they had no idea what I meant.

I told them anyone who enters the sheep pen by the gate is the shepherd, but anyone who climbs in another way is a thief or a robber. The shepherd calls his sheep by name, they know his voice, listen to him and follow him. They will never follow a stranger. The Pharisees still looked confused.

I told them I was the gate for the sheep. The ones that came before me were thieves and robbers, and the sheep didn't listen to them. But anyone who enters through the gate will be saved because I provide life to the fullest. I'm the good shepherd and I will lay down my life for my sheep. I further explained that like the good shepherd, I know my sheep and they know me, just as my Father knows me and I know Him. I have other sheep from different sheep pens whom I needed to bring too. They will listen to my voice, and there will be one flock and one shepherd.

There was a division amongst the crowd that gathered. Some thought I was a raving mad lunatic, while others acknowledged I had to be genuine since I had performed so many healings. The Pharisees left together, asking each other if I was suggesting they were guilty of sin.

Later this evening as we were eating, someone asked me to expand upon the comments I made to the Pharisees. Oh, will they never understand? I explained that physical blindness only means a person can't see. However, the Pharisees are blind to the truths of God. They think they know everything and don't listen, learn and grow. If someone is truly blind to the truth, they can't be considered guilty of sin because they have never had the truth presented to them. However, I've given the Pharisees the truth many times. They have heard me talk and witnessed my healing, yet they continue to reject the things I teach. Therefore, they are guilty of sin.

I told them that the reason my Father loves me is that I will lay down my life for him and I will take it up again. Surprisingly, none of them asked me about laying down my life. I don't think this is a subject they are very comfortable with as yet. Neither am I, frankly. The truth is I try really hard not to think about it, although maybe my Father is telling me I should. I try to enjoy life each and every day.

Shalom.

154 Loneliness

I find myself struggling with loneliness again. Some of this is because so many of my followers have been off on their own and I don't have as many people surrounding me as I used to. Curious, not that long ago, I was secretly glad to see them go so I could have a little more peace and quiet, but now I'm longing for them to return.

I'm also struggling with trying to understand my Father's plan. I imagine it's tied to my loneliness somehow. At times, I'm afraid of the future, while at other times, I'm glad at the idea that I will rejoin my Father completely. I'm concerned my followers haven't yet understood enough to be without me. This makes me feel like I'm a failure. I've tried my best to open their hearts to my message, but I might not have been successful.

Today we met up with many of my followers that were travelling on their own. Their enthusiasm was contagious. They were able to heal many, and people responded well to their preaching. They said they felt even the demons were subject to them when they used my name. I let them know that it wasn't me who delivered these things, but my Father. I don't even remember all the other things I said, since I was so excited to see them, and even more excited that my Father was again able to heal me of the different things weighing me down. He was able to address my loneliness and my concerns over how well my followers understand me. My concerns over my future have also vanished, at least for the moment.

Shalom.

155 Judea

I've been travelling through Judea lately. All of my followers have now returned. It's funny how quickly my feelings of loneliness have changed again to being overwhelmed and wanting fewer people around me so I can enjoy a little more peace and quiet.

Balance. Perhaps that's what I need in my life. Balance between loneliness and being overwhelmed. Balance between being secure and comfortable with who I am and being prideful. Balance between helping others and taking time for myself. Balance between teaching and healing. Balance between so many things, which, at times, seem to tear me in opposite directions.

Father, I thank you for the many gifts you have given me. Today, I ask for balance in my life. Help me find the balance I need to keep me from vacillating from one extreme to the other.

Shalom.

156 Feast of Dedication

Time seems to be moving so fast lately. It seems the Feast of Tabernacles was yesterday, and now it's already winter and time for the Feast of Dedication. I returned to Jerusalem for this feast.

Today, many of my fellow Jews asked me to tell them plainly if I was the Messiah. I said I had told them already, but they were reluctant to believe. I told them my Father and I are one, but they still don't see it. They aren't my sheep. My sheep listen to my voice; I know them, and they follow me.

Some of them asked me to tell them more. I did. I gained quite a few new believers and possibly even some followers. But as the discussion continued, some scribes and a Pharisee came over. When they overheard that someone referred to me as Messiah, one of them picked up a stone and the others quickly followed. Fortunately, the crowd quickly gathered around me to protect me. I asked them for which of my good works were they stoning me. They said it wasn't for my good works, but for blasphemy because I'm a mere man but claim to be God.

Feeling safe because of all the people surrounding me, I was a bit bolder than normal in my response. I pointed out that the Scriptures call people "gods." I also told them that even if they don't believe me, they should believe my works. I pointed out all the people following me, and the many healings I've performed. I told them the Father is in me and I am in Him. They tried to seize me and called others to help, but the crowd protected me so I could get away.

Father, I understand this tension is all part of your plan. I know it will climax soon. Today, you protected me from this growing sentiment. In the meantime, I still have your work to do and, as always, I promise I will perform it to my fullest. I feel that continuing to work in your name, especially around here, is akin to walking into the lion's den, however, it's a path I must follow. Please grant me the courage and strength to do so with the best of my ability.

Shalom.

157 Perea

I'm now in Perea, where we continue to preach and heal. After the Feast was over, I decided it would be best to leave Jerusalem for a while. Actually, one of the Pharisees came to me quietly and suggested I leave since Herod wanted to kill me. I find it amusing he was brave enough to warn me, but not brave enough to acknowledge it was his fellow Pharisees who wanted me killed. I told him he should tell that fox that I will keep driving out demons, healing people and preaching. I referred to him as a fox since he was unclean and a coward. I mentioned that Jerusalem was trying to kill the prophets and stone those who were sent to her. I told him I longed to gather Jerusalem's children together just as a hen gathers her chicks and protects them with her wings. I was hoping he would relay my message to his fellow Pharisees, but I have no way of knowing.

Shalom.

158 Sabbath Healing

Once again, it's the Sabbath. A local Pharisee invited me to dine with him, and once again, there was a person in need of healing. This time it was a man whose body was abnormally swollen. I asked the Pharisee and his entourage of scribes and others knowledgeable in the law if it was allowed to heal on the Sabbath. Receiving no answer, I asked them if anyone would hesitate to save a child who fell into a well on the Sabbath. No one challenged me about healing, at least this time, so I healed the man.

I found it annoying how the guests of the Pharisee at dinner were squabbling over sitting in the places of honor. I always find it amusing how we Jews need to be recognized. My followers always seem to squabble over who is the greatest. Does that mean others are supposed to feel like they are less?

As I was watching the events unfold, my Father filled my head with a lesson, which I quickly shared. I told them that when they were invited to a wedding, they should not take the place of honor since someone more distinguished may have been invited. They should take the lowest seat instead, so the host will ask them to move to a better place. Then they will be honored in the presence of the other guests. Anyone who exalts themselves will be humbled, and those who humble themselves will be exalted. I don't think anyone understood the message, except John and James, who were dining with me this evening.

The dinner was quite eventful with a lot of bickering amongst the guests. A few even commented on the quality of the food because they expected something better. It seemed everyone was complaining about everything – the weather, their family, their friends, taxes. The list seemed endless. I could tell the host was growing quite embarrassed and frustrated over the antics of his friends and neighbors. I leaned over to him and told him that when he had a luncheon or dinner, he should not invite his friends or family or wealthy neighbors, but the poor, lame and blind. Although they would be unable to repay him, he would be blessed abundantly. He smiled and thanked me.

One of the other guests overheard me and said the one to be truly blessed is the one who will eat at the feast in the Kingdom of God. He was challenging me since I had put him down. I told him a story of a certain man, who was preparing a great banquet and invited many guests. But when his servant went to tell them they should come, the guests began making excuses. When the servant returned to tell his master no one was coming, the master became angry. He asked the servant to go quickly into the streets and alleys and bring the poor, crippled, blind and lame. When they did this, there was still room, so the master directed his servants to go out into the country and compel people to come so his house could be full.

Most of the guests ignored the story and returned to their own discussions. However, the one who commented initially demanded to know what I meant. James spoke up for me. He said God has prepared a great banquet for all His children. It's a feast beyond imagination. However, the most distinguished guests all have excuses for not coming. So, God reaches out to everyone else because His banquet hall isn't full and there is enough to serve everyone. James said he found it so sad that many people, especially those in positions of esteem, reject God's invitation to the feast.

The man rose and left in a bit of a huff and another followed him out. The rest decided they would stay and eat the food they didn't like rather than leave with an empty stomach. Oh, blessed humanity!

159 The Pharisee

While teaching today, I asked, "If you had one hundred sheep and lost one, would you not leave the ninety-nine and go after the lost sheep until you find it? And when you find it, wouldn't you joyfully carry it home and ask your friends and neighbors to celebrate with you? Or suppose a woman has ten silver coins and loses one. Doesn't she light a lamp and search carefully until she finds it? And when she finds it, won't she ask her neighbors to rejoice with her since she found her lost coin?" I told them heaven rejoices more over one sinner who repents than over ninety-nine who don't need to repent.

While I was preaching, I noticed the Pharisee we had dinner with last night. Today, he looked a bit different to me. His face seemed calmer and he was truly listening to my words. When I finished preaching, I asked if anyone was in need of healing. A few people did, including the Pharisee. I hadn't noticed anything wrong with him yesterday, so I was curious as to why he felt the need for healing. My followers helped with the healing process, but I made sure I went to see the Pharisee directly.

He told me he was in need of healing in his heart. He had allowed his heart to be hardened with the teachings of the law. He was sure the teachings were valid, but last night my words about inviting guests to a banquet really resonated with him. He could see the truth in my words. He told me he felt like the lost sheep I talked about. His friends were always trying to look the best and the greatest. They didn't really care about the poor and only wanted the best for themselves. He said he realized my teachings were from God. He asked me to help him open his heart to my words.

I told him he was healed since he had already opened his heart to me. We hugged and he wished me well. He said he knew most of his fellow Pharisees were afraid of me, just as he was before last night. He was concerned about how much anger and violence might be in store for me, but he assured me he wouldn't be a part of it and would try his best to subdue the Pharisees' anger.

Father, thank you for this day. You know I sometimes wonder how much of my message is heard. I'm concerned your children will never truly learn, that the old way is too ingrained to be overcome. Yet, again and again, you show me you have everything under control. I'm concerned your children can't put aside their humanity enough to see the divine spirit residing within each of them, and yet, here I am, oftentimes guilty of the same thing. I'm truly the Son of Man.

Shalom.

160 Crowds

I've been amazed at how many people in this area are following me. It seems my followers have doubled over the last week. I think many aren't sincere but have merely been caught up in the excitement that surrounds me. I don't need more followers, especially ones who aren't genuine.

I started preaching to my followers every evening to explain the costs of following me. The journey may be exciting, but it's certainly not for the weak and weary. I told them my followers need to put aside their mother, father, brother, sister, and even their wife and children. In fact, they need to put aside their own life. Anyone who doesn't carry their own cross can't be my disciple.

I likened it to planning to build a tower. First, they need to sit down and estimate the cost to make sure they have adequate funds to complete it. People will ridicule them if they lay the foundation and then have to stop. I likened it to a king about to go to war. He must first consider whether his troops are large enough and equipped well enough to be victorious. If not, he must send a delegation while the enemy is far off to seek terms of peace. In the same way, they must look at themselves to evaluate if they have enough to be victorious. Following me isn't easy, and I have no doubt it will become even more difficult in the weeks to follow.

Some leave, some stay. Many talk to my other followers about our life and the difficulties we encounter. It's funny that no one really asks me. I don't know if I intimidate them or if they fear I'm too busy with other things. But none of the new people talk to me directly. Part of me wants to shake them and ask them why they don't seek me first, while another part of me celebrates the fact they don't bother me so I can have my own time to pray and relax. Again, I find myself being pulled in opposite directions at the same time. It seems my Son of Man part is constantly seeking something different from my Son of God part.

Father, please help me find the balance between being the Son of Man you have created me to be and the Son of God who I am as well. So often, these two parts seem to be in conflict with each other. I know you made me the Son of Man so I can relate to your children better, to understand the many complexities of life first-hand. However, at times I find the nuances of being the Son of Man are difficult and weigh me down. Father, as always, I place my being in your loving hands.

Shalom.

161 Parables

The days proceed pretty much the same, walking, preaching, and healing. My Father has given me an increasing number of parables to help explain my message. I still find parables a delightful way to preach since the examples help explain things better than mere words. Again, at John's suggestion, I will record some of them.

One of my favorites is about a man who had two sons. The younger son was a bit wild and always got into trouble. He begged his father to give him his share of the estate, so his father divided his property between his two sons. The younger son took all his possessions and set off for a distant country where he squandered his wealth. After he spent everything, a severe famine engulfed the whole country. He had to hire himself out to a citizen of the country, who sent him to feed pigs. He was so hungry he longed to eat the food he was serving the pigs.

Finally, he realized his father's servants were treated far better than he was, since they always had enough food to eat and even a surplus. He decided to return to his father and acknowledge his sins against heaven and his family. He realized he was no longer worthy to be called his son, and he would beg to be one of his hired servants.

When his father saw him, he was filled with compassion, ran to him, threw his arms around him, hugged him and gave him a kiss. The son said that he was no longer worthy to be his son and asked for a position as a servant. But the father didn't listen. He quickly called his servants to bring his best robe for his son, a ring for his finger and sandals for his feet. He asked them to bring the fattened calf and kill it so he could have a feast and celebrate.

In the meantime, the older son got angry and refused to attend the celebration. His father went to him and pleaded. The son said he had been slaving for his father and obeying him for years. Yet, his father never gave him as much as a young goat to celebrate with his friends. But a fattened calf is killed for his brother, who squandered his inheritance on prostitutes, drinking and gambling. His father assured him he was always with him and everything he had was also his, but he had to celebrate because his brother was dead to him before, and now he is alive again. He was lost, and now he is found.

I've found my followers don't always understand the meaning of parables, since they often ask me afterwards. I tell them there is usually more than one meaning; they should think about it and consider what it means to them. Sometimes I even ask them if anyone has an idea about what the parable meant, like today.

Judas said it was the same message I had been preaching all along. God celebrates the return of one sinner, one lost sheep, and one lost coin. No matter what our past was like, God is waiting for us with open arms. Thaddeus said he often felt like the older brother who felt slighted. Several others agreed. I guess they are feeling frustrated that they've known me so long, and yet, the new followers seem to enjoy a better relationship with me. This isn't true, but I understand the frustration.

I assured them my love for them was beyond imagination. I cherished all the time we shared in the past. To a large degree, each and every one of them has helped me grow personally and in my ministry. I would be a mere shadow of who I am today without them by my side. Yes, all the people who follow me now have been sent by God and are part of who I am, but I will always hold a special spot in my heart for those who have followed me and helped me the longest.

Shalom.

162 Another Parable

I especially enjoy parables when they help me point out the shortcomings of the Pharisees indirectly. Today, when the Pharisees were listening, I told the story of a rich man whose manager was accused of wasting his possessions. The manager was concerned for his future because he wasn't strong enough to dig and he was too proud to beg. He found a way to ensure people would welcome him into their homes: He called each of his master's debtors, asked them how much they owed, and then reduced the amount. If they owed nine hundred gallons of olive oil, he told them to take the bill and make it four hundred and fifty. Another that owed thousand bushels of wheat was told to take the bill and write eight hundred. When the master discovered what had happened, he commended the dishonest manager because he acted shrewdly.

The manager was obviously not someone who could be trusted. If someone wasn't trustworthy in handling worldly wealth, who would trust him with true riches? If someone wasn't trustworthy with someone else's property, who would give him property of his own? I pointed out that no one can serve two masters. You can't serve both money and God.

The Pharisees started sneering at me since they knew I was directing a lot of this towards them. I told them they justified themselves in the eyes of others, but God knew their hearts and what many people value is really detestable in God's sight. Pharisees have made money their God and have neglected their responsibilities of teaching about true riches – joy, peace, understanding, love, and forgiveness, none of which can be measured in wealth. And then they try and put themselves above everyone else by claiming some sort of superiority based mostly on their earthly wealth.

I went on and on about this for far too long. I finally noticed some of my followers were closing their eyes and realized it was getting far too late. I closed with a prayer and sent them off to bed. Mary came to me afterwards.

"What is troubling you?", she asked.

"The Pharisees, of course!" I responded. "They are turning people against me and they aren't even teaching the scriptures properly."

"Are you sure that is all there is?"

"Isn't it obvious?", I responded, perhaps a little too forcefully.

"Perhaps." she replied gently, "But I really think you should look a little deeper beyond the obvious."

With that she gave me a kiss and a hug with a loving look and left.

She's right. Something is troubling me deep inside, and it isn't the Pharisees. I think perhaps I, too, am guilty of missing the point at times. I don't treat money as my God, like the Pharisees, but I do find myself falling into the hole of pride all too often. And still, the issues I'll be facing in the future gnaw at my insides. I would like to believe that if I don't think about them, they'll go away, but this isn't the case. Trying to put a barrel over the issues to hide them doesn't make them any less real.

Oh, Father, help me overcome my prideful behavior. I know as your son I'm more in touch with you than your other children. But I can't act superior to them, I'm here to serve and teach, not lord over them. Isn't this what the Pharisees have done? Father, help me remove the barrels I've installed to hide from my future. I need to fully embrace it, not hide from it. Thank you, Father, for today, your parables, my followers and again your ability to teach me the things I need to learn.

Shalom.

163 The Rich Man and Beggar

Today I overheard someone ask how they can be convinced if my teachings are truly from God. God gave me a parable about a rich man and a beggar named Lazarus, who was covered with sores and longed to eat from the rich man's table.

When the beggar died, the angels carried him to Abraham's side. The rich man also died, but he was sent to Hades, where he lived in torment. He looked up and was able to see Abraham far away with Lazarus by his side. He begged Abraham to send Lazarus to dip his finger in water and cool his tongue because he was in agony. Abraham told him he received many good things during his life, while Lazarus received only bad things. Now Lazarus was comforted and he was in agony.

The rich man then begged Lazarus be sent to his family so they wouldn't come to the place of torment. But Abraham told him that they had Moses and the prophets for guidance. The rich man said they would listen and repent if someone returned from the dead. But Abraham said if they didn't listen to Moses and the prophets, they wouldn't be convinced even if someone returned from the dead.

I don't know if anyone understood the message, but if they can't understand the truth as I proclaim it, there's nothing more I can do or say. Again, I find this message is for me as much as for them. I've been feeling responsible for my inability to get everyone to hear my message. I know my message will fall on rocks as often as fertile soil, but I still feel a bit of a failure when I encounter rocks. Thank you, Father, for the reminder.

Shalom.

164 Marriage

Once again, the Pharisees tried to trip me. This time they asked about divorce, wondering if I thought divorce was lawful. Divorce is certainly not something my Father prefers. He wishes a man and woman would choose each other for the remainder of life, not until a problem arises. Again, conflict creates opportunities to grow. Everyone can learn and grow so much from difficult times. However, there are certain behaviors that would make life too difficult to live through, such as infidelity or physical abuse.

Therefore, divorce has become a necessity for the human condition. However, except in cases where divorce is reasonable and lawful, a person who re-marries commits adultery. We must protect against situations in which divorce is merely convenient and one or the other person simply chooses to dishonor the relationship. These things can't be easily described, but must be judged on a case-by-case basis.

My disciples were concerned when I responded so harshly against divorce. They indicated I was basically saying it's better to not marry at all. Adultery doesn't stop simply because a person isn't married. I know that it would be impossible for most people to choose a life of never being married. But if anyone can accept such a serious discipline, they should accept it. After all, such a condition would only be granted by my Father in cases He calls them to such a life.

I'm still thinking about these last words. It's so difficult not to know a woman, to choose not to be married. At times, my humanity longs for the specialness of a relationship only possible through marriage. A part of me wants to be on a pedestal because I've chosen a life without a woman. Actually, my Father has chosen it for me. I often pray it was different. From what my Father has revealed to me, it would be wrong for me to get married. I travel a lot, and she would be alone too much, or I would have to diminish my preaching. Also, I know my life will end soon, which would mean she would be alone.

However, I still long for the ability to have a child. I see the joy a child brings to so many people. Some people don't appreciate their children. Nothing saddens me more. I think having a child, the chance to be parents ourselves, may be the greatest gift of my Father. I often think children teach adults more about being adults than adults could ever teach children.

Sometimes I examine the loneliness that periodically tears at my soul. How much of it is because I can't enjoy the simplicity of life like my own parents had? I want a life of togetherness, raising a family, sharing with one special person. I've been able to accommodate those needs somewhat by sharing as much of myself as possible with my disciples. They have been my companions. But they still have families and other priorities.

Oh, Father, there are days like this, when loneliness overtakes my soul. I yearn for the joys of humanity I simply can't experience. Most of all, I yearn for the type of loving relationship I have with you, but in the form of a person. Someone I can share all my dreams with, someone I can share my love for you with, someone who understands the things I understand. Please, if it be your will, send that person to me. If it isn't your will, help me use my loneliness to get to know you even better.

Shalom.

165 Children

Today of all days, child after child was brought to me. Last night, I longed to be a father to a single child and now my Father sent me dozens. They all looked at me as they looked at their own father. The parents brought them to me to cure whatever ailments they had. Some brought them for a general blessing. Some even brought them so they may be dedicated to my Father. The children all accepted me with open arms. God gave me a day to play daddy to many children; boys, girls, infants, toddlers, children of all ages. The disciples first tried to rebuke the parents for burdening me with mere children. I smiled and said, "Let the children come." I told them that the Kingdom of Heaven belongs as much to these children as it does to us adults.

I played all day with them. We chased each other around. The parents watched for a while, and then, one by one, they left to talk to my disciples. One woman hung around the longest. It was as if she could sense my joy. I noticed a beaming smile in her eyes every time I looked at her. She never interfered, she was simply enjoying the moment as much as I was.

I left them when evening started to fall and quickly wandered off myself. I can't believe the day I had. I asked God to comfort me, and once again He delivers in grand proportion; the laughter of the children, their openness to me, the smile of a loving young mother. It was fantastic to take a break from the long days of preaching, teaching and healing and allow myself to be a child again.

Perhaps this is one of my biggest problems. I'm so caught up in being God's son, being the savior of the earth, needing to follow things perfectly that I forget I, too, am a child, God's child. I also need to romp, play and enjoy the day sometimes. I felt I had the gift of being a father today, knowing what it was like to have children of my own and, just as importantly, to be a child again.

There was one sad piece of news today. I heard my dear friend Lazarus took ill and was near death. His sisters, Mary and Martha, sent word for me to come quickly, but I couldn't bear the thought of leaving those children. I needed time to rest today and freshen my spirit. I will take leave soon. I'm sure Lazarus will be fine.

Dear Father, please don't allow me to lose the gift of play, and thanks for the gift today.

Shalom.

166 More Play

I was so happy playing with the children that I decided I needed another day. Today, I was able to get most of my followers to join in. John was the first to start playing. He had little choice. He was coming over to tell me something, and a few of the children jumped on him until he was down on the ground. He then freed himself and started chasing them. He was never quite able to catch any of them. I'm certain he let them get away each time.

One by one, the rest of the men started playing as well. We surely needed it. About halfway through the day, we thought we would need to stop to prepare a meal. Right about this time, several of the parents came by with a feast for a king. We ate heartily. We needed it, too. I don't remember playing being quite so tiring.

After eating, the children rested. I gathered the parents around and shared some of my thoughts with them. I told them that I was very lonely in life, and I missed having a wife and a family. I let them know how happy I was that they allowed me the great gift of these children. In some ways, I felt they were all mine.

The parents thanked me for taking the time to share with their children. They were so grateful I put aside time from healing, especially my dear friend Lazarus, to spend time with them. They said I made the children feel very special.

We played some more after they woke and then shared another meal. When it got dark, we all gathered around the fire. We sang songs and told delightful stories. All in all, it was another wonderful day.

Father, thank you for helping me reunite with my own inner child. I had almost forgotten how to have fun. Amen.

167 Lazarus

I received word from a traveler that Lazarus died after I wrote the last entry. I was most surprised. I was so sure my Father wanted me to stay with the children to rekindle my own spirit. How could He have allowed this to happen?

By morning, I realized this, too, was part of God's wonderful plan. Lazarus was asleep, just like the official's daughter. I told my followers we should go since Lazarus was asleep. They didn't understand. I later told them the "sleep" I was referring to was death. I also told them I was happy they would witness this with me.

The journey was mostly uneventful, so I had a lot of time to "talk" to God about the things swirling around in my head. Since we were moving pretty quickly, there was little time for the crowds to reach us. A few people found us along the path, and my disciples were able to help them. Ever since they returned from their own mission, they have been more helpful.

I saw Martha when I first arrived today. She told me she believed her brother wouldn't have died had I arrived early enough, but she said she knew it wasn't too late. I was amazed at her faith. When I discovered Lazarus had been in the tomb for four days, I doubted he could simply be asleep. Then Mary came and chastised me for being late. Her words were quite cruel and hurtful. I began doubting my Father's plan and myself. I was a bit perturbed and even shed some tears thinking I may have played with the children too long. I could have come sooner. I may have helped.

But then Martha's words echoed in my head again. I asked my Father if it were His will to bring Lazarus to life again. I was certain it was. When I came to the tomb, I stopped for a moment to pray before I went in. Martha knelt beside me, then Mary did too. I prayed quietly to myself. Then, to my surprise, I heard Thaddeus praying aloud.

He prayed for faith and understanding. He prayed for inner peace regardless of the situation. He prayed for all present to have the power to believe. He said if we prayed together, our Father in Heaven wouldn't be able to deny us. I cried, not because of Lazarus, but because of Thaddeus' prayer and the solemnity of all of us kneeling on the ground outside the tomb. It was a truly moving experience. I felt the presence of God all around me.

Re-energized, I rose. I asked Thaddeus to help me roll away the stone, as it was a bit too large for me. Martha said she was worried about the stench. When we rolled the stone away, I was certain our prayers were answered, because the smell was a musty but pleasant one. I simply cried out for Lazarus to come out. He appeared with his hands and feet bound in burial cloth.

The reunion with Mary and Martha was most incredible. They hugged each other for what seemed like forever. Then we all gave Lazarus a hug. Some asked him how he felt. He responded he was a little weak, thirsty and hungry. We returned to his home where my followers made a wonderful meal. Neither Mary nor Martha volunteered to help; they felt their place was with their brother. And so it was. I guess some of my lessons are understood after all since Martha allowed others to serve her for a change while she sat with her brother and sister.

What an incredible day. Once I was able to get past my initial reaction and have faith in Abba, I was able to be completely in touch with my inner spirit. I am incredibly energized. My doubts about everything have completely dissipated, at least for today. Thank you, Abba.

168 God's Kingdom

Today the crowds seemed more festive than usual. The atmosphere was one of celebration. The children seemed to laugh and play more, and the families joined in. About midway through the day, a young man came by on his camel. He was obviously wealthy and a little arrogant. He asked me what good he could do to enter the Kingdom. I'm sure he was taunting me a little, thinking he was "good" enough already.

I responded a bit harshly, asking him why he asked about "good," since there was only one who was good. However, if he, or anyone else for that matter, wished to enter the Kingdom of Heaven, they should simply keep the commandments. He asked me which ones. I said, the basic commandments of Moses; he should not kill, steal, or commit adultery, he should honor his parents and love his neighbor as himself. The arrogant young man retorted that he had done all of these things, what next. He believed he was above all others and was a picture of perfection.

This is pride, which is perhaps the greatest of sins. Pride gets in the way of our ability to see our own sin. It's incredibly difficult to correct something when you refuse to believe there is anything wrong. I recommended that if he truly wanted to be perfect, he should sell everything, give it to the poor and come follow me. He left with his head down. He thought I would use him as a model for others. I may or may not have opened his door to see his own pride. My Father knows. I don't.

The crowd seemed stunned after the young man left. It was obvious they felt he was somewhat better than they were. I told them the man was full of pride because of his material wealth. This pride caused him to think he was certain to enter heaven. Many of the wealthy have the same shortcoming. They envision themselves as superior and perfect. That's why it's hard for the rich to enter the Kingdom of Heaven: Pride will stand in their way, as pride is akin to someone being rich in a personal spirit. The Kingdom is for those who are poor in spirit, the ones who recognize that God, and God alone, is the ultimate source of the Kingdom. It isn't something we can gain by earthly goods or possessions.

Even my disciples, recognizing the young man was truly one of the more generous wealthy landowners in the area, were somewhat stunned. They seemed certain the young man would be saved, so they asked me who, then, could be saved. I explained salvation isn't something man can do. We can't simply fulfill a quota of good works to be saved. There is no set amount of religious observance that will save someone. There is no special formula for being saved. The commandments provide guidance, but they're only a guide. Entering the Kingdom of God depends on giving one's spirit over fully and completely to the Father, which is only possible with God's help.

Later this evening when we were alone, Peter was feeling somewhat slighted, hurt and confused about my earlier comments. He and the others had given up all they had to follow me. What will be in store for them? It seemed they felt they had wasted their lives following me when they could have been with their family instead. They needed some reassurance from me. They were still trying to understand my lessons in their head instead of their heart. They are genuinely trying hard to be poor in spirit as I explained, but they are not yet completely there. So many things are in the way – loneliness, hurt, resentment, anger, even pride. I think a few, like Judas, think being my follower makes them better than everyone else.

I know my Father won't abandon these men. They have clearly demonstrated a sincere longing to understand God and enter His Kingdom. I assured them they would achieve the comfort they sought, and when the Son of Man was seated at the throne of glory, they would be seated next to me in twelve thrones, each one judging a tribe of Israel. Everyone who abandoned homes, parents, spouses or children for my sake will receive a hundred times more and will inherit the gift of eternal life. I told them many who are first in this life, such as that young man, may end up last in the next.

Father, giving up everything for you, abandoning all we are is incredibly difficult. The young man this morning couldn't bear the thought of parting with his earthly possessions. Others, such as my disciples, gladly depart with their physical belongings, but cling to their inner possessions. When one looks at what they can do to better themselves for God, the answer is to give up their inner self. Humans only stand in the way of God. They try to use their mind to understand you, Father, which won't work. Your laws are written in the heart, not the mind. We have to overcome the thoughts of who we are to allow you to enter our hearts. We must give our hearts over to you so you can fill them with your love.

You sent me to teach them these very truths. But the job you give me seems hopeless at times. Even these men who have been so loyal, who have been earnestly trying, don't quite understand. They keep falling into the same pits they had before. Their hearts don't quite seem to open to you. John especially seems to have moments of great understanding, as do the others, but then they revert back to their old selves quite often.

Father, you want me to show them the way and help them recognize that the path will be long and arduous. Ultimately, you'll find a way to bring the entire human family to your Kingdom. After all, we are all your children, and like any loving parent, you want the best for us, you won't abandon us, and you'll always keep trying. You will also let us grow and be on our own to make our own mistakes. That, too, is part of being a loving parent. A parent must be careful not to hold onto a child too long, or it will dash the spirit and cause rebellion. That's just like you. We, your children, have grown to a point you had to let us go. Sure, we make mistakes, which is part of growing. But sooner or later, the understanding will come. After all, we have you for a teacher.

Thank you, Father, for revealing so many of your mysteries to me and mostly for allowing me to open my heart as fully as I can to you.

Shalom.

169 The First Is Last

It seems that when I told my disciples yesterday that the first would be last and the last would be first, I added more confusion than clarity. I still can't get them to understand the things of God are unlike the things of this world. God doesn't necessarily care about who is the wealthiest, strongest or smartest. It's up to us to use His gifts to the fullest. God doesn't see the gift of leadership as more important than the gift of singing. Nor is the gift of wealth better than the gift of compassion. And the gift of intelligence isn't cherished more than the gift of carpentry skills. All gifts are equally important.

But these brothers and sisters of mine seem to be caught up in being better than the next. My disciples, because they believe me to be the Messiah, think they are somehow the best in God's eyes. Everyone wants to be the first or the closest. They think their role here will bring special favors for them in the following life. Certainly, they are incredibly special to my Father; after all, He chose them for me, and me for them. But all humanity is special to my Father.

Today I told them a story about a landowner who had great need in his vineyard for harvest one day. He sent his servants out to the village at dawn and hired laborers at the customary daily wage. About nine o'clock in the morning, his servants found more workers standing idly about, so they hired them too. Again, at noon the servants went out and found still more people standing around, and they were sent off to the vineyard as well. At five o'clock, the servants still found others standing around. Upon asking why they were still standing there idly, they responded no one had hired them. They, too, were sent to work in the vineyard even though the sun was growing low.

When evening came, the landowner asked his servants to summon all the workers. He paid those who had started at five o'clock first and paid them the usual wage for an entire day's work. He paid the rest the same amount as well. The workers who were there all day grumbled that the last ones who worked only an hour earned the same as they did even though they were working hard all day, especially through the intense heat of midday. The landowner replied that he paid them the wage they had agreed upon, therefore, they should accept it without complaining. It's up to him to pay the others whatever he wanted since it was his money to do as he pleased. He then asked if they were envious because of his generosity.

Again, the disciples didn't quite get the point. I asked them to let me know what they thought it meant. Thaddeus explained that the landowner promised the first group a reasonable wage and paid it. They were jealous because they expected even better treatment when the last ones received a full day's wage. Judas further explained that the landowner was right to be generous as he saw fit, after all, some people give to the poor with no requirement for work at all. Thaddeus added Judas was right because God asks us all to be generous, and giving alms is part of our heritage. Everyone agreed.

I asked what this told them about my Father. Peter blurted out, "God is like the landowner, giving generously to those who need it." James added that the landowner required no more from anyone than the willingness to work, just like God only requires a willingness to follow him.

John spoke up. "Don't you understand? We are like the first workers of the day. We believe we deserve some special privilege because we were first to follow, and we've worked longer and harder than anyone else. But God's rewards are the same, regardless of how soon we decide to follow him. Even those who follow him at the last moment of life will receive the reward of heaven. It's the only reward He has. He can't give us more than the rest. The promise of heaven is complete, and there isn't anything greater for God to offer." Then he added that because of their need to hold onto petty jealousies, they would become the last to enter. He said they should all be ashamed of themselves.

John turned to me with eyes full of tears and fell prostrate on the ground in front of me, begging forgiveness. Peter followed immediately and then the rest followed one by one. I was going to ask them to rise because their understanding was sufficient vindication, but I felt God's hand upon my shoulder and a gentle voice in my head told me to give them some time.

After a short while, I went to each in turn and knelt beside them. I said a short prayer, asking for our Father's forgiveness for the sin of pride and jealousy. I asked Him to truly open our hearts more each and every day. I thanked God for the gift He gave me to have these men as disciples. I told my Father they were truly wonderful followers of mine, who somehow managed to teach me many lessons I would otherwise miss. I hugged each one as they rose. Most left silently with tears in their eyes. John's hug seemed to be endless. It was as if his energy flowed into me and recharged my inner being. I'm so used to that being the other way around.

Father, thank you. Sometimes I think a hug is enough of a prayer. It certainly was for me today.

Shalom.

170 Peace

After the events, I left silently to find a place to rest my head. I couldn't sleep. The stars in the sky were a true sign of God's glory that night. There were no clouds or any lights from adjacent campfires or nearby villages. The stars twinkled and gleamed. I saw one, then another shoot across the sky in front of me. The second one was even brighter than the first. It was so peaceful. I can't remember the last time I felt so full of the power of my Father. It was as if He and I were one with this earth, the sky and the stars. I felt as if nothing could ever come between Him and me, nothing could ever break this bond. I can't really explain the sensation. It's my special time with my Father. It's almost as if telling someone will ruin it.

As I lay there, soaking in God's majesty, a warmth enveloped my body. It filled me with a peaceful yet energetic calm. I closed my eyes and lay there in perfect tranquility. I've been keeping quite a daily pace lately. The disciples can't understand how I can get up and keep going. They all work hard, but they know they aren't going quite as long and hard as I am. They wonder what my secret is. Well, this is it. These moments of rest are far more refreshing to my body, mind and soul than even ten hours of sleep. Sleep followed not too long afterwards, a deep restful sleep.

I was up and running again as dawn broke. I caught some fish and cooked breakfast before anyone else rose except for John and some of the women. John must have experienced a little bit of the same thing last night, because he looked so refreshed.

Father, thank you for the special gift of your presence with me. I especially enjoy those quiet moments together when I feel as if the whole world was just you and me alone, and nothing else is needed.

171 Inner Yearnings

It seems every time I get close to my Father, whenever I feel the two of us are in complete harmony, something happens to change things. Lately, I have found myself unable to share those special moments of utter tranquility with my Father. As a result, I'm tired and irritable. Today I insisted we find a place to rest. I know my followers were surprised. At first, they thought something was wrong, but then they merely said thanks for the gift of rest.

It was so refreshing to not be walking all day in the dust. We were also lucky enough not to have too many people around. It seems as if the numbers have been reducing every day anyway.

I tried unsuccessfully to rest. Then I took a little walk. I overheard Matthew and Judas talking.

Matthew, who rejoined us a few days ago, asked "Has Jesus mentioned anything about dying while I was gone?

"No, nothing at all." Judas responded. "I certainly hope whatever it was has passed since I still can't believe God would be taking him away from us so soon. He has touched just about everyone we meet, and I know I still have a lot to learn."

"I know what you mean. I can't believe God would be calling him to die at all, especially not now since I, too, have a lot to learn. I also can't believe he would have to suffer with what to me might be the worse type of death anyone can imagine. It simply makes no sense."

I felt as if a dagger had pierced my heart. How foolish I've been. We're heading towards Jerusalem to my death, which remains the one thing I still don't fully comprehend. As much as I've asked for a full understanding, all I get is silence. I worry about failing. I asked to understand my inner discontent and my Father quickly provided the answer.

I sat in the shade alone and prayed. I again asked Him to explain my trip to Jerusalem. I listened intently. Suddenly, my head was filled with words. He said I'm going to Jerusalem where I will be handed over to the chief priests and scribes, and they will condemn me to death. I will be handed over to the Gentiles, who will mock me, scourge me and then crucify me, but I will be raised on the third day. I imagine, deep down, I was hoping for a different answer. Just like Matthew and Judas, I was hoping this was all a misunderstanding, and there was really another reason to go to Jerusalem. There isn't.

Later this evening, the disciples asked me what was wrong. I told them the Son of Man was going to Jerusalem to be put to death. I hung my head low and asked them to pray for me to have the strength to deal with it. As reluctant as they were to hear this, as much as they wanted me to be wrong for once, as much as these words stung them, they prayed for me. Each and every one prayed for me. They had such beautiful words to say. My beloved John went last. He didn't have much to say, but what he said was the most powerful of all. He said, "I love you. No matter what, I will always love you." Peter added, "We all do, Jesus, we all do."

Father, I love them, too.

Shalom

172 Love

What is this thing we call love? Some people look at different types of love, communal love or charity, physical love, the love of a spouse, parents, or children. In reality, there is just one type of love, since true love isn't a feeling, but a state of being in complete oneness with God, who is love.

Love is selfless, since there is no room for one's own wants, needs, or desires in love. The only focus of a person in love is joyful giving of one's self. Love is fearless, since fear limits one's ability to give and be of service to others. Love is blissful, since when one is capable of completely emptying one's self, all that remains is the spirit of God. Love is energizing, because opening up one's self completely diminishes the fear of being hurt. All of these work together to create a state of internal peace that's full of joy and energy.

As I grow in my ministry to God's people, I find my love for them also grows, as does my understanding of love. I have a difficult time expressing my understanding of all God has given me. I know this is part of His message I am to bring to his people. To explain such a radically different philosophy of something so basically ingrained in human beliefs will be difficult at best. How do you separate lust and passion from love? How do you explain children are unique and special individuals, not another hungry mouth to feed? And worse, how do I explain a state of being that exists only by a complete emptying of everything of seeming importance. Forget family, forget friends, and forget food and drink. Give everything up so God's spirit can take its place. Family, friends, food, and drink will all remain for they are also a part of this life, but the attachments to them must be laid bare.

How do I express this thing called "love"? I know all I can do is to be love itself and to explain love not by words, not even by actions, but by my total state of being. I'm certain this is what draws some people to me. God called me to be a physical representation of His love here on earth.

Shalom.

173 Ephraim

Today some of my followers overheard a plot by the Sanhedrin to kill me. I know we've discussed this before, but they weren't ready for this news. It seems hearing it has made it more real. I'm still a little weary from all the travels; my inner soul seems to be up one moment and down the next, unsettled with my doubts and fears of the future. I decided we should go somewhere and rest for a while. As before, the crowds seem to be lessening anyway, and I think I'm not the only one who could use some rest.

Bartholomew had a relative in a town nearby named Ephraim. He was sure we could all stay there for a while, so we decided to head there. We arrived near dinnertime and were amazed at how welcoming Bartholomew's family was. They heard of our travels, healings and preachings and were so excited to see us and proud of Bartholomew for being a part of it. I knew God had directed us here. It's close to Jerusalem and yet far enough to offer some much-needed rest for all of us.

Thank you, Father, for your incredible ability to plan. Here I am, far from home and years into my ministry. Yet, you knew when Bartholomew first joined us that we would someday need this place to stay. You touched the hearts of his family to be open to us and gave them an abundant harvest this past year to have sufficient food to sustain all of us. You are truly amazing in all things.

Shalom.

174 Lessons of Life

Sometimes I wonder what it means to be the Son of God. How do I describe to others the points of living with God as the sole source of strength? It's easy to say: love one another. But how do I explain what love is? It's easy to describe attributes of love, like kindness, loyalty, honesty, etc., but what steps can a person take to attain these qualities on a daily basis? This question has plagued me for quite some time. I think it would do me well to sort out my thoughts one by one.

First on the list (although not necessarily in any order of importance) is to live in the moment. God gives us every moment of every day as a special gift. Sometimes humanity doesn't fully appreciate this. Even I, in my humanness, have experienced times when I've been too preoccupied with thoughts about some past event, like the death of my cousin John.

I also frequently find myself looking to my future, which doesn't make complete sense yet. At those times, I can't truly love anything other than my own inner spirit. I'm not present to my disciples and find myself carrying out half-hearted conversations and not really listening. True love would require me to be fully present to whomever I'm with. Certainly, this isn't always possible. At times I find myself being pulled in two directions.

One example would be when I received news of Lazarus dying while I had unfinished business where I was. Part of my human side wanted to drop everything and rush to my friend's side. However, after trying to get in touch with my godly spirit, I realized true love required me to finish the task at hand and, at the same time, rely on Abba to provide for Lazarus. Hearing about his death, my first thought was that God had abandoned me. On second thought, I was sure that

Abba could never let me down. I was certain God had not intended for Lazarus to be dead.

I even found myself neglecting my carpentry at times since I was so wrapped up in something else. What does that say about my love to the person I was supposed to be working for? I wasn't giving them the best product possible when my mind was wandering elsewhere. That too, as small as it may seem, is a part of love.

Live in the present, in the moment you have. If it's a moment of anger, be angry. Celebrate grief, joy, pride, sadness and every other emotion God gives us. Being truly alive requires us to live in the here and now. God will give us ample time in our schedule to reflect on the past in order to sort out our feelings, emotions, problems, or to fully enjoy a particularly happy occasion. Even though we also need to plan for upcoming events, we must never selfishly deny the moment we are in to ponder the past or future.

All too often, I meet people who are so wrapped up in things – even good things like trying to provide for one's family – that they are never really present to anyone else. They never really listen to their wife or children whom they are supposedly working so hard for. They seem like empty bodies. Their eyes have no fire. I see other people who drink to mask their lifelessness. They resort to drinking to fool themselves into thinking they are happy. But drunken people never live in the moment because they are not even sure what the moment is.

One definable quality of love is to live in the present. Recognize every moment is a gift from God and celebrate it fully. This is the only life you have. Live it fully and completely, moment by moment. Immerse yourself in the life God has given you. It's the first step to love all those around you.

175 Time for Reflection

Another thing someone must do to be a loving person is to make time for personal reflection. This may seem selfish at first, but it's absolutely necessary for love. First, we must have some quiet time to ourselves. It's almost as important for life as air, water or sleep. In fact, it's even more important. If we don't create time for ourselves to reflect on the majesty of God, the limitations of our inner self, or the trials and tribulations of life, we won't be able to live in the moment and be truly present to anyone else. We'll always have issues haunting our insides, frequently making us tired or ill. They'll eat at us, thereby limiting our ability to love others in the truest sense of the word.

We may find ourselves "going through the motions" of a loving parent or a good friend, but it won't be real. Irritability, anger and all sorts of other negative emotions won't be far behind. We must set aside time for ourselves to reflect on things. Personally, I've found writing this journal very rewarding since it gives me a chance not only to take some time for reflection, but also to sort out my feelings and thoughts. Writing, being such a tedious task, helps my thoughts slow down enough for me to catch them and really ponder them.

There is however yet another important reason to take time for reflection. Love is an all-inclusive term. By this I mean no one can truly love someone else if their love doesn't include themselves. Certainly, in today's world a mother may be too busy raising and teaching the children, cooking food, and mending and washing clothes to take time for reflection. A father may be too busy working in the fields, repairing broken tools, hunting for food, and disciplining the children to take time for reflection. This isn't only a big mistake, it's a lie. God will provide ample time for all things to be done. Live in the moment and God will ensure there are plenty of moments for reflection. It's an imperative part of true love for each and every person to take time for personal reflection. No one can truly love someone else if their love doesn't include themselves. As an act of loving yourself, you must make time just for you.

Lastly, a time for personal reflection is a time to get closer to Abba, our God. Always include God as a living and real part of the process when you take some time for personal reflection. Talk to him, or better yet, talk *with* him. As I follow my own precepts, I find it easier and easier to communicate with God during these private reflection times. Other times, God simply fills my head with knowledge. This is the most amazing type of communication. In a split second, my head is filled with His message and something previously confusing suddenly crystallizes into absolute clarity.

Reflection is a very important time to extend your love to God, and conversely, for God to extend His love to you. No love can be complete if God isn't an integral part of the equation. I'm convinced my personal communication with God isn't reserved for me alone. In fact, my dear mother and my beloved apostles have had similar experiences. As they take time for personal reflection, prayer and communication, they've been able to demonstrate the real love they have.

Shalom.

176 Service

Another lesson of love is to be of service. All too often, we are too tired or lazy to help another. We think that if they want something, they should be able to get it themselves. But we miss the opportunity to love when we act selfishly.

Love is selfless. When we are in love, we never worry about providing for the object of our love. We would always have the energy to assist them when needed. In fact, we are frequently able to anticipate the needs of another and respond before we are even asked.

I remember a time from my carpentry shop. I was fashioning a table for a customer. When he came to pick it up, he was upset because the table was too high for him. He told me needed it lower because his wife was a cripple and could only work on a low table. I was a little distraught because I had spent a lot of time crafting the legs of that table. Despite my anxieties, I was able to accommodate his request.

When he returned a few days later, he brought his wife. She sat next to the new table, which was just the right height. You could just see the joy in her eyes because it was a perfect fit. And the other table legs became part of another table, which I made for my mother. She was so thrilled with it. And you know what? It was the perfect height as well. I would have missed two wonderful opportunities to express my love for my fellow humans if I wasn't accommodating.

Service is difficult, especially for people like me who are called to be leaders. I sometimes think others need to serve me because of who I am. My time is more valuable, my needs and wants come first. This is another easy hole for me to fall into. However, the sign of a true leader is to lead by serving others. That's how we can truly express our love. It's also through serving that we can teach others. It's another paradox of love and life. To serve is to lead and to lead is to serve.

Father, thank you for these days and the ability to share some of my thoughts in this journal. I ask you to give me the ability to serve these disciples well so they may serve others in turn.

Amen.

177 Honesty and Integrity

Two other characteristics of love are honesty and integrity. We must never be afraid of the truth. We need to live and speak the truth. I find this very difficult. I'm God's son, yet, I fear speaking the truth will lead me to harm. I'm afraid people will rebuke me. I'm afraid I will be ineffective. However, I do live the truth of who I am, but I don't express myself verbally. My followers have acknowledged I'm the Messiah because I live life in a manner befitting my inner soul. I don't pretend to be something I'm not.

All people should live honestly. Sometimes it's difficult to know the truth inside. In these times, we must turn to prayer. Ask God what the truth is and listen openly for the answer. Openness is another characteristic of love. We must be open to God, open to His message, open to His love. We have a tendency to hide from God because we don't think we are worthy of His love. Or even worse, we think we already have all the answers. It's critical to remain open and receptive to God's word.

Perseverance is another key ingredient to love. We'll all be faced with difficult times in our lives. It could be the death or severe injury of a loved one. It could be famine or illness. We must trust in God, believe in Him, and let Him work His miracles. He will take care of all of our needs.

Father, thank you for the insights into love. I see how you are love, plain and simple. I thank you for all those times in my life you have gifted me with your love, the kind that's complete, non-judgmental, selfless, honest, open, and without conditions. Your gift of love is truly the most wonderful experience of life.

Shalom.

178 Meeting Disciple's Mother

I've never seen two people so happy as James and John today. Their mother arrived to fill them in on news of the family. Their sister was expecting a child soon, and everyone was happy and healthy. James and John were delighted to see their mother, as one might expect. They filled her in on our travels and some of the things they had learned. We shared a wonderful meal. We all talked about life and love and God. They left for a while to spend some time alone with her.

Later, she approached me with her sons and fell prostrate in front of me. She started talking so fast I could hardly understand what she said. It seemed the boys had convinced her I was the Messiah. She had a favor to ask of me; she asked me to command her two sons to sit with me on the throne, one at my right side and the other at my left. I was a bit stunned, and I could tell that John and James were surprised as well. Just a short while ago, we discussed the very issue of wanting to be the greatest on this earth. I responded that granting the wish to be seated next to me wasn't mine to grant. James and John begged pardon and tried to talk to their mother about what she requested.

As usual, the others overheard the conversation. Naturally, they misunderstood the situation, thinking that the request came from John or James and not from their mother. They thought the two of them plotted to have their mother ask for them, since I would surely listen to her beg for her sons.

By evening, the news spread throughout our camp and everyone was indignant with John and James. Luckily, I quickly understood what was happening when I witnessed the way the rest of the disciples treated the two of them. I called the rest over after we ate. I told them the Gentiles were great in having rulers lord over people and make their authority known. However, this isn't the way for them or for God. To be great among my disciples requires service. We are here to serve, not to be served. They are to learn and act as the Son of Man, who comes to serve all people. He also comes to give his life as the ransom for many.

At first, they didn't understand what I was saying. I reminded them again that the first will be last and the last will be first. The route to becoming the greatest lies in submission to the will of the Father, and submission to the Father's will means service.

Shalom.

179 On to Jerusalem

We broke camp today and left Jericho on our way towards Jerusalem. A fairly large crowd followed us again. The mood was a bit tenuous. My disciples were still displeased with James and John and refused to listen to me. They each felt they should be my most beloved and they somehow each deserved to be on top. I decided it would be best to remain silent and let God work His miracles.

I found myself using the travel time to pray, and I walked along paying no attention to the events around me. I was talking to Abba about the events of yesterday, and I asked Him what to do. He assured me He would handle it. I asked Him again about the upcoming events in Jerusalem, and He tried to explain His plan to me. I was interrupted by loud shouts from two men sitting on the side of the road who hollered out, "Lord, Son of David, have pity on us!" I inquired as to the nature of their plea. They responded that they were blind and asked me to help their eyes be open.

I was instantly rewarded with the depth of my Father's plan. I kept returning in my prayer to the question, "How are you going to help my disciples see the light?" And here are two blind men! Unlike my own disciples, these two men realize their blindness and sought help. My disciples are unaware of their own blindness. They're still too worried about the splinter in someone else's eye to see the plank in their own. I knew God would use this example for me to help them understand.

I simply touched the eyes of the two blind men, and they were able to open them and see. One had been able to see before, and he marveled at being able to see again. He had a little difficulty with color at first, but after a short while, his vision returned in full.

The other man was blind from birth. Watching him as he began to see was incredible. At first, things were cloudy. After a while, things began to focus more and more. He put his hands on my face and told me he could feel how special I was and wanted to put his feelings to his sight. He then proceeded to touch everyone's face around him, at least those who didn't pull away. His eyes sparkled with joy and his enthusiasm was endless. We stopped for a break and to let him take in the beauty of the countryside and the people around.

I discovered the blind men had been calling me for a little while, but I paid them no mind since I was deeply entrenched in prayer. My followers assured them I wasn't to be disturbed and asked them to be quiet. In the course of their power quest, my disciples have forgotten the need for service, the need to heal, the need for me to be God's Son and to follow His plan. I called them aside and asked them if anyone realized why God sent the two blind men at this time. None of them had anything to respond. I told them to think about it, and we would discuss it again before we retired this evening.

After dinner I called the twelve aside again and asked if anyone had any idea as to the significance of the blind men. Oddly enough, it was quiet and unassuming Andrew who responded after a long silence. "My Lord," he said, with his head bowed low in shame. "God sent us the two blind men as a symbol of our own blindness. We've all become so obsessed with greatness, being at the top, being first that we've missed our true mission."

I was more than surprised. He truly understood the meaning of this encounter although I was certain I was going to have to beat the meaning into their heads. I smiled and I praised Andrew for his insights and asked him to explain further.

He reminded the others that my mission was to serve, not to be served. He said he had realized healing was one of the duties of our ministry he enjoyed the most. He said it gave him great joy whenever I healed. He added that the few times he was able to share in the ministry were incredible, but because of greed they almost passed the opportunity to serve others. He then shamefully expressed his sorrow and called himself a failure.

I assured him he was no failure nor was it any mere coincidence those men were there today. We all have lessons to learn and God uses all means available to point them out to us, me included. We simply have to consider everything. If we remain open to His infinite methods, we'll be constantly aware of His presence and His lessons. Peter, not to be outdone by a younger brother, or anyone else for that matter, jumped up and begged forgiveness. He went to John and James and asked them to forgive him as well, since he, too, was concerned with them being the first. The evening ended with a lot of hugs and camaraderie, and the disciples were as close-knit a group as ever. Praise God!

Shalom.

180 Zacchaeus

As we were travelling today, I saw a man in a sycamore tree. Bartholomew was walking next to me and told me he was Zacchaeus, the chief tax collector in the region and a very wealthy man. When I reached the tree, I stopped and told him we needed to stay at his house. He came down and welcomed us enthusiastically.

As we were walking towards his house, I overheard some of the local people mumbling because they all considered tax collectors sinners. Zacchaeus obviously overheard them as well, and he told me rather loudly that he had decided to give half of his possessions to the poor, and if he ever cheated anyone out of anything, he would pay back four times the amount. I told him salvation came to his house because he was truly the son of Abraham. I also told him I came to seek and save the lost and was glad we met.

I then told a parable about two men who went to the temple to pray. One was a Pharisee and the other a tax collector. The Pharisee stood by himself and prayed, thanking God he wasn't like other people – robbers, evildoers, adulterers – or even like the tax collector standing close to him. He honored himself because he fasted twice a week and gave a tenth of all he received.

In the meantime, the tax collector stood at a distance, unable to look up to heaven. He beat his breast and asked God to have mercy on him. I assured them that the tax collector, not the Pharisee, was justified before God because all those who exalt themselves will be humbled, and those who humble themselves will be exalted.

I followed this with a parable about a man of noble birth who went to a distant country to have himself appointed king. He called his servants and gave them ten minas each and instructed them to put the money to work until he returned. When he returned, he sent for his servants to see how they fared with the money he had given them. The first said he earned ten more. The master was happy and gave him charge of ten cities. The second said he had earned five more. The King said he would give him charge of five cities.

The third servant proudly returned the original ten minas because he had kept the money safe. The master asked why didn't he put the money on deposit so he could at least have earned some interest. He then asked the servant to give his mina to the first servant, who already had ten, stating that to everyone who has, more would be given, but from he who has nothing even what little he has will be taken away.

This is a wonderful parable. First, it shows God doesn't look at things the way humans normally do. He's concerned with things of the heart. God gives everyone gifts, and while the gifts differ, they are all of equal importance. God also rewards those who generously use their gifts, especially to further His Kingdom on earth. The more the gifts are utilized, the more God will give. However, if someone just sits on his gift and simply protects it, the gift will ultimately be taken away.

This parable was in part for my followers, who have to understand the need to utilize their gifts, especially after I'm gone. It was said in part to Zacchaeus to make him understand how much more he can do to further God's Kingdom. It was in part for the people who were concerned that I accepted a "sinner" like Zacchaeus.

God gives everyone gifts, sinners and the righteous alike. It's up to us to utilize whatever gifts we have, and it's never too late to do so.

Shalom.

181 Final Stage to Jerusalem

We drew near Jerusalem today, and I decided to camp on the outskirts of the city in Bethpage. My emotions have been going crazy today. In fact, as I look at it, my inner turmoil has been growing for quite some time. I'm not at inner peace, not at all. I feel a bit weak physically, too. In fact, my physical energy always relates directly to my inner peace and my oneness with Abba. Whenever everything is in harmony, my energy is boundless. Of course, I still need sleep, but I need a lot less, and my ability to share, teach, preach, heal, and simply be fully with whomever I'm with is endless during waking hours.

Today, I find myself wanting to be alone, wanting to pray. Yet, every time I try to pray, my mind races with the things my Father has revealed to me about Jerusalem. I know it's right, I know it's time. I know I'm to suffer and die here. I know I'm to free my fellow brothers and sisters from sin. I'm to somehow herald in a new era, a new understanding of God and His wonders.

How will God use that to implement his plan? With me gone, He'll have only these disciples. They aren't ready. Just a few days ago, they were still fighting over being first. They almost walked past two blind men and refused to help them. I've preached and taught everything I know to these men, and yet, their understanding is still lacking. The lessons seem to be borne in their heads, not in their hearts. I've seen glimpses of true understanding of love, inner peace, forgiveness, and the awareness of God's presence within each of them. But they always revert to their former childlike manner.

My Father has told me the men will deny me, and one will even betray me. After all, if no one betrays me, He'll be unable to implement His plan. Most confusing. I try to find peace, but it simply doesn't come. I try to tell myself this is His plan, and He has every detail determined to be perfect. Yet, my human side still doubts. I'm truly the Son of Man. Even though I experience perfect love and forgiveness at times, today I'm fully human, complete with all the shortcomings.

Oh, Father, please help me to regain my inner peace. In my mind, I've reviewed all the events of my life, especially the past few years. Mentally, I know this must be you because if it isn't, then everything has been a complete lie. I must be your son, I must have been sent by you to teach your good news, and I must follow through with your plan in Jerusalem. To do otherwise would destroy all you have created, I would deny my sonship.

I also know you've laid out a course for me, which I must follow. I know in my head I must go on, and I know I will go wherever you lead. Father, I ask you now to help me understand. I ask you to remove my fears and doubts. Please, help me, your only son, to follow this most incredible and difficult path.

Shalom.

182 Entry Into Jerusalem

Last night I found little rest. I tossed all night, trying to talk to Abba and allowing my imagination to run wild at the sbame time. As morning approached, I was finally able to quiet my anxieties enough to listen to my Father. He reminded me of a passage in the Scriptures from Isaiah and Zechariah prophesying that the king will come meekly and riding on an ass. This Scripture repeated over and over in my head, and I realized my Father placed it there. He wanted to reveal something to me.

I was able to quiet myself long enough to understand I was to enter Jerusalem on an ass, just as the prophecy suggested. I demanded to know where we would get an ass, since our treasury was almost bare. He responded I was to send Thaddeus and Judas Iscariot to town ahead of me to retrieve an ass that would be tethered there. I asked what should be done if anyone questioned this, since it could easily be construed as stealing. God responded that if anyone asked, Thaddeus and Judas should simply respond, "The Master has need of it."

I have to admit, I questioned Abba somewhat about the choice of Judas. He has not quite seemed himself lately. He has left camp for long intervals, presumably because he was the keeper of the treasury, but these things never took quite so long before. He also seemed distant. I questioned him, and he assured me nothing was wrong, but I can see that something is. I know God told me I'm to be betrayed and denied. I'm certain Judas will be one of them.

It's unfortunate, really. Judas is by far the most intelligent of the twelve. Perhaps it's his intelligence that stands in the way of understanding; he tries to understand things through logic alone. I keep telling him the answer is love, and love is of the heart, not of the mind. He intellectualizes the lessons I teach, and I see few signs of the inner understanding the others have all shown.

Nonetheless, early in the morning I repeated the instructions to Thaddeus and Judas. Thaddeus pulled me aside before they left and questioned me as to the choice of Judas. It appears I'm not the only one beginning to wonder what is wrong. I told Thaddeus that this was God's decision, which we must respect. Then the two of them left to go on their mission. Things went just as God instructed. They soon returned, towing an ass.

At this point, I turned to the crowds and told them simply, "It's time." Peter exclaimed, "No, Lord, it must not be." I assured him this was my path and we all had to follow God's way. I saw tears in his eyes. In a show of respect, he laid his cloak on the ass, as did Thaddeus. As I sat upon the ass, John looked me straight in the eye, then simply nodded and turned away. Then, in what I found to be one of the most loving gestures imaginable, he laid his precious cloak, a cloak he had just received from his mom, right in front of the ass. I was a bit stunned, but he motioned for me to start.

Before I could take a step, the remaining disciples laid their cloaks along the path in front of me one by one. The remainder of the crowd ran ahead, and one by one, they all laid their cloaks upon my path. Those who didn't have a cloak cut branches nearby and laid them down instead. The ass stepped upon each one ever so gently. It was almost as if it knew how incredibly special this was. He seemed to move along with a certain pride and dignity. I'm not sure who it was, but the chanting started soon thereafter. "Hosanna to the Son of David, blessed is he who comes in the name of the Lord, Hosanna in the highest." I had begun to see only the beauty of God's plan with the magnificent entry, the chanting and the belief in me. The entire procession overwhelmed me.

We entered Jerusalem this way, slowly and solemnly. It seemed as if the entire city was shaken at its foundation to observe such a sight. Some asked who it was that caused such an incredible reaction. The crowds told them it was Jesus, the prophet from Nazareth. We headed straight to the temple. I could see the crowd swell as we continued on our journey. At least half the people of Jerusalem joined us, some no doubt simply caught up in the moment.

As we approached the temple, I saw the money-changers and people selling doves for sacrifice. They ridiculed God's people and turned our customs into profit. I was beside myself. The temple is intended to be a place of worship, not worldly gain. I jumped off the ass and ran up the temple stairs. I don't even remember the exact words I hollered, but I told them to stop stealing and cheating my brothers and sisters. I told them this was a house of prayer, not a den for thieves. I turned over table after table.

Needless to say, this caused quite a commotion. Most of the people gathered what they could find and moved on, but a few went to find the chief priests and scribes. My disciples stood speechless while I moved through the temple area and drove out all the merchants. Philip came to me, hugged me and told me it was all right. He asked me to quiet down. He said they were all emotionally unstable and my being out of control wasn't helping. I assured him I was far from being out of control and I was completely righteous in my doings. He simply smiled and said, "I know."

I guess I had that coming. I have to admit that Philip was right; I was just a little bit out of control. I found all of my emotions out of control today. The inner peace has been replaced with inner turmoil. As the Son of Man and the Son of God, I've gone from high to low to high to low. The highs are incredible, well beyond the highs I've experienced in the past, but they seem to give way to a new low.

Not long after Philip sat me down, a lone person came to me. Actually, he crawled up the steps. He was crippled, his right leg badly mangled and withered. He asked me to heal him. What a high again! In spite of my behavior, he was willing to believe in me – it was incredible! I cured him, and more followed, crippled, blind, deaf, and mute. I healed them all. The high of being the Son of God enveloped my entire being. I felt as if I was on a cloud again.

Not long after, I realized the chief priests and scribes had arrived in a large group. By then, the children were again singing "Hosanna to the son of David." The priests were indignant and demanded to know if I was aware of the words they were singing, as if I was somehow to blame. I have to admit to being a little less than loving in my response, since their interference triggered the onslaught of a new low.

I asked them if they had ever read that out of the mouths of infants and nurslings God has brought forth praise. They started to offer rebuttal, but Philip whispered gently and wisely to me that it was time to go. I wanted to lash back at them, but I knew Philip was right. I again thanked Abba for teaching my disciples so well. Whenever I'm truly in need of something, one of them rises to the challenge. We walked right out of Jerusalem, Philip and I leading the rest. We came to Bethany, where we spent the night.

Father, again and again I beg you to help me understand the events about to unfold. I ask you to help keep my human side a little more in control. I beg you to help me resume my sonship fully. I know I will need to be your Son fully, without the bondage of human shortcomings to rise to the coming events. I must not embarrass you or myself with my temper.

Oh, yes, and lest I forget, thank you so much for these disciples. It's days like today, when I find my strength through them, that I realize they will be fine when I'm gone and you have chosen well. Be with them one and all.

Shalom.

183 A Long Day in Jerusalem

I awoke this morning after a less than restful evening. We had only a little to eat last night, and my stomach was growling. I was quite hungry and still tired. I know this is because my whole being is simply out of peace. I'm changing from being incredibly close to my Father to being unaware of His real existence. My emotions are still high one moment and low the next. I feel as if I'm spinning out of control.

When we woke, I had to urge my disciples to return to Jerusalem. They still think they can change the things I need to do. They still question whether I understand what God wants of me. I know I'm unable to stop the inner forces that push me towards the path my Father has set out for me, even though part of me wants to turn around and run the other direction.

I had been praying, as much as I'm able to pray at this time, for a little food to stop the pains of hunger and provide some strength to pass the day. Not long after my prayer, we passed a fig tree. I ran over to it, since I wanted the first fig or two for myself. I wasn't thinking of sharing the fruit. When I got to the tree, I discovered it had not one single fig on it. Nothing except leaves. I cursed the tree and declared it should never bear fruit again.

To my surprise, it withered immediately. I was a little shocked, but then my high returned. I'm God's son, the Son of Man, the Messiah. If I chose to curse a mere tree, wouldn't my Father respond immediately? This was one of those little things He does to make certain I understand that no matter what, He is always by my side; He's always there for me. Besides, if I am hungry and tired, my followers are likely also tired. I should know enough to not put myself ahead of them. Another simple reminder that I can't focus on myself.

Philip came over and asked me how the tree obeyed me so quickly. I'm amazed he waited just long enough for me to process my own thoughts before he raised the question. Perhaps they're all learning my little signs of when they can and can't disturb me. I was a little surprised at my own confidence as I replied. I told my followers that whoever has faith and doesn't waiver will be able to do more than I did with a fig tree. With faith, they could move mountains. I explained to them that whatever they ask for in complete, unwavering faith, our loving Father would answer them abundantly.

When we arrived at the temple, I began teaching. I was amazed at the number of people who listened. I could tell by their intense gaze that they were listening not simply with their heads but their heart, too. In fact, even the children were sitting quietly. They were almost mesmerized. After some preaching, I was challenged by the chief priests to explain by what authority I was teaching. I knew they were trying to trap me. I knew they would use any answer I gave them to try to discredit me in front of the people. Luckily, God immediately gave me a response in the form of a question. "By whose authority did John the Baptist preach?"

I knew as I asked the question that Abba gave me the best possible response to their question. My cousin was well loved by these people, much respected and recognized as the prophet he was. The priest couldn't say his authority was from God, because they'd have had to concede my authority was also of God. They couldn't say his authority wasn't of God because they would discredit themselves in front of the crowd. They responded they didn't know. I said if they didn't know, I wouldn't answer them. They left murmuring to themselves. The crowd seemed to know the answer.

I was given many parables by Abba to teach today. I told them about two sons, one, who agreed to everything the father asked but did nothing, and the other, who complained and argued but followed the father's wishes. They recognized it was the latter son who really served the father.

I pointed out to them that the scribes, Pharisees, priests, and possibly some of the crowd were like the first son. They listened to the Father, they said yes to everything, but when it came time to follow, they didn't do it. On the other hand, there are many tax collectors, prostitutes and other sinners who have said no to the word of the Father but are doing the things He asks of them. When John the Baptist came, some of the priests listened but didn't follow him, while the tax collectors, prostitutes and other sinners believed. Unfortunate are the ones who witnessed this but still chose not to listen.

Another of the parables I used was about the tenant farmers. I knew the priests were standing around pretending not to hear me but intently listening. I told the story about the rich landowner, who left his vineyard for tenant farmers. When harvest came, he sent his servant to collect the rent. The tenant farmers seized and killed the servant. The landowner then sent numerous others. They were all treated similarly. Finally, he sent his beloved son thinking they would surely not harm him, but the tenants seized him as well.

I saw the looks of the priests. They knew this story was intended for them. They wanted to arrest me and throw me in prison for heresy, for claiming to be God's son. They knew I was using this story to proclaim my heritage. They wanted to interrupt me, but their first attempt failed, and they couldn't risk another attempt in front of these believers. The crowd was obviously impressed by my words.

I asked the crowd what they thought the landowner would do to the tenant farmers. The children yelled out the loudest, "The wretched tenant farmers would be put to death!" I pointed out some passages in our Scripture that prophesied such things, like the one about the stone that the builders rejected and later became the cornerstone. I let them know that the Kingdom of God would be taken away from the builders and given to those who will produce fruit.

I knew most of the adults listening understood what I was saying. They realized God had left the earth in the care of his priests. They also realized the priests tended not to listen to the prophets such as John. They also recognized I was God's son and the same fate would await me.

I think it may have been the first time some of my own disciples realized God had to follow through with His plan. These priests were out of control, and the only way to institute a new idea was to thoroughly demonstrate the existing powers weren't in keeping with the true understanding. The parable of the tenant farmers was yet another clever way for God to have every group hear the message intended for them.

Another of the parables was about a wedding feast. The thoughts of the wedding in Cana flooded my being. I told them the Kingdom of Heaven could be likened to a king who gave a wedding feast for his son. The king sent his servants to bring the guests to the feast, but the guests refused to go. He sent the servants a second time, but some guests ignored the invitation, while others mistreated and killed the servants.

The king was enraged and sent his troops to destroy the murderers and burn their cities. Then he commanded his servants to go out to the main roads and invite anyone they found to the feast. The servants gathered all they found, good and bad, and the hall was filled. But when the king met the guests, he noticed one who came without a wedding garment. The man offered no response, so the king asked his attendants to bind his hands and feet and cast him out into the darkness. The king said many are invited, but few are chosen.

I couldn't believe the energy and zeal I had after the restless night I had last night. I was on fire ever since Abba spoke to me at the fig tree. I never felt God's presence this strongly before. It was *my* mouth and *my* voice, but the words seemed to come from a source outside me. It seemed as if I could say nothing wrong at all. The disciples were silently listening to everything I said with attentiveness I haven't seen in a while.

The crowds grew. The Pharisees went off about noon. I knew they wanted to arrest me, but their fear of the crowds prevented them. Sure enough, shortly afterwards they sent a few young men to me, some of their prodigy. One young man in particular stood out among them, but not physically, as he was of medium height, balding, his legs were set apart and he had large eyes. However, I could sense he was astute and intelligent and obviously had leadership skills. His best quality was his zeal for God, albeit in the wrong manner.

They challenged me by asking if it was lawful to pay the temple tax. Again, they thought they had me trapped. At first the panic at not having an answer almost filled me, but when I opened my mouth once again, words from Abba flowed out. I simply pointed out to them that Caesar's image and inscription were on the coin. I told them they should give to Caesar what was Caesar's.

The Pharisees started to leave. The one young man I had noticed, Saul, looked at me. I felt he may have wanted to stay, but the others urged him on. I could see the Pharisees filling his head. What a shame. That young man could do so much for my father.

Later, the Sadducees tried to trap me with a question concerning the resurrection, doubting life after death exists. They asked me who a woman would be married to in heaven if she married seven brothers in this life. Full of assurance from above, I told them that they were missing the point. Marriage, houses, clothes, food – these are all things of this world, not the world beyond. People need not be married in heaven, as they are simply in a state of extreme bliss.

The Pharisees again returned to try and stump me. This time, they sent another young man to me. I was so impressed with him. As timid as he was, he was able to come. As much as the Pharisees influenced him, he still called me a teacher. He asked meekly which commandment was the greatest. I put my arm around his shoulder. "My brother," I said, "the greatest commandment is love. You shall love God with all of your heart, all of your soul and with your entire mind. This leads to perfect harmony with Him. This is the first and greatest commandment. The second is to love your neighbor as you love yourself."

I told him – and everyone else – that the whole law, the teachings of the prophets, and all of my own teaching is embodied in these two commandments. I was simply astounded by these words. For years, I've been trying to teach people the way of God, the things I was sent to teach, to bring a new understanding of God. Here, my Father gave me the whole of His teachings in two simple commandments. I was absolutely amazed. I need to preach nothing else but to love. To love God first and to love thy neighbor, meaning all of our fellow humans, as you love yourself. If I say nothing else that stays with my followers, I hope they can place this simple message into their hearts and repeat it to everyone they meet.

Then I questioned the Pharisees' opinion of the Messiah, asking them whose son he is. They said David's. I asked them if the Messiah was David's son, then why would David call him "Lord"? The Pharisees had no answer. After this, the Pharisees and scribes left.

A few in the crowd insisted that the commandment of love, the one I had just stated, was essentially what the Pharisees taught. I assured them they could indeed listen to the teachings of the Pharisees, as these men taught the Torah, the commandments, and the truths that have been revealed throughout the ages through the prophets. The problem with the Pharisees wasn't their teaching, but their doing. They taught one thing, but their example said another. They were hypocrites.

I went on to prove the Pharisees' their hypocrisy with several examples. I think perhaps I was a little strong in my rebuke. I could see that my words were no longer words of love, instead, they were like swords, and people started to walk away. After a morning of awesome insightfulness and crowds listening intently, here I was again, allowing my hurt, anger, frustration and doubt to block the flow of words from above. I failed again. As I talked, I kept thinking about the inequity, questioning the reality of my own impending death. I again slipped into a bit of despair and doubt.

I left the temple area suddenly. The disciples followed me and pointed out buildings, stating there were still many people in there, ready to listen. I again answered harshly. I told them that of all the buildings they were pointing out not a stone would be left. They were puzzled. Frankly, so was I.

I told them I simply needed to be alone, to have some prayer time. I went off alone to the Mount of Olives, where I started recording the events of my day.

Again, I find recording things like this are a special manner of prayer for me, even though it takes long. I look at these events and see the hand of my Father guiding me. This morning, when I really needed some comfort, He was there. He was there when I was preaching in the temple. The words were flowing out of me, parable after parable. I was saying all the right things. I allowed my spirit to be given over totally to Abba and it was incredible.

Then the thoughts of the Pharisees and of the future I must soon bear started to enter. This caused doubts, and the human side of me took over again. The words were wrong. They weren't words of love – they were words of anger. I turned so many people away. Oh, Son of Man that I am. I understand the reasons my fellow humans fail. Even I, Son of Man, can fail.

No! I know I will never be able to completely fail my Father. I know whatever His plans for me are, I will follow. I can't turn away from Him. But on occasion, the Son of Man returns. In a way, I enjoy it. I enjoy the anger, because I can compare it to my joy. I would be less if I didn't understand the struggles my fellow humans face. I know that only in rare moments can humans experience the same connectedness I experienced with my Father this morning. I know that as mankind grows and matures, individuals will be able to open themselves enough to have similar experiences. I'm here to show them a new way of understanding the ways of God, the ways of our loving Father.

Just like any parent, He must start with close loving care, constantly watching over us, and providing our every need. Then, as we mature, love needs to allow us to learn for ourselves, to make mistakes, to grow on our own. After a while, we are ready to go out on our own. And once we are truly mature, we will be able to experience love, true love, a lot better. But as with human life, the process of maturing is long, arduous, and full of lessons, wrong turns, and mistakes.

I thank you Father for this new understanding. I'm here to show people a better way. I understand I can't stay too long or I will be in the way of their personal growth. They will rely too much on me and not experience the maturity themselves. I'm here to free them from the bonds of childhood so that they are able to continue into adolescence. They must face things alone now.

Oh, and don't let me forget, I love you.

Shalom.

184 Futuristic Thoughts

After I finished my first entry today, I felt quite relaxed and at peace once again. I've learned my inner peace can be defined as being at one with my Father. Whenever my humanity takes over, inner peace retreats. Whenever my godliness takes over, peace returns. I relaxed and entered a prayerful moment alone with my Father. I asked Him about my future and the future of mankind. He told me things He had never told me before.

I understand now that I won't die in the sense people understand death. Death isn't complete elimination. We simply pass from this mortal existence. Since I'm God's Son, I won't exactly die in the mortal body. It won't exactly be like the little girl or Lazarus, either. For all real purposes, my time as a human being will end on the cross, but my spirit will remain here on earth for a short while to help the disciples understand what's going on. I also understand that as humanity continues to grow, I'll somehow return. But the growth of humanity won't be without difficulty.

Many will rebuke my earthly existence and me. Many others will fight to prove I was the Son of God. People will fight to be right; people will fight for territory. All of these things are part of the process of maturation. After humans reach adolescence, they need to assert themselves; they care little for their fellow man. They always need to be right, and they think their parents are all wrong. They think they can't be destroyed. They oftentimes try to stop anyone who dares challenge them. They are quick to fight. All these things will be true as mankind matures.

A few of my disciples returned as I was deep in meditation about the future of the world. They asked me when the end of the times would come and what signs there would be. I first explained the signs as I see them. Wars, famine, earthquakes, pestilence. I pointed out the signs would be as sure as the signs of the fig tree that bears leaves in the spring. We can always tell when spring is coming, so, too, should we be able to read the signs of the future. As to the hour and the time, only my Father knows for sure. I see a lot of the things going on in the present day that may indicate the reaching of maturity is at hand. I told them to remain awake because the hour could be at any time. It could be swift and sudden.

I was able to utilize parables to teach them about being prepared and about the rewards for prudent service. I told them they had been given many talents, which they had to utilize wisely for the Kingdom of God. Timothy asked about judgment. I told him I would come again in glory a second time to gather up all those who lived in accordance with the understanding of God written on their hearts. He asked me how we would recognize when people had the spirit of God written in their heart. I explained it would be easy, for whoever saw me hungry and fed me, or saw me naked and clothed me, or visited me in prison would be the ones I would gather up on my right side. They asked when they would see me hungry, naked or in jail, so I explained that whenever they helped any of their brothers and sisters, they were, in fact, helping me.

After this, Judas Iscariot questioned my going into Jerusalem. I explained that it would be Passover in two days, and I, the Son of Man, would be handed over at that time to be crucified. I was a little amazed because this time none of the disciples seemed to doubt or question the plan. They seemed inclined to blind obedience.

We had a quick dinner as it was getting late. They all fell fast asleep. I lay down, too, but the energy within was burning, so I decided to journal some of the later events of today. I also reread my earlier entry. Everything about my life, the life of humanity, my presence here on earth is starting to make sense. I understand at some level, although not fully, what my Father is doing.

Father, thank you for this time of inner peace. I know I've been full of your spirit and aware of my sonship at times, while at other times, I'm more acutely aware of my humanity. I'm a simple, humble man, and I'm thankful for every moment you graced me with to share in this existence. I understand so much now about my fellow brothers and sisters. I understand their shortcomings, appreciate their struggles, and rejoice as they grow in their awareness. Father, yours is truly a great plan. You are full of wonder and awe, even for me, your Son, who lives in you and reigns in you. I love you. Amen. Alleluia.

185 Anointing

Tomorrow is the Passover. I know it will be full of prayer and traditional moments with my faithful companions. Afterwards, things will become a lot more tumultuous. I feel a sort of excitement within me to watch the events unfold according to the will and plan of my Father.

Today was sort of a lazy day. We spent most of the day quietly. We talked some. I tried to explain some of my parables and teachings to my disciples again. We ate a hearty breakfast, actually it was more like a lunch because we all slept late. We even played a few games. It was just such a warm, wonderful day. It was as if we were all part of the same family, sharing our lives and truly enjoying each other's company.

In the meantime, Judas was checking the treasury. He was complaining all day that there was hardly any money left. He was worried how we'd eat. I assured him not to worry because God provided for us all these years and it was up to us to simply trust Him.

Later on, we went to dinner at Simon of Bethany's home. He was a leper I had previously cured. He heard we were in town and begged us to join him for a meal. Needless to say, when the invitation arrived, we all told Judas to see how our Father will and does take care of our needs. This did not seem to elevate his mood.

While at dinner, a woman came up to me. She was clothed in a ritual dance dress and her face was covered. She danced a while, and we all enjoyed it. It was obvious Simon arranged this performance.

At the end of the dance she whispered into my ear that God had directed her to end the dance in a special way. She then pulled out an alabaster jar filled with expensive perfume and poured it onto my head, three times. As she poured it, she placed her hand on my head and whispered again that God, our Father, was proud of me and my ability to follow Him in all things. She whispered that I must continue to have faith in Him and follow the path even when it becomes more difficult. When she poured it a third time, she simply said, "Abba loves you."

I was overwhelmed by this entire performance. I was amazed at my Father's ability to touch people. First Simon, and now this woman. Through them, He encourages me and assures me all is within His plan. I was still deep in my own thoughts, thanking the woman, when all the disciples started complaining about the money wasted on the perfume. It seems they had allowed Judas' comments to diminish their faith.

I was again full of the spirit of my Father as I spoke. The words were kind and loving. I merely pointed out this woman was sent by my Father and was preparing me for the things to come. Furthermore, although she could have used the money for something else, she chose to use it for me as directed by my Father. As for them, they should have the same faith as she does, since I wouldn't be with them much longer.

Needless to say, Peter immediately changed his tune and asked if there was any more oil or perfume so he could anoint me too. Andrew laughed and teased Peter, which made everyone laugh. The evening continued full of warmth, calmness, and fellowship. We lost track of time and left late into the evening hours.

Father, I know the days for me here on earth in this shell called a body are drawing to an end. I thank you for this day of joy, peace, and love. I also thank you so much for anointing me through your beautiful servant. I know whenever I need you, you will always find a way to be there for me. Please help me to keep these memories alive as the events unfold.

Shalom.

186 Passover

Again, we slept late. Little wonder, as we went to bed only a little before the sun rose. When we got up, the disciples approached me to find out where we would celebrate the Passover. It's one of the greatest celebrations of our religion and they were concerned over the plans, or should I say, lack of plans. But after last night, most seemed to have some inner trust all would be right.

I told Thaddeus and Bartholomew they should go into the city to a man named Cephas, who would be standing in front of the fifth house and carrying a jar of water. They should tell him the teacher says the appointed time is near and ask him to allow us to celebrate the Passover in his house. He'll prepare the upper room. I directed them to help him.

I went to a spot on a hill in the woods and prayed almost all day. My spirits were high after the peace and the amazing anointing of the evening before. I focused on God's plan. I understood that after the Passover tonight, one of my faithful twelve would betray me. They'd all deny knowing me. I would be turned over to the Sanhedrin and accused of blasphemy. I also perceived this would be my last evening with these men, the most faithful of all faithful followers.

I understand I'm to die in this human form, so my Father can somehow raise me up again. God will use me as a sacrifice for humanity. Through Adam and Eve, sin entered the world. I've been sent to free people of sin. I've been sent for them to enter into a new relationship with God; an understanding wherein God calls them all sons and daughters and loves all people everywhere. He even loves those who don't believe in Him as well as those who believe in multiple gods. He'll use my suffering, death and rising from death to teach them there is life beyond this vessel called a body. The soul is created by God and it survives death. I must sacrifice my body and blood so they might gain understanding. It all seems somewhat confusing, but for now, I seem to be at peace with it.

As I record this entry, I know tonight's meal will be my last. I know it will be something special. As I try to sort out all the thoughts and details of the events about to unfold, I find myself weakening in spirit. I don't want to die. There is so much left for me to live for. I don't want to suffer. Who would? I'm thankful for this time of peace, quiet and aloneness.

There are so many things to sort out, so much my Father says to me that first makes some sense, but then it doesn't. Can't there be a better way to have these people, my very own brothers and sisters, understand the message? I'm sure they don't grasp all the things my Father has sent me to teach. I'm sure there are still so many lessons to learn and even more to reinforce. At times, I feel I've failed.

I know tonight's dinner will be the most special Passover of my life. I only wish my Father would also consider allowing me to continue in His name. Perhaps He will. After all, it's customary to allow one prisoner to be freed. I'm sure God will protect me and will be able to influence the crowd to ensure that. In the meantime, I will have a long night tonight and an even longer day tomorrow.

Father, I ask you to continue to reside within me. Help me say the things I need to say tonight. Help me remain true to you in my time of the greatest challenge. Help me follow the path just as you desire. If you call upon me to deliver my body and blood to death, then so be it. Whatever is your desire, help burn it deeply within my soul.

Shalom.

187 Prayers in the Garden

This evening, I felt the weight of the world again upon my shoulders. I've taken my last supper with my disciples, the last supper of this earthly existence. I'm so full of emotions it's hard to describe. I will try to write my feelings down to sort them all out.

First and foremost, I feel fear. I'm so afraid to die. I'm still a young man, and I know I have so much more to offer my Father. I can't believe it's time for me to go home. I know I'm to be the source of a major change in the history of the Jews and of Gentiles as well. Yet, my own Pharisees plot to take my life. How can it be?

Perhaps God is calling me home because I'm a failure. I've done whatever I could in His name, but I don't feel like a miracle worker and certainly not the savior I had believed myself to be. Yet, God tells me all is fine and I should find peace in these my last moments, as I've done my job well. What job have I done well? I've healed many, but they don't follow. Many seem to have a new light within, but they return to their homes and their customs. Nothing really changed in their life. I have a meager band of followers, with one who will betray me. Oh, and one who will deny me is the one God has chosen to be the leader, the rock, upon my leaving. How can this be?

This leads to another one of my feelings – confusion. On the one hand, I'm certain this is the path God has chosen for me. I feel certain I've followed His every desire. But I'm equally certain God has chosen me to help lead my fellow

Jews as well as people throughout the entire world to know the God I know a little better. How can I do this if I am to die?

Fear comes back to me again. This time, oddly enough, it isn't a fear to leave, but rather a fear to stay. Part of me is tired of this journey, and the thought of reuniting with my Father has a lot of peace attached to it. Part of me no longer wants to fight. I can't seem to get people to truly understand all I have to say anyway. Leaving this world right now seems good; I can use the rest. I'm truly tired; I'm losing my inner spark, my candle is flickering.

Loneliness. I've felt lonely most of my life, even though I'm surrounded by many who love me. My first thoughts turn to my mother, lovely Mary. She's stayed with me, prayed with me, encouraged me and lifted my spirits. Then my thoughts turn to my beloved John. At times, he is the closest to being able to comprehend the love within me. I definitely feel we share the same spirit of love. But neither my mother, nor John can fully understand me. They can't truly comprehend the confusion, fear and anger inside me this evening. I am an island. I'm so far away and simply alone.

I mentioned anger. This is even more difficult to explain. I hesitated as I wrote it down because I don't really understand my anger at all. In fact, I would deny I had anger, except it is obvious that anger is raging within me. All my life I've fought with my inner anger, which sometimes tends to boil over, like the day not long ago in the temple. For some reason, I don't believe that God's son should ever get angry. But anger is just as valid an emotion as any of the more positive ones I experience. Oh, precious anger!

But what is the source of my anger tonight? I'm angry with Judas. He will be my betrayer. I loved him as much as any of my followers. I entrusted him with our treasury. Yet, he steals it! I know his heart is sort of in the right place, since he will use the money for the poor, or so he thinks. But stealing is still stealing, and betraying me is still betraying someone you supposedly love. I know Judas is merely following his script in the grand and glorious plan of my Father, but a part of me is still undeniably angry with him.

That leads me to my anger over my rock, Peter. While his transgression to deny me isn't as great as a betrayal, I'm even angrier at this thought. To think one of my closest followers, one of my most trusted confidants, one who is chosen to carry on in my spirit after I leave will simply deny he knows me! But to be honest, Peter hardly knows me. As much as I've tried to give him my knowledge, my peace and strength, he simply fails to understand who I really am. That's one of the reasons for my loneliness.

Sorrow. I feel sorrow for my mother. In some ways, I wish I could lift this burden from her. I don't understand why my Father has chosen to let her stay and suffer with me. I can't comfort or relieve her sorrow any more than she can relieve mine. We both know this is the path I was destined to walk, but we both suffer. I'm so sorry for what burdens she has borne for agreeing to bring me into this world, and the worse is yet to come. Oh, wouldn't my Father lift this cruel burden from the shoulders of my beloved mother? I wish I could.

Joy. Another one of the odd feelings I have is joy. While I'm confused and angry over this path, I find joy that I've accomplished whatever plan my Father has set for me. I'm glad that the plan is in its final stages. I often feel I'm but an actor in a carefully planned drama, one God has skillfully manipulated all my life. So, here I stand at the last scene, waiting with joy, anticipation and excitement for the finale.

How will this drama end? Or will it? Maybe this isn't the end at all, but a new beginning.

I'm both exhausted and energized. I'm full of joy and full of sorrow. I'm angry and at peace at the same time. I guess this is another source of confusion. It seems as if all my emotions have merged into one giant mass of conflicting feelings. Perhaps this is God's way for me to fully realize this experience. I'm full of grief and full of joy; tired, yet full of life. I'm alive and fully human. I'm the alpha and omega. *I am*. I simply am.

My writing has again helped sort out some of these feelings. I know God is in control, and all of the feelings are wonderful expressions of being human. I'm certain God's plan, so magnificently created, included this final night, this full cycle of human emotions. Name one, and I feel it. All of them. Greed – yes, a part of me wants to be the King of the Jews. Jealousy – a part of me is jealous of almost anyone else, anyone who hasn't been given this blessing or curse of being God's son. Hurt – how could I not be hurt over the course two of my followers will take? Depressed – the thoughts of dying, the suffering of my mother, the denial of my followers, the physical pain I will endure tomorrow and the thoughts of my own shortcomings – and possibly failure – all make me feel depressed.

Love. Oh, sweet love. In some ways, I've never felt love more powerfully than I feel it this evening. I almost wept with love for all my friends and followers as we dined this evening. Even though most have no clue of tomorrow's events, they all know the end is near. They've given up their lives to follow me, to try and understand the new word of our Father, to watch me heal people. They've left their homes to pursue a dream. I'm at the center of their dreams. I'm at the center of their lives. I never felt as close to them as tonight.

Oh, sweet love! Tonight, I truly felt most of my followers experienced a glimpse of pure love, the kind of love only found within the deepest recesses of their own hearts. Hopefully, it will be enough to nurture them through the events of tomorrow. Hopefully, it will continue to nurture them through the days after I'm gone. If they could feel only one fraction of the love within me, they could carry God's message of love and forgiveness to the ends of the earth.

Oh, sweet Father, my love. That's your plan, isn't it? It's me, your son, who has the message. I can't, however, carry it throughout this world. You have given it to me to give to my followers, and they shall be commissioned to go out to the entire world. What a beautiful and wonderful plan! If only I had realized it sooner.

I feel myself growing in strength as I write this. My doubts and fears for the most part have been cast away from my body. I'm again certain of the plan God has laid out. I must follow. I've spent a long time in prayer in this wonderful garden. I will go now and check on the followers God has given me.

Shalom.

188 More Prayers in The Garden

Fools! I'm not sure who is the bigger fool – them, for being so inattentive and distant, or me, for actually thinking they could be part of God's plan for creation! Can you believe they were asleep? Asleep! Here I am, facing the most difficult time of my life, struggling with matters of earth-shattering importance, and those three men who I consider my closest and most loving followers and friends fall asleep! Obviously, I'm the greatest fool. To think my Father could actually use these men to bring about a major change in the whole human race. Preposterous!

God has given me the gift to perform miracles. But I can only perform the easy miracles of the flesh. I can make the lame walk, the blind see, the deaf hear. I can even raise some from the dead. What I can't do is change a man's heart. I can't open up the heart for the love of God or instill the spirit of God into a soul. That would be a true miracle! Making others understand the loving nature of my Father, their God, is completely beyond my control. Yet, this is the mission God has sent me to perform – to open the souls of mankind to His love.

He gives me a mission and no ability to perform the miracles it takes to complete it. After years of trying, of preaching, of performing physical miracles, of being a representation of God's love in flesh, all I can do is sit here in my last hours and see failure. I can't change the heart of any other person. The key to the miracle of opening one's heart and soul to freely let God in belongs to each individual, and that individual alone. Perhaps this is why my time has come. Perhaps I've finally learned the last lesson of my own journey.

Oh, dear Father, please remove this yoke from my shoulders. I learn more and more of your infinite love and lessons of life, but I can no longer carry the weight of the world on my shoulders. Lift this burden from me. Take it away. I'm simply not strong enough to be all you ask me to be. I can't crack the hearts of these men; they alone must do that. If this is truly your lesson, why do I have to suffer so? Help me find the peace I lack right now. I vacillate from doubt to confusion to fear to pain to brief glimpses of hope, and then right back to doubt.

If you must take me, let it be done. I won't back out on my commitments to you, I will follow the path you lead me down. But Father, dear God, please release me from the torment of my soul. Free me from the doubts. Remove the weight of the world from my shoulder. Allow me the privilege of opening just one other soul to have one tenth of the understanding of your love and compassion I have.

Please, take this burden of failure from me. Let me complete the mission. I've truly served you to the best of my capacity, I've given all I have to give. I've endured the torments of some of my fellow Jews, and I know many more will follow tomorrow. I've been left here in my greatest hour of need to suffer alone through my innermost agony. All in the name of your love. All to bring the gift of salvation, your love and forgiveness to your people, to my brothers and sisters.

Father, don't let me die a failure. But as much as I plead for your intervention in my fate, I ask first and foremost that your will, not mine, be followed. I won't, I can't, let you down. Give me the perseverance I need to face the challenges you have in store for me. I will remain true to you in all things.

Shalom.

Epilogue

I've just read in amazement the journal of my wonderful and blessed son, my wonderful baby boy. Jesus was wrong about having no more lessons to learn after he wrote his last entry the night before last. He agonized so much over his failures, not realizing that to follow God's plan is never equal to a failure, even if it seems so.

He also agonized over leaving me, even more than the writings reveal. I must admit I was worried about how I would be able to cope with the loss of this very special gift from God. He has been so much of my life. But Jesus was able to give me the gift of understanding to help me cope with his passing. I'm not at all scared or lonely or afraid. I don't even miss him, at least right at this moment. I feel like I will turn around some day and he will be smiling at me and hugging me again. It's a feeling I can't explain. My reactions are so different from what I would have envisioned.

But the greatest gift Jesus gave me was also the last lesson of his life. As he was hanging on the cross, my wonderful son, delivered his spirit over to God. Not a part of it, but all of it. In his last moment, he gave all of his doubts, fears, confusion, loneliness, sorrow, agony, and pain to God. And God rewarded my son with his last wish, which was for God to remove the yoke on his shoulder.

I know my son, at times, felt that the weight of humanity was on his shoulders, that the very future of the world rested on him. However, that isn't really correct. As much as my son was God's son, God never really gave Jesus a yoke to carry. Jesus perceived what in reality never existed. Jesus may have felt the weight of the world upon his shoulders, but in truth, it was always carried by God, and only God himself.

Once Jesus was able to fully deliver his spirit to God, the perceived burden of his life was removed. I saw the greatest peace and understanding befall my son in that moment. I felt the spirit of my son rise from the body that limited it. It was an indescribable moment. I felt not sorrow but joy as my son died. What a wonderful gift. He was so worried about me, and yet he was able to give me the ultimate gift of faith and the knowledge of God. This gift that was able to turn a mother's sorrow into sheer joy and elation. I can feel the spirit of God all around me.

There is a hush in the air. We are all waiting in silent anticipation of something grand and glorious. I don't have any specific knowledge of God's plan, but one thing I do know is Jesus accomplished exactly what he was sent to accomplish. I also know my spirit lies firmly within the palm of God's hand, together with the spirits of everyone else.

Shalom.

Deborah Ayars

ACKNOWLEDGEMENTS

This book would not have been possible without all the people mentioned in the dedication. A special shout out is due for my daughter Laura, who also helped by utilizing her artistic talents to create the illustrations. In addition, I would like to acknowledge some good friends, Donna Garvey and Cynthia Shafer, who read the manuscript and offered words of encouragement; and Joe Sosnowsky who not only offered encouragement, but also made a number of suggestions, comments and questions, which helped improve the overall manuscript. A very special thank you goes to Charlotte Kardokus, who not only was the first to read the manuscript and offer encouragement, but as a published Christian writer herself, was able to provide invaluable assistance in moving this manuscript towards publication.

I'd also like to acknowledge my editor, David Ferris, who helped streamline the manuscript, making important adjustments, offering suggestions and overall helping the final product be a worthy work of literature, while at the same time treating the subject matter with the respect and reverence it warrants.. And finally, another special thanks to my cousin and publisher, Carol L. Rickard, who provided me invaluable assistance throughout the publishing process.

ABOUT THE AUTHOR

Deborah Ayars began this manuscript in her early 30's soon after she experienced a life-changing awakening of her indwelling spirit. Since then she has been very active in a number of religious and spiritual activities, including: serving as a lector and Eucharistic Minister; supervising the church youth activities; being a member of numerous prayer groups, Cursillo, Credo, the Veteran's Home Ministry, and The Troubadour's; making Rosaries; and development of an eReflection Ministry. While the initial part of the Journal was written while she was in her 30's, the manuscript was put aside until her retirement, when the Spirit prodded her to finish it after a bout with breast cancer.

Deborah is a licensed Professional Engineer by trade but is currently retired. She is living in Oahu, Hawaii with her husband, Steven, and her daughter and son-in-law, Lisa and Willie Velez, and their two children, Tre' and Lorilai.

I'd love to hear from you. Please feel free to reach out if you have questions or comments!

Email: JournalofJesus@gmail.com

Or like us and leave a comment on my Facebook page - The Journal of Jesus.

FROM THE ILLUSTRATOR

When I was first contacted by my mom to create the cover art, I focused on making it fit the story. I didn't want yet another picture of Jesus, there are so many. I wanted it to be simple, yet powerful. Then if hit me, a simple drawing of Jesus' hand actually writing on a scroll. I researched what the pen and paper would look like along with the actual letters He would have used. For the hand, I couldn't think of a better hand model than my husband, Dave. I knew if I used his hand, that my love for him would reflect in the finished product. I thoroughly enjoyed drawing the hand because I love realism and trying to capture it for this book which I knew was so important to the author.

For the rest of the drawings, I focused again on simplicity and making them fit the story. Pictures that someone might doodle in an actual Journal. The little girl was fun and happy. The wedding couple was so special since I recently got re-married. The young Jesus working with Joseph made me think of my son working with his new dad. I hope I was able to capture the love Jesus had for the lost sheep, which is my personal favorite. I also hope I was able to capture the power and torment of Jesus as He prayed in the garden. I hope my sketches enhance the overall impact of this incredible book.

Made in USA - North Chelmsford, MA
1203514_9781947745285
12.01.2020 1719